LEAD the WAY

Also by
JOHN J. (JACK) NORA

One Way

Transforming the Workplace

LEAD the WAY

JOHN J. NORA

PLYMOUTH PROCLAMATION PRESS, INC.
West Bloomfield, Michigan

Library of Congress Control Number: 2006934073

Cataloging-in-Publication Data Block:
Nora, John J.
    Lead the way / John J. Nora
    p. cm.
    Includes bibliographical references and index.
    ISBN-13: 978-0-9788960-0-3
    ISBN-10: 0-9788960-0-9

    1. Management. 2. Leadership. 3. Organizational effectiveness.
  4. Industrial productivity. I. Title.

    HD57.7.N665 2006   658.4
                                  QBI06-600350

Printed in the United States of America.

For more information or to order *Lead the Way,* please call, write, e-mail, or fax:
    Plymouth Proclamation Press, Inc.
    5340 Isle Royal Court
    West Bloomfield, Michigan 48323
    (248) 851-4200 (phone)
    (800) 783-2026 (phone)
    (248) 851-5266 (fax)
    mlbrose@workplacetransform.com
    Web site at: *www.workplacetransform.com*

Contents

Acknowledgments

I would like to thank my wife Ellen-Mary for putting up with eight years of book writing without once complaining. I would like to thank Amanda Nora, a colleague who designed the cover and did a much needed edit of *Lead The Way*. I would also like to thank my colleagues who reviewed the book and sent ideas, especially Nancy Ryan, Julie Anderson, and Patrick Nora. I would like to thank all of the effective leaders who previewed the book prior to publication and sent quotes found on the dustjacket of *Lead The Way*. Finally, I would to thank all of the clients of Workplace Transformation, Inc. for giving us the opportunity to learn while we helped you on the journey to high performance.

Guide to Acronyms and Terms

CI: Formal Continuous Improvement Process

JOBS Training, Verification, and Versatility System: Job identification; Operator guidelines; Basic training; and Skills verification

Five E's of Leadership Direction: Envision, Example, Encourage, Enable, Empower

Five V's of High Performance Employees: Valued, Versed, Verified, Versatile, Vitally Engaged

Four O's of Positive Union and Management Relationships: Openness and honesty; Objectives understood; Obstructions eliminated; and Ongoing support and involvement

Four T's of High Performance Structure: Tailored, Tactical, Trim, Team-oriented

PRIDE Short-term Improvement Process: Series of sequential steps (starting with P, R, I, D, and E) that are necessary when performing a high performance, short-term directed improvement initiative

4-S Cleanliness, Orderliness, and Safety Process: Select area and team; Sort, clean, and straighten out; Safety and ergonomics assured; Sustaining the process with Continuous Improvement

TECS Technical Employee Training, Verification, and Versatility System: Tasks and skills needed; Establish levels of skills; Create operating guidelines; Skills verification

D1, D2, & D3 The Three Styles of Leadership: D1, Directing people; D2, Delegating analysis or involving people; D3, delegating authority or empowering people

LMQ: Leadership Maturity Quotient

Introduction

At this critical time when:

- The skeletons of once vibrant companies are desperately chasing one gimmick after another in a futile attempt to survive.
- Longtime giants, such as General Motors and Ford make cut after cut, employee buyout after buyout, and become smaller and not stronger while wondering if industry consolidation is the only way to survive.
- Rapidly emerging competitors from Eastern Europe, China, India, and Russia, dominate growth in basic manufacturing, while the vital manufacturing base, where one job creates ten others, continues to erode in developed countries.
- Electronic outsourcing of services like technical phone support, accounting, programming, CAT-scan reading, and tax preparation moves jobs from developed countries to developing countries.
- Unethical leaders at companies like Enron mortgage their company's future for selfish gain.
- Wall Street analysts act as the judges of business success and stock options, or "golden parachutes," provide incentives for self-serving executives to manipulate results.
- Top managers impose one unrealistic, short-term objective after another, reduce capital budgets, and brutally grind up the people reporting to them in their lemming-like drive for short-term results at the expense of long-term success.
- Manipulating the quarterly balance sheet takes precedent over product development, crucial capital investment, and acquiring critical resources needed for long-term competitiveness.
- Ill-conceived manpower cuts, done without fundamental changes in the way business is done, leave companies smaller and weaker.
- Companies, unions, and employees in developed countries struggle aimlessly and unproductively as developing countries rob them of vital manufacturing content and associated jobs.
- Companies, unions, and employees in developing countries struggle to find lasting competitiveness under the burdens of corruption, bureaucracy, government regulations, and inefficient structures.

Lead the Way offers real and lasting answers to achieve success in today's world market. Written by John J. (Jack) Nora, the author of *One Way* and co-author of *Transforming the Workplace, Lead the Way* will put you on a path that invariably delivers quick results, continual improvement, long-term profitability, and growth. Fundamental, clear, simple, and proven, *Lead the Way* describes how to lead a fundamental change in the way you do business.

In 1718, Matthew Prior wrote, "The end must justify the means." What Prior could not have known, is that in business, the means determine the end. It is time to stop spinning your wheels. Stop manipulating the results for the short-term appearance of gain. Stop tightening your belt because it will not cause you to lose weight, just as across-the-board cost cutting does not lead to success. Stop trying one shortcut program after another as they only lead to frustration and failure. It is time to change the way you do business and achieve real and lasting success.

Lead the Way will show you how to develop the leadership skills you will need to engage your workforce in becoming a high performance organization. Learn to lead the way and enhance short-term performance, while at the same time ensuring long-term growth and security.

Here are some suggestions on how to read *Lead the Way*. First, do not read it to see if you agree. There is no need to agree; *Lead the Way* is not theoretical or an experiment. It offers a proven road map that has worked for decades in many industries and many countries. You do not need to know how far you want to go. You must only choose to let *Lead the Way* put you on the proper path and to persevere. This path will get you there and beyond. The French novelist Marcel Proust said, "The real voyage of discovery consists not in seeking new landscapes, but in having new eyes." You may sense a bit of arrogance, but I assure you that arrogance has no place in the values or principles of high performance. When something works repeatedly, cross culturally, and in so many different industries around the globe, you develop complete confidence that it will continue to work.

Second, *Lead the Way* is not a "speed-read." Leading a company to high performance, like reading this book, is a journey—not a race. Relax, slow down, and enjoy the message. Though *Lead the Way* presents basic and proven methods, full understanding is necessary. Underlining, highlighting, scribbling in the margin, and rereading the key points will help you to fully absorb the message.

Third, do not become overwhelmed as you read *Lead the Way*. This one book presents real answers and provides the many pieces necessary to complete your puzzle. At times, you may feel lost as you read the material in Chapters One through Twenty-nine. Do not worry. It is essential first to see all the pieces: the needs, and the answers. Part Seven, "Putting it all Together," will clarify how to sort through all the pieces and put them together in the proper order for your unique organization.

Fourth, do not despair when reading *Lead the Way*. Many of you will ask yourself, "*What have I done?*" Some of you will say, "*I should have started years ago.*" Even worse, some of you will say, "*I think it is too late!*" The truth is that you can only affect the future, not the past. Even if you think it is too late, the only hope to forestall continued frustration and certain failure is to begin to lead the way. Often, individuals and organizations are on the brink of failure, facing severe survival challenges after trying several shortcuts, before they find the will to make the fundamental changes described in this book.

If you find yourself thinking, "*I cannot do this,*" take heart. No one has to make this journey alone. You will gain supporters as implementation progresses. You can bolster your efforts by using allies and trained experts both within and outside your company. This is not to say that just anyone has what it takes to lead the way. Many people, because of a lack of integrity, courage, or energy, will choose not to even try.

If you have the will and the courage, but do not yet have the position to take charge, do not sell yourself short. You can learn to lead at any level in the organization and for your own team, even if your leader is ineffective. Almost all who lead the way must at times ask for forgiveness, rather than permission, and shelter the move to high performance from those higher in the organization. Former U.S. Secretary of State Colin Powell said, "So the moral is: don't ask. Less effective middle managers endorse the sentiment, 'If I haven't explicitly been told "yes," I can't do it,' whereas the good ones believe, 'If I haven't explicitly been told "no," I can."

One certainty is this: if you choose to lead the way and persevere, you will achieve rewards beyond your wildest expectations.

PART ONE

The Need and The Answer

1

Complex Challenge, Simple Answer

Toto, I've got a feeling we're not in Kansas anymore.

Dorothy from the movie, *The Wizard of Oz* (1939)

The opportunity to work in many different countries and cultures has helped me to understand that everyone must change to survive and prosper in the new world market. The reasons that change is necessary are different depending on where you are, but everyone must change, and the changes that everyone must make are the same.

Those of us in the United States must change to meet the competitive challenge from developing countries and the huge market force blossoming in China and soon to blossom in India and Russia. Lulled into the entitlement mind-set of the 1950s, 60s, and 70s, the United States was without competition as the only industrial power not destroyed in World War II. We grew accustomed to working less and getting more, year after year. Beginning with the onset of competition from the newly rebuilt Germany and Japan, followed by the emergence of Mexico, we started losing our dominance in the world market. Recently, with the emergence of Eastern Europe and now, the explosive growth in China, our manufacturing base has eroded and our average manufacturing wages continue to plummet. Our service industry is under attack as job after job moves to Eastern Europe and India. What is the answer?

In Western European countries, the challenge is to change or else watch the standard of living dissipate. High social costs and restrictive rules make manufacturing uneconomical. Nations in the eastern sector of the European Union, with their low wage rates, are eyeing Western European markets and taking Western European jobs. Protecting industries by restricting the growth in the East will only delay needed industrial and social changes and widen the competitive gap. Every day, Western European companies shrink and move operations to Eastern Europe or the Far East. What is the answer?

Mexico recently had the worldwide competitive advantage because of a comparatively low labor rate. Now, Mexico must change tactics or witness the continued exodus of foreign companies and investment. Today, large developing countries with even lower wage rates than Mexico's are capturing manufacturing jobs. Companies are pulling up stakes and moving elsewhere. Just when Mexico's standard of living was rising, the world changed. Now, almost everything in Wal-Mart and Home Depot says, "Made in China" instead of "Made in Mexico." Mexico has not developed the infrastructure to be an economic power. What happens when India and Russia join China and Eastern Europe in rapid development? What is the answer?

In Eastern Europe, which recently escaped the suffocating grip of communism and dictatorships, workers became conditioned to entitlement from years of employment for the sake of employment. Those countries' laws and rules were designed to create employment for everyone, not to encourage competitiveness. Continual improvement and high performance are foreign concepts to Eastern Europe, and the excessive bureaucracy chokes potential progress. Corruption still infiltrates the government and business. What is the answer?

In the oil rich Middle East, leaders either are or are controlled by Islamic extremists who wish to keep the general population centuries behind the rest of the world in terms of personal freedom. People who desire safety, security, and free choice are exploited for the financial well-being of their leaders or for the cause of world-wide terror. What is the answer?

In companies all over the world, unions fight to preserve unproductive work practices, protect non-performers, and resist technology and upgrading the skills and versatility of the workforce. They cling to an old model that worked in the 1950's, dooming them to irrelevance in many developed countries. They do not understand the economic reality that the well-being of their membership depends on the financial success of the business. What is the answer?

Workforces cling to the belief that they can simply come to work and avoid contributing value for major portions of the working day. They fail to realize that it takes performance to stay in business and that job security only comes from working for a profitable company, becoming engaged, and increasing their individual skills. What is the answer?

Company leaders still believe they can take huge bonuses while the frontline worker has their numbers and compensation reduced. These leaders do not believe in equality of sacrifice or in setting the example. They fail to realize the workforce will not cooperate with a false leader and that their shortsightedness will put the company out of business. What is the answer?

By now you may have guessed the answer—effective leadership. By effective leadership I mean, leadership that is able to unite diverse groups and engage them in the pursuit of a common purpose. Effective leaders are those who lead the way, understanding what is needed, why it is needed, and how to put it in place.

Dorothy in *The Wizard of Oz,* after dropping from the tornado, realized that she and her dog Toto were not in Kansas anymore. The world is changing faster than a tornado. Like Dorothy and her friends, the Tin Man, the Scarecrow, and the Cowardly Lion, you will need direction, heart, wisdom, and courage to adapt and survive. Like Dorothy and her friends, you must learn that there are no wizards and no shortcuts. The ultimate wake-up call comes from understanding that the key to business success resides within. Are you ready to lead the way, or are you simply going to skip along down the yellow brick road to failure?

➲ We must change for different reasons, but the changes we must make are the same.

➲ The only answer is: effective leadership that engages others in the pursuit of a common purpose.

➲ Effective leadership starts from within.

2

The High Performance Organization

Do, or do not. There is no try.

Yoda from the movie, *Star Wars:*
Episode V—The Empire Strikes Back

There is no alternative but to meet the competitive challenge of the world market. Most people now understand that the survival, growth, and security of a company depend on whether the company can become a **high performance organization— one that can compete successfully in the global market**. Taken to a higher level, entire countries are beginning to understand their economic future depends on their industries' capacity to become high performance.

In his book, *The World Is Flat,* Thomas L. Friedman quoted an African proverb he saw hanging in the office of an auto parts manufacturer Chairman and CEO in China. The proverb stated:

> Every morning in Africa, a gazelle wakes up.
> It knows it must run faster than the fastest lion or it will be killed.
> Every morning a lion wakes up.
> It knows it must run faster than the slowest gazelle or it will
>   starve to death.
> It doesn't matter if you are a lion or a gazelle.
> When the sun comes up, you better start running.[1]

Friedman then writes,

> Or, to put it another way, if Americans and Europeans want to benefit
> from the flattening of the world and the interconnecting of all the

markets and knowledge centers, they will all have to run as least as fast as the fastest lion—and I suspect that lion will be China—and I suspect that lion will be pretty darn fast.[2]

There is little mystery about what a high performance organization can achieve. Like fast lions and gazelles, high performance companies survive, grow, get stronger, and are secure. The only alternatives are either a quick death or a painfully slow one. The mystery lies in how to build a high performance organization. Most companies have tried programs, shortcuts, and cost reductions in the pursuit of becoming a high performance organization. Such companies unfortunately find that there is no program or shortcut for becoming a high performance organization. They also learn that you cannot cut or buy your way to competitiveness.

The mission statements of most companies contain a description of what a high performance organization can achieve. Ironically, most companies touting such mission statements are clueless about how to become a high performance organization. Paraphrased from the mission statements of many companies, a high performance organization will:

- Be cost competitive while having the highest quality goods and services in its market.
- Anticipate, innovate, and make strategic changes necessary in products, processes, people, services, and markets to distinguish the company from emerging global competitors.
- Continually improve quality, productivity, cost, service, delivery, safety, and environmental compliance, faster than the competition.
- Develop and hire the strongest, high performance leaders and the most skilled and versatile workforce.
- Engage everyone to improve performance faster than the competition.
- Grow at a financially responsible rate to capitalize on the improvements made.
- Preserve an acceptable rate of return while improving the security and standard of living of those actively contributing to the organization's high performance.

A high performance organization is not simply one that is profitable. Understanding what a high performance organization can achieve is different from understanding how to make it happen. Understanding how to build a high performance organization begins with understanding what constitutes high performance. Defining high performance begins as follows:

> A *high performance organization* has five key, adaptive, and integrated systems that improve performance to the levels necessary to compete, grow, and secure the organization today and into the future.

The five systems that comprise a high performance organization are "key" systems because each system is indispensable. If any of the systems are missing, the organization is vulnerable and will not reach, preserve, or continually improve the results necessary for ongoing success. Many companies have implemented one or more of the five key systems necessary, only to fail to achieve long-term security and growth because of the lack of one or more of these systems.

The systems are "adaptive" because they change focus and evolve based on data and changes in the competitive environment. A high performance organization can respond to different challenges and threats, without the need to change its fundamental systems or approach. Add a new tool to one of the systems as needed, but the key, adaptive systems that comprise the companies' overall approach are constant.

The systems that comprise a high performance organization are "integrated." This means that they are interdependent and work in a synergistic manner. One thing leads to another, as the old adage has it. The timing of implementing the systems according to the needs of each company is critical. The prerequisite building blocks from one system must be in place before building the next.

The five key, adaptive, and integrated systems of a high performance organization do not simply fall into place. Effective leaders implement the systems in a disciplined manner that engages the entire workforce in the pursuit of high performance.

High performance organizations achieve results. However, understanding how to become high performance has nothing to do with the results. It has everything to do with how you achieve the results. A simple example will explain the difference.

One company unexpectedly has three injuries this month. This company has:

- top leadership that is passionate about safety and a clean, orderly workplace, not only to reduce cost and improve quality and productivity, but mainly because the leaders care about the well-being of their employees.
- leadership that sets an example for safety by performing daily observations to spot potential hazards and assure corrective actions before injuries occur.

- Operators involved in ongoing housekeeping audits and improvement efforts.
- Operators verified in effective and enforced safety practices.
- a data-driven Continuous Improvement process focused on continually reducing injuries with committed leadership and engaged Operators.
- leadership that is sensitive to the environment and strives to improve environmental compliance.

Another company has zero injuries this month. This company has:

- leadership that talks about safety but accepts a dirty, unorganized workplace, because the leaders do not care about the employees' well-being.
- leaders that simply walk past safety hazards every day.
- an unengaged workforce that is not involved in housekeeping and safety.
- no operator guidelines, let alone systematic operator training and skill verification.
- no systematic Continuous Improvement process to reduce injuries.
- no sensitivity to the environment or interest in compliance.

Where would you rather have your son or daughter work? Which company is the high performance company when it comes to safety? Is it the company with three injuries or the company with zero injuries? The clear answer has nothing to do with last months results. Even with three injuries this month, the first company has committed leadership, a safety system, and an engaged workforce in place to improve safety. The company's leadership, systems, and engaged workforce are the means to assure future results for safety and every other performance measure.

> In a *high performance organization,* effective leadership engages the entire workforce in the disciplined implementation of the five key, adaptive, and integrated systems necessary to outperform the competition and secure the organization and the workforce today and into the future.

Almost everyone will agree that leadership is the key. Almost everyone will agree that systems fail without proper leadership. Almost everyone will agree that engaging the workforce depends on leadership. Unfortunately, few understand the leadership skills necessary, and how to develop the skills at every level of the organization. Company after company is full of apathetic employees and frustrated Managers, who either never knew or have forgotten how to develop leadership!

This is why the results of a high performance organization are clear, while the way to build a high performance organization is so obscure and universally misunderstood. Those occupying leadership positions fail to realize that every morning when they shave or put on their make-up, they are looking at the answer. They are the reason their company is or is not a high performance organization. What escapes them is that they will not find the answer on a benchmarking trip, from 30 black belts, or in any new program. Positive change must start within them and then spread to those around them. No program, consultant, or process can accomplish this; it must start within the leader. Sadly, looking within can be the last place people in leadership positions want to look.

An old saying in the Upper Peninsula of Michigan, where I grew up is, "If you don't know where to start, try the beginning." Becoming a high performance organization starts with leadership, when people at a company decide within themselves to become leaders. In our lifetimes, we consciously or subconsciously answer one or two questions. The first question is, "Should I step up and become the leader?" If the answer to the first question is "yes," the second question is, "What kind of leader shall I become?" If your answer to the second question is, "The kind of leader who makes a positive difference," you are about to become armed and dangerous!

To demystify high performance, it helps to understand that the five systems of a high performance organization have not changed in over twenty-five years of both implementing them and helping others in their pursuit of high performance throughout the world. I believe that they will never change. This is why we call them and picture them as the **Pillars of High Performance.** The pillars are the foundation supporting high performance in any business or industry. Build your high performance organization on the rock of these five pillar systems.

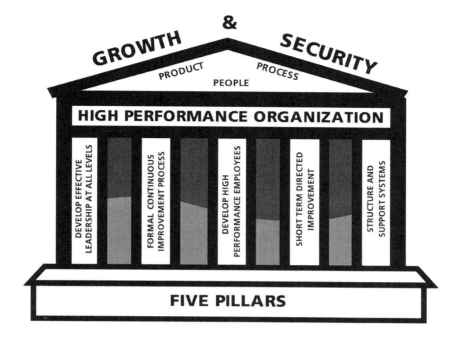

The **Principles of High Performance** cement the pillars together. The principles help leaders make decisions when implementing the five pillars.

PRINCIPLES OF A HIGH PERFORMANCE WORK ENVIRONMENT
True high performance and strategic leadership must be developed at every level, there is no room for ineffective leaders.
Everyone must join at least one natural work group pursuing continuous improvement with aligned measures and objectives.
The company must fundamentally change products, processes, and markets before the competition.
The workforce must gain a broader range of skills, be more versatile, and more engaged in Continuous Improvement than the competition.
The organization must be properly structured and efficiently staffed and non-performers must be handled consistently.
Proven systems, tools, and processes must be implemented and everyone must consistently use them wthout exception.

The **values** supporting a high performance organization are all about people:

VALUES OF A HIGH PERFORMANCE ORGANIZATION

1. People are the only lasting competitive advantage.

2. Continuous improvement and innovation come only from people.

3. Effective leaders are required to engage employees in the pursuit of high performance.

4. All employees must enhance their skills and pursue performance improvement to secure their own future.

The pillars, principles, and values of high performance have led to both short-term and long-term improvement, growth, and security in the United States, Mexico, South America, Australia, Europe, and Asia. They apply to every industry in the manufacturing and service sectors.

At first glance, it may appear that the pillars, principles, and values of high performance are simply common sense, and that any company would naturally outperform the competition with the following characteristics in place:

- Stronger leadership at every level than the competition
- Strategic leadership that out-anticipates the competition and develops new processes, products, materials, locations, markets, and people faster than the competition
- Everyone engaged in improving cost, quality, productivity, safety, orderliness, training, and environmental compliance, with aligned key measures, through a systematic, data-driven Continuous Improvement process, and improving faster than the competition
- An operating workforce making products or providing customer services that is more skilled, versatile, autonomous, and engaged than the competitors' workforces
- An effective and quick method to reconfigure uncompetitive, wasteful, and inefficient product families or administrative services, when exposed by a sudden change in the world, industry, market, customer, or competitor, and proactive waste reduction as high performance systems and structure spread throughout the organization
- A structure that supports the direction of the company and the development of its workforce with efficiently staffed teams linked together to pursue common objectives
- Support systems to assist and encourage leaders and employees

when implementing high performance, and sound operational support systems to assure safety, quality, and productivity

What makes you think that doing this takes anything but common sense? Yet, how many people truly understand the pillars, principles, and values of high performance, let alone how to implement each system? How many people have the discipline and courage to live by the principles of a high performance organization? How many leaders are engaging the entire workforce in the common fight to improve faster than their competitors? How many companies have a clear common objective of growth and security, as opposed to cutting, alienating, and disenfranchising employees? We have not yet found the leader or organization that suffers from having too much common sense.

Although defining the characteristics of high performance seems like common sense, exemplifying those characteristics is more complicated. Implementation is difficult. Values, commitment, energy, personal involvement, patience, perseverance, and courage are the essential ingredients for achieving high performance.

Yoda, who trained Jedi warriors in the movie, *Star Wars: Episode V—The Empire Strikes Back*, scolded a doubtful Luke Skywalker by saying, "Do, or do not. There is no try." When it comes to choosing high performance, there is no room for doubt and no acceptable alternative. *Not* to succeed is terminal. Leaders must trust in the force within themselves to become true, high performance leaders. They must use their lightsabers, the pillars of high performance, to win the day. Choose to lead the way for your organization, and do not let anything stop you.

⊃ High performance organizations achieve results; however, how they achieve the results defines them as high performance.

⊃ High performance organizations have five key, adaptive, and integrated pillar systems, principles, and values to secure the organization and workforce into the future.

⊃ Effective leaders implement high performance in a disciplined manner and they engage the entire workforce in pursuit of common objectives.

Notes

1 Thomas L. Friedman, *The World Is Flat* (Farrar, Straus, and Giroux, 2005).

2 Ibid.

PART TWO

Effective Leadership

3

True Leadership

Your motives, not your methods
determine if you truly lead.

Many efforts to achieve high performance fail because they do not begin with leadership development. Many committed and well-intentioned top leaders fail because they do not recognize that developing effective leadership at every level before beginning implementation of the other key systems is a prerequisite. They mistakenly believe that they can supply all the needed drive and energy it takes to achieve high performance. No matter how committed the Plant Manager is, if a Supervisor does not support the direction, all the people working for that Supervisor will fail to implement the systems necessary to achieve high performance.

The first pillar of a high performance organization is leadership development. One matching principle is: to develop true, high performance, and strategic leadership at each level. The second matching principle is: there is no room for ineffective leaders in a high performance organization. The corresponding value is: effective leaders are required to engage employees in the pursuit of high performance.

To develop effective leadership at every level requires an understanding of effective leadership. Only when all the ingredients of the leadership required to lead the way are understood, can they be put into place. This applies to leadership of a company, a union, a church, a school, or a country.

The first ingredient of effective leadership is *true* leadership. True leaders guide others to achieve a particular outcome. Not just any outcome, *true* leaders guide others to outcomes that will make a positive difference in the lives of those they lead. To lead the way to success requires high performance, strategic, and above all, *true* leadership. Slobodan Milosevic, President of Serbia and Yugoslavia, and

Saddam Hussein, President of Iraq, were leaders, but certainly not true leaders. Their motives and means were to further themselves, not the people they led.

In my company, Workplace Transformation, Inc., we teach leaders to become high performance and strategic every day, but we cannot externally teach or cause leaders to be true. It is impossible to teach the proper values and motives, and instill integrity. So how then do people become true leaders? They make a fundamental decision, deep within themselves, to make a positive difference in the lives of others. Whether you are a leader starting a major change, or have decided to take a leadership role in helping other true leaders implement a major change, the choice is the same. Only when people understand and accept the underlying moral imperative of true leadership, can they make the critical choice to *truly* lead.

True leadership emerges from many different circumstances, places, and people. Consider the following:

- The President of a United Steelworkers local who did not want to let the copper mine close down and hurt the economic future of his community: he ended a three-year strike, promoted employee ownership, and set up high performance systems, despite management interference.
- The School Superintendent who would not allow cost pressures to adversely affect the academic curriculum or sports program of his school system: he started leadership training, strategic planning, and continuous improvement in the face of political pressure in a small town and reduced cost, while at the same time improving the curriculum and rebuilding the sports program.
- The new Complex Manager of an engine and car assembly complex in Mexico: he decided the Mexican workforce could outperform any in the world and recognized that they deserved a future and a higher standard of living.
- The Purchasing Director who recognized the urgent need to streamline his non-competitive organization in Eastern Europe, burdened by wasteful systems, inefficient staffing, and buyers who were merely performing clerical roles: he made the difficult decisions to achieve competitiveness and at the same time had the values and courage to set up systems to retrain and reward the buyers who remained, and reduce the impact on the workforce.
- The steel mill President who relied on workers in Eastern Europe, despite years of communist influence: he gave them a chance to

compete in the world market and bring lasting prosperity to their communities.

- The union President who risked his reelection, and the new Plant Manager who risked his future career growth, to join in promoting radically new work practices and compensation systems in a failing industrial film factory in the northern United States: they put themselves on the line to attract investment and new products to save the jobs of their co-workers.
- The company President who is the grandson of the owner: he would not let family wealth seduce him from working twelve-hour days, striving for worldwide competitiveness to ensure the jobs of his workforce in South America.

TRUE Leaders Hold the Well-being of Those They Lead Above Their Own and Recognize that They Build People not Products.

True leadership begins the moment people accept a calling that is bigger than seeking their own comfort or gain. This is the real meaning of the often misused and misunderstood phrase, "principle based leadership." A true leader may wish to be corporate President, reelected, or independently wealthy. However, the true leader's *primary* motive is to better the lot of those they lead. True leaders will forego the promotion, the reelection, or the money, if their individual reward would cause them to sell out the success of those they lead. These leaders most often become legends, inspiring those that follow.

As outlined in the next chapter on High Performance Leadership, leaders must achieve results and the organization's performance must improve. However, advancing the company by achieving results is the vehicle, not the primary motive.

Even Jim Collins in his book, *Good to Great,* missed the meaning of true leadership by one step, when he wrote,

> Level 5 leaders channel their ego needs away from themselves and into the larger goal of building a great company. It is not that level five leaders have no ego or self-interest. Indeed, they are incredibly ambitious—but their ambition is first and foremost for the institution, not themselves.[1]

Jim Collins seemingly missed the fact that the first ambition is to build people, not to advance an institution. The institution is only the means used to advance people. Companies are to serve the needs of people, not visa versa. Caring for the well-being of people drives true leadership. Building the institution is the vehicle through which the leader can provide that well-being. The team must sense the coach is mainly interested in building them as players and people, not that his or her primary motive is to have the program prosper, irrespective of whether they are sacrificed or not.

Trust this. The people who work for you know whether you are a true leader. If you are, they will follow you relentlessly. If not, they will only tolerate you. To engage the workforce in the pursuit of high performance, the workforce must view you as a true leader. You cannot fake it. You must become a true leader. Employees determine whether a leader is true, based on how they are treated. The words and deeds of true leaders communicate to employees that they are valued as the only lasting competitive advantage.

If you ask a true leader, "What do you make?" The answer will be, "I build people who make the best products or who provide the best services in the world." If you ask a true leader, "What would you like to achieve?" You will not hear a sum of money, a career objective, or a plea for early retirement. You will hear, "I would like to make a positive difference in the lives of those I lead. If you compliment a true leader for a job well done, the response will not be "Thank you" but rather, "It wasn't me, it was my team."

Lead the Way explains all the leadership skills necessary to assure business success. All of these skills are learnable. However, you must initiate the most important requirement to lead the way: true leadership. If you need encouragement, the intrinsic rewards that come from true leadership will far outweigh and outlast any extrinsic reward you can achieve through the pursuit of individual glory. People forget false leaders as soon as they leave; however, they remember true leaders for generations. As social critic John Ruskin said, "The highest reward for a person's toil is not what they get for it, but what they become by it."

True leaders accept the "Stewardship of Leadership," meaning that they place the gain and benefit of others ahead of their own gain and benefit. Stewardship means that the leader serves those they lead, not vice versa. True leaders recognize the key to success lies in building the skills of those they lead and making them successful, autonomous, and responsible for their job, not in focusing on a leader's individual expertise or achievements.

Many believe true leadership is dying. Daily publicity highlights false leaders in business and government. With examples like Enron and Dafur, is there any reason why employees, unions, investors, and citizens have become cynical?

Short-term results drive most false leaders. Their motive is to make themselves look good and achieve quick wealth, most often at the expense of long-term performance and growth. They hope to achieve short-term success by cutbacks and manipulating rather than by building the ability and capacity of the organization. These false leaders hope to be gone with their stock options and wealth when the impact of their shortsightedness comes to bear.

It has gotten so bad in business and the pendulum has swung so far one way, that people are writing books about how to do it. The following appeared in a 2002 business book, perhaps aptly entitled *Execution*: "Execution is now tested on a quarterly basis and not just by the numbers. Security analysts look to see whether a company is showing progress toward meeting its quarterly goals. If they think it isn't, their downgrades can wipe out billions in market capitalization."[2]

True leaders know they cannot effectively lead to impress the security analysts. In pursuit of quarterly results, some companies will delay developing critical new products, buying needed tools and equipment, adding critical talent, and even doing needed upkeep and maintenance. Companies will split orders to book sales in this quarter, only to suffer double shipping and packaging cost in the next. Companies build excessive inventory to absorb costs in this quarter only to assure poor cost performance in the next. Companies offer huge discounts to book sales in this quarter, only to erode margins and ruin future sales results for the sake of today's figures. As the impact and futility of their shortsighted decisions come to bear, such companies get more desperate and pursue even more manipulation. In far too many cases, they move from "manipulating" to "cooking" the books.

The newspapers are full of stories about companies who make cut after cut to reduce cost in the short-term, only to get smaller and weaker. All too often, those performing a value-added service lose their jobs, while their false leader hides and takes a huge bonus for cutting costs that quarter.

Why are there so many false leaders? The barriers blocking true leadership are ignorance, arrogance, selfishness, insecurity, laziness, and impatience.

- Ignorance: Many leaders do not understand that they have a choice. Choosing to build strong people, systems, and organizations that will provide long-term profitability and growth is an alternative to short-term greed, manipulation, cost-cutting, or unfettered growth. All of the latter can lead to bankruptcy. Often leaders do not recognize their ability to make a huge positive difference and receive the satisfying extrinsic and intrinsic rewards that await true leaders.
- Arrogance: Some leaders are so full of themselves and ego-driven that they believe they are better, smarter, and more deserving than those they lead. Blinded by an inflated image of themselves, they think they alone can make a lasting difference and see no need to act in concert with others. What do they think they will leave behind whether their choices work or fail? Do they even care?
- Selfishness: Some leaders' need for personal position, wealth, or power drives short-term cost cutting at the expense of long-term growth and security. They rush and scramble to take financial advantage of the moment. They comfortably increase their bonus and lay off the workforce, while their family flies on the company jet to another vacation destination.
- Insecurity: Some leaders are insecure personally and thus lack the courage or confidence to pursue a difficult and unpopular path, or make the tough decisions associated with high performance leadership. They refuse to stand up for those they lead and make a difference, they simply buckle under. They usually end up hating their company, their job, and sometimes even themselves.

- Laziness: Some leaders do not step up because true leadership requires commitment and boundless energy. Some do not have the will to make the sacrifice of time and energy required. They do not have the "fire in their belly" to succeed. As English philosopher Edmund Burke said, "All that is necessary for the triumph of evil is for good men to do nothing."
- Impatience: Some leaders are unwilling to spend the years, not months, that it takes to make a difference and lead the way to assured success. Lacking perseverance, they hop from program to program and never achieve any lasting success.

Working with clients at Workplace Transformation, Inc., we believe that true leadership burns inside as many people as it ever did. Now is the time for the pendulum to swing away from the false leaders to the true. It is clearer and clearer every day that simply cutting back only makes companies smaller, not stronger, and short-term decision making only produces results lasting a short time. More and more investors, boards of directors, companies, and leaders recognize there is no easy way out. Whether out of desperation or desire has come an awareness of the need to change and lead the way to lasting success.

True leaders who rise above the selfish mass and reassert themselves, can positively influence the lives of thousands. Bill George, former CEO of Medtronic aptly said, "We need authentic leaders, people of the highest integrity, committed to building enduring organizations. We need leaders who have a deep sense of purpose and are true to their core values. We need leaders with the courage to build their companies to meet the needs of all their stakeholders and who recognize the importance of their service to society."

President John F. Kennedy said, "It is time for a new generation of leadership, to cope with new problems and new opportunities, for there is a new world to be run."[3] His words are more appropriate today than they were four decades ago when North America still ruled the industrial world.

Workforces around the world are resilient. They have not been disappointed to the point that they will not respond to true leadership. If you resist and reject ignorance, arrogance, selfishness, insecurity, laziness, and impatience, you could be one of the lucky ones: a true leader who can make a huge and lasting difference.

What makes a leader "great" is how that leader treats the "ordinary." I believe football coach Vince Lombardi said it best. "The new leadership is in sacrifice, it is in self-denial. It is in love. It is in loyalty, it is in fearlessness. It is in humility, and it is in the perfectly disciplined will. This is not only the difference in men; it is the difference between great and little men."[4]

⮕ The first part of effective leadership is true leadership.

⮕ True leaders hold the well-being of those they lead above their own and recognize their success comes from building others.

⮕ True leaders become legends.

Notes

[1] Jim Collins, *Good to Great* (New York: HarperCollins Publishers, 2001).

[2] Larry Bossidy and Ram Charan, *Execution: The Discipline of Getting Things Done* (New York: Crown Business, 2002).

[3] John F. Kennedy, Television Address, July 4, 1960.

[4] Vince Lombardi, Jr., *The Essential Vince Lombardi: Words & Wisdom to Motivate, Inspire & Win* (New York: McGraw-Hill, 2002), 103.

4

Understanding High Performance Leadership

You *manage* systems and processes, you *lead* people.

To be an effective leader and to implement the systems of a high performance organization takes more than true leadership. To be effective, a **true leader** must also be a **high performance leader**. There is a big difference between a true leader and a true, high performance leader. Your motives determine if you are a true leader, your methods determine if you are a high performance leader. Every true leader can learn to be a high performance leader, but a false leader can never last as an effective leader. To lead the way you must be **both**, a true and a high performance leader.

I remember debating Irving Bluestone, former Vice President of the United Auto Workers and one of the most intelligent leaders I have worked with, about the motive behind effective leadership that engages the workforce. Bluestone argued for the moral imperative behind true leadership, while I argued the economic imperative of high performance. In retrospect, of course, we were both right. It takes both true and high performance leadership.

A true but low performance leader is just another bleeding heart who wishes he or she could have made a difference for those they may have loved and led. You must have both the heart of a true leader and the mind and will of a high performance leader to achieve lasting success. For all the right reasons, you must relentlessly push and engage the entire workforce in the pursuit of high performance.

In professional sports, how often have you seen a "players" coach fail? The players love and respect the coach and believe the coach has their best interests at heart. However, the team lacks discipline and accountability and performance suffers. No results means it is just a matter of time before there is a new coach. On the other hand, how often have we seen a high-intensity X's and O's coaches fail because they become bigger than the program and the players? Even though they demand execution, discipline, accountability, and have a proven system, they fail because they don't keep the loyalty and commitment of the players. Only a true, "players" coach and a high performance, "X's & O's" coach combined can sustain results long enough to become legendary.

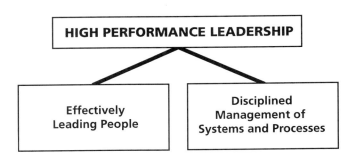

High performance leadership has two parts: leading people and managing systems. There is an age-old debate about the difference between leading and managing. The answer is that you manage systems and processes, while you lead people. There is also an age-old debate about whether you are born to be a leader or learn to be a leader. The answer is that you may be too selfish, arrogant, ignorant, insecure, impatient, or lazy to be a true leader, but you can learn the skills to be a high performance leader.

Learning to be a high performance leader is not theory. Consider that loading and cleaning your rifle are survival skills in the army. Learning to lead people and manage systems are survival skills for effective leadership.

In 1972, I was the only Supervisor on Cadillac Motor Company's Final Assembly line with a college degree. As a result, I received a promotion at a very young age to lead seven much older Supervisors. Three of the men resented me because I was young, inexperienced, and had passed them in the organization. I later learned that they vowed to cause me to fail and prove to the organization that my promotion was a mistake. They refused to carry out the directions I gave and their quality, productivity, housekeeping, and relations with the union and workforce declined. I was constantly in trouble because of their lack of performance. I secretly called them "the terrible three."

Three of the older Supervisors performed well and followed through on most assignments even though they felt that they were passed-over for my position. They had clean and orderly areas, quality and productivity were high, and grievances were few, resulting only from the union protecting those who clearly did not want to perform. I attributed their performance to a sense of professionalism and called them "the terrific three." Finally, I led one Supervisor who was sitting on the fence, waiting to see what would happen before deciding which camp to join.

The terrible three performed so badly, that I had to do something or risk losing my job. One night it hit me, I would switch the areas of the terrible three and the terrific three. I figured the terrific three would clean up the bad areas that were causing me to fail while the terrible three would learn how nice it was to work in a clean, high-quality, productive, and harmonious area. Then, they would change.

Six months later, I was in the same jam as before with three good areas and three horrible areas. The only difference is that they had switched places; the terrific three fixed the bad performing areas, and simultaneously, instead of learning and changing, the terrible three destroyed the good performing areas. I was learning some important principles of high performance leadership at a very young age. The first was that no matter how committed I was as a General Supervisor, performance in an area would always match that of the Supervisor, or the immediate leader.

My next step was one of survival. It was either give up or stand up. I did something uncommon in the Big Three, in the 1970s. I built a case of insubordination and unauthorized absence from the plant and fired a Supervisor, the worst of the terrible three. He was fifty-two years old and had twenty-four years of service. I did not sleep at all that night, thinking about the family of the dismissed Supervisor and how despised I would be.

To my surprise, the next day during the morning tour of the line, several of the hourly employees shook my hand and told me just how bad it had been working for the man I had fired. Three days later, the terrific three came to me as a group, shook my hand and said, "Perhaps the company was right when they promoted you." Most incredibly, the remaining two of the terrible three as well as the fence sitter changed their ways and performance improved in their areas. I realized that being an effective leader is not easy, but at the same time, there is no alternative.

To get high performance, a leader must demand accountability, make tough decisions, and address performance issues as they arise. But first, leaders must have confidence in themselves. As Adlai Stevenson, the two-time Democratic Presidential candidate, once said, "It is hard to lead a cavalry charge if you think you look funny on a horse."

➲ Effective leaders combine true leadership with high performance leadership to achieve results that secure the organization and the workforce into the future.

➲ High performance leaders effectively lead people and implement systems in a disciplined manner.

➲ High performance leaders demand accountability, insist on performance, and develop leadership at all levels.

5

Effectively Leading People: Direction and Style

Prophet, salesperson, guide, role model, driver, authoritarian, cheerleader, coach, teacher, listener, instigator, disciplinarian, integrator—which describes an effective leader of people?

The answer to the question posed above, of course, is: all the above. Understanding how to lead people starts with understanding that your role as a leader must change as people develop through each stage of the journey to become a high performance organization. Since few of us are "naturals" at effectively leading people, fundamental skills of Direction and Style must be learned and applied sequentially, as if from a recipe. There are many leadership theories; however, the basic survival skills of high performance leadership are not theoretical. High performance leaders fulfill specific roles and meet specific leadership expectations.

In review, the first critical ingredient to effective leadership is **true** leadership. The second critical ingredient is **high performance** leadership. High performance leadership has two major parts: **effectively leading people** and **managing systems and processes in a disciplined manner**.

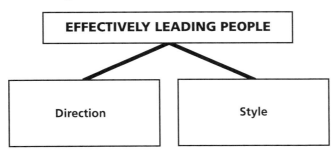

Effectively leading people also has two interdependent parts: **Direction** and **Style**. Using them properly will enable a leader to fulfill various roles for leading people and avoid destructive behavior along the way.

Leadership *Direction* is a set of techniques that a leader must master to spread understanding, earn credibility, build enthusiasm, develop skills, and foster discipline and responsibility in others. Leadership *Style* is learning when and how to use three fundamental leadership Styles as groups and individuals move from understanding, to participating, to learning, and finally to taking responsibility for implementation themselves.

LEADERSHIP DIRECTION

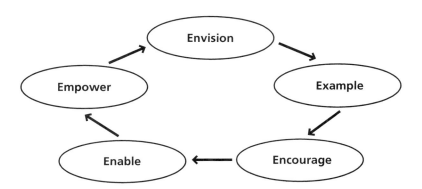

The techniques for providing leadership Direction fall into five categories called the five E's: **Envision, Example, Encourage, Enable,** and **Empower.** If you follow the five E's in a sequential manner, starting with Envision, you will move from talking about the future, acting in accordance with the future, getting others to act consistently with the future, preparing others to take responsibility for the future, and finally to turning over the future, piece by piece and person by person, to those you lead. During this final growth step, your direction for the future becomes their direction for the future.

Leadership Styles move from D1, directing people; to D2, delegating analysis or involving people; to D3, delegating authority or empowering people. The correct leadership Style for each situation is dependent upon several established variables. Just as important as knowing when to use each Style, is learning how to use each Style to achieve results through others.

The five E's and Styles D1, D2, and D3 work together. As the leader moves past Envision and Example, to Encourage, Enable, and Empower, the predominant Style gradually changes from D1, to D2, and eventually to D3. Consistent Direction and correct Style are the fundamentals for effectively leading people. Together, true leadership, leadership Direction, and leadership Style, naturally yield another E: an **Engaged** workforce. An engaged workforce is the mark of high performance and a company's only lasting competitive advantage. It cannot be bought or threatened into existence; it happens only naturally, as leaders like you lead the way.

➲ Effectively leading people is comprised of two parts: providing consistent leadership Direction and using the correct Style to achieve that direction.

➲ Consistent Direction is the sequential implementation of the five E's of leadership.

➲ Leadership Style is using D1, D2, and D3 at the right time and in the correct way.

6

Leadership Direction: Envision

People do not follow those who do not know
where they are going.

The first "E" of the five E's of leadership Direction is **Envision**. It requires the leader
to understand and picture what high performance would look like far before it becomes a reality. *Envision* has four major parts.

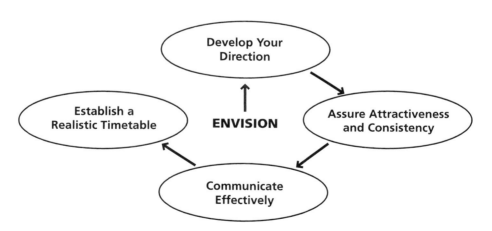

As with the five E's, these four parts of *Envision* work sequentially. First, you
must develop your direction. Second, you must assure it is attractive and consistent.
Third, you must effectively communicate your direction. Fourth, you must set up a
realistic plan and timetable. Your initial role is to be both prophet and salesperson.

Most people wander through life and business passively letting things happen to
them. They are looking for, if not craving, leadership they can believe in and follow.

However, to assume a leadership role, as the opening quote to the chapter infers, you have to know in what direction you are going. The late Theodore Hesburgh, former dean of the University of Notre Dame, knew the importance of clear leadership Direction when he said, "The very essence of leadership is that you have to have vision. You can't blow an uncertain trumpet." As the leader, you must describe a new and exciting future.

Several years ago for Christmas, I bought two jigsaw puzzles for my three children. One depicted a snow-covered mountain scene and the other a farmhouse at sunset. In my usual compulsive manner, I picked up the wrapping paper, ribbons, and empty boxes as my children tore open their gifts on Christmas morning.

The next day when my children gathered to build the puzzles, they decided to start with the snow-covered mountain. They found the open box with all the pieces, but not the top of the box with the picture of the snow covered mountain. Unfortunately, I had burned the box top in the fireplace in my rush to clean up. The children tried to piece the puzzle together for hours, but made little progress, the pieces would not fit together to form a picture. Finally, my then four-year-old daughter, Amanda, looked up at me with a look of total frustration and said, "If we can't see the picture, we can't build the puzzle."

My children switched to the farmhouse at sunset. While examining the picture on the box top, they made steady progress. They started with the boundaries where there are straight edges. Then turning to the colors and patterns, they filled in the center. The snow-covered mountain puzzle ended up in the land of misfit toys.

Leaders must paint a clear picture of the future so their team can help put the pieces into place. Not just any picture, but one that is both attractive and consistent. Having a consistent direction means that your direction is consistent with the direction of the company and consistent with the pillars, principles, and values of high performance. Having an attractive direction is complementary to the values underlying true leadership as the picture must benefit those who come together to make it a reality. Your leadership Direction must be in the best interest of those who buy your products and services, your company, and your employees.

Internal and external customers both want quality, cost, service, delivery, and innovation. Make all of these elements part of your direction. The company wants profit, so improved cost performance must be part of your direction. Employees want to be safe, secure, involved, developed, and responsible, so these outcomes must be included. If you satisfy your internal and external customers' needs, you can expect more business. If you satisfy your company, you can expect more capital and freedom to run and grow your part of the business. If you satisfy the needs of your employees, you can expect continuing performance improvements in quality, cost, service, delivery, and innovation. Consistent and attractive direction leads to more satisfied customers, more business, more profit, more capital, and new opportunities to involve the workforce in continuous improvement. Thus, you start a cycle of success that begins with involving the workforce in continuous perform-ance improvement.

Once you have developed an attractive direction you must communicate it with enthusiasm at the beginning of the change process, and then reinforce it every day. Effective leaders refer to the direction at every opportunity. Communicating your attractive direction does not mean that people will immediately embrace you or your direction. President Harry S. Truman said, "A leader is a man who has the abil-ity to get other people to do what they don't want to do and like it." A high per-formance leader accomplishes this by sequentially following each part of *Envision*, on the way to completing all five E's.

In more than two decades of consulting, I have found that those holding leader-ship positions either lead or occupy space. The quickest way to find out whether a person is leading or occupying space is to ask three random people who work for the leader the following questions: "Where is the leader leading your group?" "What will it look like when you get there?" "What steps are you doing now?"

If the answer you get is a blank stare or "I don't know," the leader is occupying space. If they answer, "It changes every week based on the hot topic or which book the leader has read," the leader is occupying space. If all three employees consis-tently describe a high performance group satisfying the customers, then you have found a capable leader.

One skill we have to teach many leaders is basic communication. It is amazing how many leaders do not know how to run a meeting or use their voice, hands, eyes, and presence to effectively communicate with enthusiasm and sincerity. Effec-tive leaders realize when engaging others, how they communicate is just as impor-tant as what they communicate. The late author, aviator, and wife of Charles Lindbergh, Anne Morrow Lindbergh said, "Good communication is as stimulating as black coffee and just as hard to sleep after."[1]

Once you have developed your complete direction and communicated it effec-tively, the last step needed in *Envision* is to establish a realistic plan and timetable. Most leaders commit a fatal error by underestimating the time needed to make a substantial change in the way they do business. They fail to realize that when people are presented with an attractive direction and vision, they want it to happen quickly and painlessly. Without a well-thought-out plan and timetable, people will lose confidence based on the slow pace of change. They will turn on the leader at the first sign of trouble.

Great leaders throughout history have made this mistake. The best example is former Soviet President Mikhail Gorbachev. He had an attractive direction, a colorful vision, and he communicated it well. Why did he fail to carry out his social and economic reforms? He could not lead his country from communism to free enterprise fast enough to satisfy the masses, and he lost his leadership position.

If Gorbachev had laid out a twenty-year plan and timetable with clear milestones each year, he may well have succeeded. Then his people would have judged him on the timely implementation of the plan. If Gorbachev had offered a well-communicated timetable, perhaps Russia would still be a unified nation today. By now, Russia could have been a huge economic power exploiting its assets of people, land, and natural resources. Untold human suffering would have been avoided in that part of the world.

Leading the way to a high performance organization takes years, not months. The time required depends upon the size of the company, current competitive position, amount of resistance, systems in place, and the leader's resolve and autonomy. Leaders should do a diagnosis of the forces helping and hindering the move to high performance before finishing their plan.

Most importantly, the plan must have a realistic timetable and logical sequence. Furthermore, the pace of change should be fast enough to allow visible progress and results, but not so fast so as to overwhelm the organization. For example, if a new or changed labor agreement is necessary to involve the workforce, it will take several months to gain support and develop the needed changes. The early focus should be on leadership development, a management-driven Continuous Improvement process, improving safety and housekeeping, quality improvement, and removing process bottlenecks. Visible progress and performance improvement will help build support as the leader works on labor contract changes.

In many cases, the leader may choose to involve others in developing the plan and timetable to gain support. This technique is helpful when implementation requires the buy-in of others independent of the leader. A joint participative planning process can lead to support of the plan and timetable. However, the leadership Direction is not negotiable.

When developing an overall plan, it is important to have clear and visible milestones along the way. Most people do not respond to the promise of a long-term change. To stay motivated on a long journey, people must see visible short-term progress. For example, in a three-year change plan, the first six months should be full of specific scheduled steps, the next six months with several steps listed, and the next two years with a general description of steps and timing. An updated plan continually shows accomplishments and specific steps that will occur in the next six months.

Like a prophet, high performance leaders confidently and enthusiastically communicate their vision of the future. Like a salesperson, they convince others that there is no alternative. Like the careful guide, they develop and involve others in developing the plan to get there.

If you have not put substantial thought and time into working on your statement of direction and you have not developed and communicated a plan and timetable, then you are not leading. You are simply occupying space.

➲ *Envision* means effective leaders develop and communicate an attractive direction for the team they lead.

➲ The direction must be consistent with becoming a high performance organization and be attractive to the company, customers, and the workforce.

➲ A realistic plan and timetable supports the direction and encourages others to give the leader enough time to succeed.

Note

[1] Anne Morrow Lindbergh, *Gifts from the Sea* (New York, NY: Random House, Inc., 1955)

7

Leadership Direction: Example

It is not enough to talk a good game;
you must walk the talk.

The second sequential "E" is **Example**. During the *Envision* phase, the leader talks a good game as a prophet and salesperson. The leader talks about being a high performance organization. Talking a good game is not enough; *Envision* connects to *Example* as the leader "walks the talk." During the *Example* phase, you must become a role model and a cheerleader. *Example* means fulfilling four specific behavioral expectations.

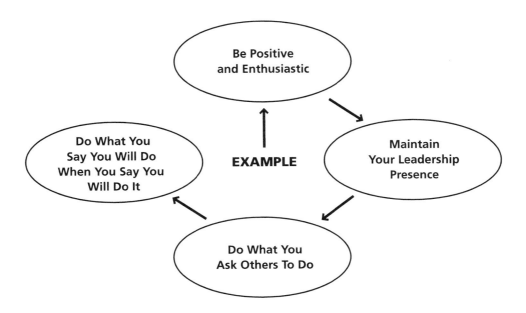

Projecting a positive attitude is the first and most often violated element in the *Example* phase. The leader must be confident the group will succeed, even in the face of disaster. Acting as the cheerleader, the leader encourages the team even when the game is not going well at the moment. After being stopped one yard short of his team's first national football league championship, Coach Lombardi's post-game speech was simply, "We will never be stopped one yard short again." He found no need to place blame. When asked about his team's devastating and sole loss of the season, suffered at the hands of the Detroit Lions on Thanksgiving Day, Vince Lombardi's reported response to the media was, "My team has never lost a game." Then after a moment to reflect, he added, "On occasion, we have run out of time."

When the pressure is on, leaders disclose their true nature. Instead of pointing fingers and seeking to place blame, effective leaders courageously work to solve problems and assure they will not reoccur. Shouting, swearing, degrading, and visibly losing control are not acceptable behaviors for an effective leader. The leader must be the role model in implementation of systems and tools, but even more importantly, in behavior. Enthusiasm should accentuate the positive, not the negative.

The second part of *Example* is to keep your composure. To be effective, you must never lament in front of the group you lead. We have heard leaders who complain and whine about the union, the workforce, the equipment, support groups, customers, their fellow leaders, the corporation, and the government. To be a high performance leader, adopt the rule, "No more whining." People do not follow leaders who whine.

Complainers suck positive energy out of an organization. By contrast, a high performance leader pumps energy into the organization. The leader must never complain publicly and must always exude confidence in the direction's eventual success. The leader's example of composure, enthusiasm, and confidence, will by example, become characteristics of the organization.

From the 1950s to the '90s, leaders were judged by their intelligence. Many people thought that technical knowledge and the capacity to learn and remember facts were the most important ingredients for success. We now realize that emotional intelligence (EI) is a greater predictor of success than a person's IQ.

John Mayer, Ph.D. and Peter Salovey, Ph.D. introduced the term "emotional intelligence" in the early 1990s, in the *Journal of Personality Assessment*. They described a person's capacity to understand his or her own emotions, the emotions of others, and more importantly, a person's knowledge of how to act properly based on this understanding. In 1995, psychologist Daniel Goleman made the term "emotional intelligence," or EI, well known in his book. *Emotional Intelligence: Why It Can Matter More Than IQ*.

In business, the most important quotient is not IQ, or EI, but what we call (LMQ) or Leadership Maturity Quotient. LMQ measures whether leaders are emotionally mature enough to know that their behavior, both public and private, will influence their success, and if they're mature enough to change behaviors that interfere with achieving their direction. Mature leaders assure that their behavior does not stand in the way of their direction and thus the well-being of those they lead.

Unfortunately, many people in powerful positions behave like little children. They throw tantrums and publicly treat others, even family and friends, with disrespect. Somehow, they mistakenly think they look more powerful when they embarrass or degrade others and act outrageously. They proudly declare, "I don't care what people think!" These immature leaders fail to realize they are only embarrassing themselves and showing their low Leadership Maturity Quotient.

Some leaders become so arrogant that those publicly paying homage, privately grow to despise the leader. Some emotionally immature leaders place themselves above moral and ethical codes of conduct and above the law. For them, the old and crude cliché holds true: "The further up the pole the monkey goes, the more of his back side shows." More often than not, leaders with a Low Maturity Quotient, not only short-circuit their direction, they lose the respect of those they lead. Eventually, as if by poetic justice, their career suffers.

Effective leaders are willing and able to control their behavior not because they are political, but because they place themselves second to achieving their direction and positively influencing others. They recognize that they must build, not break people. High Performance leaders preserve their professional leadership image with the customer, community, employees, union, and company during business hours and after business hours. They are mature enough to avoid confusing being professional with playing politics or playing "the game." Leaders who always set a good example understand cause and effect. They know that everything they say and do has an effect on others and they assure their words or actions will not negatively influence others.

Test your LMQ by choosing which behavior more closely describes yours, immature or mature. Then, ask others familiar with your behavior to score you.

LEADERSHIP MATURITY QUOTIENT

1. **Immature:** Seek personal recognition for what you do as your career comes first

   Mature: Humbly accept compliments while diverting credit to others

2. **Immature:** Degrade or embarrass subordinates in front of others

   Mature: Treat people with respect and always handle performance issues in private

3. **Immature:** Shout, scream, swear, or "fly off the handle"

   Mature: Remain in calm control and let your reason not your resonance influence others

4. **Immature:** Cut off, talk over, or show impatience with people sharing information or opinions different from yours

   Mature: Encourage dissent and listen fully to opposing views before speaking

5. **Immature:** Treat your spouse or friends rudely or as inferior in public

   Mature: Show your friends and family the utmost respect in public

6. **Immature:** Surround yourself with a group that agrees with you

   Mature: Surround yourself with those of equal or greater intelligence who have the courage to tell you when they think you are wrong

7. **Immature:** Talk badly about other leaders, those you lead, or the corporation in front of others

   Mature: Never publicly criticize or talk about others, providing only face-to-face feedback

8. **Immature:** Call people names like idiot, dumb, clueless, or useless

   Mature: Talk to others with respect; disagree with positions not personalities

9. **Immature:** Feelings are easily hurt and you pout or resort to revenge

   Mature: Have a thick skin, a sense of humor, can laugh at yourself and overlook personal conflicts for the good of the company

10. **Immature:** Fight battles just to show off and embellish your rebel image

    Mature: Challenge only issues significant to carrying out your direction or when value issues are at stake

11. **Immature:** Expect special treatment because of your position

    Mature: Resist special treatment to remain part of the team you lead

12. **Immature:** Overreact based on little or second-hand information

    Mature: React only after personally gathering data supporting action

13. **Immature:** Act immorally, unethically, or irresponsibly, share confidential information to show off

    Mature: Set an example for principled and mature behavior

14. **Immature:** Most of your friends are business associates; work is your life

    Mature: Balance in your life with family, friends, and activities outside work taking a high priority

15. **Immature:** See yourself as indispensable and the one who most often has to save the day; no one can do it like you

    Mature: Focus on building a quality team and a replacement for yourself who will be more effective than you are and delegate authority to others

Scoring and Rating:

Each instance of immature behavior has a score of minus one and each mature behavior has a score of plus one. Score your responses and compare with those of others who rated you. Then, tabulate your lowest net score to reveal your Leadership Maturity Quotient.

- If your score is plus 11 to plus 15, you are a very mature leader.
- If your score is plus 5 to plus 10, you are a mature leader.
- If your score is plus 1 to plus 4, you are immature and need to make substantial changes in your behavior before you destroy your capacity to lead as well as your own career. You need leadership coaching.
- If your score is minus 1 to minus 5, you need a complete leadership makeover. You may need a new position or company to succeed.
- If your score is lower than minus 5, you may need professional help for possible deep-seated psychological issues.

Behavioral changes are difficult to make. They require repetitive reinforcement. My oldest son, Joe, is an accomplished soccer player. When he was twelve years old and playing on an elite team, he easily led the league in scoring from his left wing position. Joe always had the strongest left leg on the field.

Joe's coach realized that for Joe to take the next step as a player, he needed to develop a stronger right foot. No matter how many times he asked Joe to use his right foot, Joe always went to his left.

The next season the coach switched Joe from left to right wing. When Joe's scoring performance suffered, we parents privately criticized the coach. As the season progressed, so did Joe's right foot. By season's end, he was a balanced threat and ready to move back to left wing as an even more imposing player. The change was painful but well worth it. True high performance leaders must first change their behavior to be a role model and then like a coach, cause others to change as well.

The third part of *Example* extends the responsibility of being a role model of the disciplined implementation of high performance systems and process tools. Leaders must do what they ask others to do and sometimes even more, practicing what they preach. St. Francis of Assisi said, "Preach all the time . . . sometimes even with words." In the same way, like a champion, the high performance leader enters the field first, demands performance through words and deeds, and leaves the field last.

The biggest step in getting others to use high performance processes and tools consistently is for the leader to be the shining example. The leader cannot be above the rest of the organization or exempt from using the systems or using the process tools. Those led must believe that they succeed with the leader, they sacrifice together, they implement together, and they learn together. High performance leaders personally lead the troops into battle, instead of sitting safely atop a distant hill and directing the battle.

India's Mahatma Gandhi said, "Be the change you want to see in the world." If the leader wants housekeeping to improve, the leader should have a clean and organized office and be the first to pick up clutter in the workplace and properly dispose of it. If the leader wishes the group to improve its skills, the group had better see the leader improve his own skills. If the leader wants the group to use the scientific Continuous Improvement process, the leader must go first.

The final part of *Example* has to do with credibility. As a leader, your word is your bond. Leaders must never make promises they cannot keep. They must follow the timeline in their plan to carry out their direction, no matter how inconvenient it becomes. People do not follow those they cannot believe or who do not follow through in a timely fashion.   .

A common pitfall is that leaders in their enthusiasm, establish unrealistic timetables, set unrealistic objectives, and make promises that will be next to impossible to keep. This is a critical error. Smart leaders will only make commitments they can keep. Then, they keep every commitment they make. It is better to promise little and deliver more. Similarly, it is better to report being early than to cancel or delay implementation steps. Remember, people do not follow leaders without credibility.

➲ Many people suck energy out of the workplace with their negativity. High performance leaders must be positive and inject energy into the work environment.

➲ Be a role model for composure, mature behavior, and use of high performance systems and tools.

➲ Promise what you can deliver, and deliver what you promise.

8

Leadership Direction: Encourage

The eager, the reluctant, and the destructive must all be encouraged, only the consequences differ.

The third sequential "E" of leadership Direction is **Encourage**. Moving from being the protagonist in the *Envision* and *Example* phase, the leader must make a transition to focus on getting others involved in the direction and then responding to how they perform. In addition to getting involvement, the leader must also listen to opposing viewpoints and consistently handle exceptional as well as unacceptable performance.

The first part of *Encourage* is getting people involved in activities in support of the direction and implementing high performance systems. Most people will initially shy away from active involvement because of their fear of failure or negative peer pressure. The leader must direct people to attend training, solve problems, share their ideas, and manage projects. In the first part of *Encourage,* the leader slowly pulls people into the direction. Playing the role of the instigator and integrator, the high performance leader assigns problems, projects, or training to every member of the team. The leader finds a role that each employee can play in furthering the direction. Nobody stays on the bench.

A major mistake of many leaders is focusing on those who willingly volunteer and habitually follow through. A high performance leader involves even those who are reluctant to get involved. Some employees will need scheduled follow-up to encourage them to complete assignments. The team will respond to the leader's vision in one of three different ways: exceed expectations, meet expectations, or fail to meet expectations. The leader will handle each response differently as a part of the *Encourage* step of leadership Direction.

The natural results of getting others involved are differing opinions and conflict. One of the worst mistakes leaders can make is to surround themselves with "yes" people. High performance leaders recognize the difference between destructive, political, self-protecting, dishonest disagreement, and good-faith disagreement, is one of motive, not content. When high performance leaders encourage people to disagree, it helps avoid making mistakes. After making a final decision, however, the leader expects support for the direction chosen, even if it is contrary to a team member's position.

In his book *The Four Obsessions of an Extraordinary Executive,*[1] Patrick Lencioni points out that the first discipline is to create a cohesive team. Three of the four steps he asserts in creating a cohesive team, are part of *Encourage*. They are: openly engage in constructive ideological conflict, hold one another accountable for behaviors and actions, and commit to group decisions.

To gain true commitment, the high performance leader must encourage dissent by asking for input, avoiding being defensive, and respecting every opinion. It is through involvement, disagreement, spirited debate, and conflict over ideas and alternatives that others begin to gain understanding, commitment, and ownership of the direction. The high performance leader must on one hand have the patience to encourage discussion, and on the other hand, have the courage to hold people accountable and insist on commitment to the direction of the team.

No leader is smart enough to be right all of the time. People must feel free to disagree and point out potential errors the leader is about to make. A leader's arrogance or brutality must not get in the way of others candidly expressing their views. The higher in the organization, the more people tend to agree with the leader rather than take the risk of voicing honest disagreement. This can prove to be fatal. High performance leaders encourage, rather than punish good-faith criticism and dissent. People should not fear good-faith disagreement with the leader. More suitably, what they should fear are the consequences from failing to speak up, failing to support the final decision following discussion, and failing to follow through on assignments in a timely manner.

Accountability is the engine of high performance. One of the most common comments heard about high performance leaders is, "They never forget anything." A high performance leader must follow-up on a scheduled basis to assure accountability from all members of the team on assigned tasks, big and small. As a driver, the high performance leader recognizes that accountability is a learned behavior, developed through dogged follow-up by the leader. If a leader does not demand accountability and demand the use of high performance systems and tools, then disciplined implementation simply will not occur. Whenever a leader asks, "Why don't my people follow through and do what I ask?" The only answer is, "You are too weak to be a high performance leader."

One of the common phrases expressed by high performance leaders is, "The train is leaving the station—either get on board or get left behind." The high performance leader is an autocrat when it comes to the overall direction, but open to suggestions on how to better get there. Following good-faith debate, team members must support the leader's decision. If not, they are making a career choice and will be left behind. In Lombardi's first speech to his new team, the Green Bay Packers, not only did he talk about the new leadership, he also said, "There are planes, trains, and buses leaving here every day. If you don't perform for me, you will find yourself on one of them."[2]

Private disagreement followed by public support and follow-through are the earmarks of an exceptional team member. The only boundaries of public support are legality, ethics, safety, and morality. Patrick Lencioni in *The Five Temptations of a CEO*[3] identifies two of the five temptations as choosing harmony over conflict and choosing popularity over accountability.

The second part of *Encourage* is formally recognizing exceptional performance. The high performance leader, in the roles of a coach and cheerleader, recognizes there is no substitute for a thank you, followed by documentation of the exceptional performance. As stated, every group has those that quickly respond, willingly get involved, follow through, and exceed expectations. The late General George S. Patton when talking to young military leaders said, "There is a short distance between a pat on the back and a kick in the pants. I suggest you use both often." Indeed, during his winter march to rescue the 101st American Airborne Division at the battle of Bastogne, Patton held countless formal celebrations where he awarded field accommodations.

Emanating from the research of B.F. Skinner (1904–1990), behavior analysts have long recognized the powerful impact of the immediate consequences on learning and performance. Skinner affirmed, "The consequence of behavior determines the likelihood the behavior will occur again."[4]

Author Dr. Dale Brethover would agree. In a passage from his book, *A Total Performance System*, he wrote, "If an individual does something that leads to a satisfying result, he is likely to do that same thing again."[5] In fact, when high performance leaders build on the strengths of their group by recognizing exemplary performance, they get results faster than from focusing on weaknesses.

High performance leaders always publicly recognize those that exceed expectations and go the extra mile. They also formally document exceptional performance to make the recognition permanent. Publicly recognizing and then documenting outstanding performance encourages continued exceptional performance from the recipient, and from others as well. Because most leaders are negligent in this area, we have created a worksheet to formalize the old pat-on-the-back called the **Human Performance Improvement Worksheet**. The completed worksheet becomes part of the recipient's personnel file to make the recognition permanent.

The impact of positive reinforcement brings a likelihood of inspiring the same positive behavior, while the opposite is true for negative reinforcement. The power of reinforcement depends on three factors: the type of the reinforcement, the frequency of the reinforcement, and the timeliness of the reinforcement.

Leaders generally do not have the means to reward each instance of exemplary behavior with a tangible or monetary reward. The best form of reinforcing exemplary behavior is public recognition. Although some people say they do not like public recognition, our experience is that this is not true. Almost everyone likes public recognition, and it also has the benefit of encouraging the same or better performance in others. Thus, when someone exceeds expectations, the best course of action is to recognize them and do so in the presence of the entire work group.

The best forms of positive recognition are permanent, meaning they carry lasting value. High performance leaders document exemplary performance on the *Human Performance Improvement Worksheet* and keep it in the employee's file. Leaders review documented recognition when there is a promotional or merit increase opportunity.

The frequency of recognition is also important. The leader should not recognize every little initiative. This will make the occurrence of public and documented reinforcement too frequent and render it meaningless. The leader should use public recognition and the *Human Performance Improvement Worksheet* only for exemplary performance, to preserve the impact of such recognition.

The best timing of positive recognition is immediately after the exemplary performance occurs. This way the performer knows immediately that the leader noticed their behavior or performance and there is no confusion about why the employee was recognized.

High performance leaders all have egos and many have strong personalities. Yet, they have the self-confidence necessary to allow them to show humility. Indeed, when praise and recognition come, the true high performance leader deflects the praise to the team and the individuals that helped the leader succeed. Phrases like, "I know perfectly well," "I did it," "I was the first to do it," and "I was the one who told them to do it," are not part of the true high performance leader's vocabulary. In high performance leaders, humility is a sign of strength and self-confidence, not weakness. Basking in glory without recognizing others is unacceptable. It costs nothing to deflect credit to the team.

The third and fourth parts of *Encourage* are more difficult. As stated, when leaders involve everyone in the direction, some will fly and deserve a pat-on-the-back, while others resist and need a kick in the pants. Leaders must deal consistently and fairly, with those who do not perform. The high performance leader must not only reinforce exemplary performance, but be a human performance problem solver, a performance environment builder, and occasionally a disciplinarian.

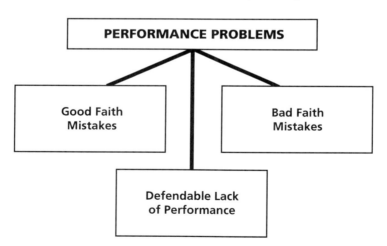

To play these roles, the high performance leader must realize that performance issues fall into three categories: **good faith** mistakes, **defendable** lack of performance, and **bad faith** mistakes. The leader must not only have the wisdom and patience to detect the difference, but the knowledge to handle each situation differently and appropriately.

An organization that continually strives to improve makes more mistakes than a stagnant organization. The trick is not making the same mistake twice. It is essential that leaders know how to identify and handle a *good faith* mistake if they seek to preserve a continuous improvement environment.

When I was the newly assigned Supervisor on the chassis line, my Utility Man was Charlie Ott. Charlie was from Harlan County, Kentucky, had not finished 6th grade, and never wore his teeth to work. Nevertheless, he was an excellent worker who always tried to help his group improve performance. One day he noticed that the people tightening the shock absorbers on each side of the line, took a long time to complete their job cycle. As a result, they were always rushing and invading the job space of the next Operator. To help them, Charlie switched the air guns to speed up the cycle time. Unknown to him, however, was that the faster guns could not achieve the torque control needed in this application.

The next week, I was called up to the quality audit area and severely criticized for many critical, safety-related, quality defects on the chassis. It seems the torque on the shock absorber connecting bolts and nuts was not correct. My boss in his usual bravado said, "Find the cause and fix it immediately, and if someone screwed up, fire them."

When I discovered what Charlie had done, my first impulse was to yell and blame him. I felt like saying, "Don't you ever change anything again without asking me first." As I approached, I could see the pain in his eyes. Charlie greeted me and said, "Jack, I guess I really messed up this time!"

My response even surprised me. I said, "No, Charlie, I want to thank you for trying to improve the job. Don't worry; I am sure you made this mistake because of trying to improve the line and out of good faith." Then I asked Charlie how the mistake happened. We discussed why he made the mistake and how we could avoid anyone else ever making this same mistake again. As a result, we identified all the torque sensitive air guns on the line with a red warning label and a start of shift check to assure proper torque. Overall torque control improved significantly.

Later that week, my General Supervisor made a rare visit to the line to ask me, "Who screwed up and did you fire them?"

I told my new boss, "It is my fault. The torque guns were changed as part of my instructions to the crew to try new methods to improve performance." I promised that we would never have the torque problem again. Charlie and the rest of the group heard him verbally attack me. From then on, I had their complete support. Charlie continued to strive to improve the line, and we continued to achieve quality and productivity records.

Almost by accident, I learned how to handle *good faith* mistakes and that most improvement follows mistakes. As Bob Jones, the so-called emperor of golf said, "I never learned anything from a match that I won; I got my golf education from drubbings."

When an employee is trying to do the job or trying to improve the job, and in so doing, takes an action that turns out to be a mistake, this is a *good faith* mistake. A high performance leader expects people to try new approaches, make decisions, take initiative, and yes, make mistakes. In turn, the leader must respond by thanking employees for their efforts, acknowledging that they made a mistake—a *good faith* mistake—and focusing energy on ensuring the same mistake will not occur again. Again, the *Human Performance Improvement Worksheet* will help uncover ways to avoid future mistakes by examining the performance environment, the clarity of expectations, the adequacy of training, and the appropriateness of the tools, systems, etc.

If a leader responds to a *good faith* mistake by embarrassing or disciplining the employee, then that employee and others in the group will stop trying to improve to avoid making mistakes. Human nature tells us that the best way to avoid mistakes is to do nothing at all. The result will be a work group that says, "I come in, do as I am told, and go home. Two years, three months, and five days from now, I can retire." This workforce will never compete in the global market.

The high performance leader must establish an environment where people freely and openly admit mistakes, knowing that if they are *good faith* mistakes, the leader will respond properly—not with negative outcomes—but with praise and a problem-solving approach.

Sometimes performance is neither exemplary nor *good faith*; it is performance that simply does not meet expectations. This is when the high performance leader becomes a human performance problem solver.

The leader must first understand there are two factors controlling performance, the performer and the performance environment. A proper performance environment consists of three components. They are: clear understanding of responsibilities and expectations, training to build the skills to fulfill responsibilities and expectations, and the opportunity to perform, which consists of time, tools, resources, and materials necessary to do the job.

Most performance problems, when actual performance does not rise to the level of expected performance, are the product of an incomplete work environment. High performance leaders recognize their role in putting a complete or proper work environment in place, to maximize the likelihood that people will succeed and meet expectations.

The high performance leader understands *defendable* lack of performance. This means that an employee has not met expectations and has not performed to expectations because of a deficiency in the work environment. The goal when actual performance does not match expected performance is to reduce or eliminate the gap. When the gap is *defendable*, the reasons for the gap in performance are due to a lack of understanding, ability, or opportunity. These are "can't do" performance issues. Such performers could not perform even if they wanted to. It is the leader's responsibility to correct the performance environment.

A *bad faith* mistake occurs when a leader or employee does not perform as desired even though there were clear expectations, adequate training, and sufficient opportunity. This is a "won't do" problem, or a *bad faith* mistake. Fortunately "won't do" or *bad faith* mistakes comprise a small percentage of performance issues. Nonetheless, it is very important that the leader address *bad faith* mistakes consistently and appropriately. There must be negative consequences for *bad faith* mistakes.

A revealing story about poor performance was told by a former United Steel Workers Local President from Northern Michigan. The story is about white rabbits. In Northern Michigan, there is a species of rabbit called the snowshoe rabbit or hare. The snowshoe is a large, fast, and tasty rabbit. In the winter when there is usually snow on the ground, the rabbits are white. In the summer when the snow is gone, their color changes to brown. Because of this change, there is a huge opportunity in March or April called "first thaw." The snow is gone but the rabbits are still white. On this special occasion, all rabbit hunters in Northern Michigan get a holiday to go hunt for white snowshoe rabbits.

Just as white rabbits stick out when they do not change color to match the environment, so do leaders and employees who do not change to adapt to the new high performance work environment. A high performance environment requires that leaders and employees be trained, verified, follow operating procedures, become involved in continuous improvement, and use prescribed processes and tools. Some naturally resist and after a fair opportunity to change, become white rabbits.

The first inclination of white rabbits in a brown environment is to hide—and they do. White rabbits hide together, eat lunch together, ride to work together, and socialize together. I remember "the terrible three" from my early job, all drinking coffee together and complaining about my promotion to General Supervisor ahead of them. However, you cannot hide from a system that demands accountability, use of visible tools, and provides informal and formal evaluation techniques.

The next inclination for white rabbits is to run. White rabbits will work harder at avoiding doing the job correctly, than those doing the job correctly. Rabbits run fast, but cannot run for long. As any experienced rabbit hunter knows, they run in a big circle. Soon they stop running and the head white rabbit, usually the loudest and ugliest of the bunch, turns and says, "On behalf of my fellow white rabbits, I am not doing it."

The role of the leader is to shoot this rabbit. If the leader makes an exception, then the head white rabbit will do what all rabbits do well. They will multiply. Before the leader knows it, there will be white rabbits popping up all over saying, "If that one doesn't have to follow standard operating practices, then why should I have to follow them?" Henceforth, the discipline needed in a high performance organization will be lost.

Handling performance issues in a consistent and appropriate manner is often the weakest skill set of leaders. Some leaders fail to recognize and formally document exceptional performance. Consequently, the exemplary performance may stop as those going the extra mile believe the leader did not notice or care. Leaders who shoot people for *good faith* mistakes create an environment where employees are unwilling to take initiative on the job. Additionally, leaders mistakenly shoot people for "can't do" performance deficiencies, when the leader fails to provide and document a complete work environment (including clear expectations, sufficient training, and adequate time, tools, material, and resources). Finally, some leaders ignore *bad faith* mistakes, which leads to rampant disregard for consistency, essential operating practices, and use of prescribed process tools. As Bob Web, the Local United Steel Workers President said to me in conclusion to his story, "Jack, we've got some leaders that are not only tolerating white rabbits, they are feeding them."

Leaders are so weak in properly handling performance issues of all kinds, that we at Workplace Transformation, Inc. developed a second function for the *Human Performance Improvement Worksheet*. Our worksheet is also one of the three tools used in the third step of the formal Continuous Improvement process, which is discussed in Part Three of this book.

The *Human Performance Improvement Worksheet* assures the leader understands and completes all parts of providing a proper work environment. It provides a way for leaders to recognize and document exemplary performance. The worksheet helps leaders react correctly to a lack of performance. When there is a performance deficiency, the worksheet asks the leader to:

- **describe** the performance issue
- **discuss** the performance issue with the employee
- **decide** whether the mistake is *defendable* ("can't do") or *bad faith* ("won't do")
- **document** the actions taken to fix the performance environment for *defendable* lack of performance or the consistent and appropriate negative consequences for *bad faith* mistakes

"Consistent consequences" means that there will be consequences every time a *bad faith* performance issue occurs. Even your best leader or operating employee will face consequences for failing to use the systems and tools or choosing not to meet expectations in your high performance organization. Putting past performance aside, any employee who does not perform to expectations by following best practices to do the job also faces consequences.

"Appropriate consequences" means the form and extent of the consequences should match the severity of the performance issue and the performance history of the performer. If a leader cancels too many continuous improvement meetings and another leader refuses to use the Continuous Improvement process at all, the consequences are different based on the severity of the performance issue. If an employee forgets to put on safety glasses and another drives a forklift truck over the posted speed and injures a colleague, the consequences are different according to the severity of the performance problem.

If a leader implements all but one of the systems of a high performance organization and another leader refuses to implement any of the systems, the consequences would be different based on the performance history of the leader. If an excellent employee forgets to do a quality check for the first time and another employee chronically forgets the quality check, again the consequences are different based on the performance history of the employee. For most represented employees, the appropriate discipline or consequences are mandated by a pattern in the collective bargaining agreement.

As with positive reinforcement, negative reinforcement should occur as soon as possible after the *bad faith* performance issue. The consequence follows immediately after the leader describes the performance issue, discusses it with the employee, completes the *Human Performance Improvement Worksheet*, and decides if the performance problem was a "won't do" performance issue.

In summary, high performance leaders have many expectations and responsibilities for employee performance in the *Encourage* stage. Leaders must get everyone involved. They must formally recognize those that willingly get involved and go the extra mile, which provides reinforcement for the performer to repeat the exceptional performance and for others to do the same. Leaders recognize and handle *good faith* mistakes properly, capturing improvement following the mistake without dampening initiative. Leaders must make responsibilities and expectations clear, document them, provide training to other leaders and employees, verify their skills, and provide the time, tools, resources and material necessary for them to perform. Finally, the leader must stand up to those who choose not to perform in spite of a proper work environment. Leaders must consistently respond to "won't do" problems in a timely fashion with appropriate negative consequences to preserve the discipline of a high performance organization.

The positive results from handling human performance correctly are enormous. Exceptional performance is more prevalent because of positive reinforcement. Continuous improvement occurs because of preventing the reoccurrence of *good faith* mistakes and correcting the performance environment to prevent defendable lack of performance. And finally, *bad faith* mistakes will soon disappear when consequences are given to the white rabbits, to either change their color or career rather than multiply and destroy the high performance environment.

➲ High performance leaders get everyone involved in the move to high performance.

➲ High performance leaders welcome feedback and good faith dissent and surround themselves with people brave enough to disagree.

➲ High performance leaders recognize exemplary performance and consistently and appropriately address mistakes and performance problems.

Notes

1 Patrick Lencioni, *The Four Obsessions of an Extraordinary Executive* (San Francisco: Jossey-Bass, 2000).

2 David Maraniss, *When Pride Still Mattered: A Life of Vince Lombardi* (New York: Simon & Schuster, 1999).

3 Patrick Lencioni, *The Five Temptations of a CEO* (San Francisco: Jossey-Bass, 1998).

4 B. F. Skinner, *About Behaviorism* (New York, NY: Random House, Inc. 1974).

5 Dale N. Brethover, Ph.D., *A Total Performance System* (Kalamazoo, Mich.: Behaviordelia., 1972) 4–7.

9

Leadership Direction: Enable

> Leaders are effective not because they are the experts but because their employees are.

The fourth sequential "E," **Enable**, means developing people by providing the training, resources, and systems necessary to prepare them to manage their piece of the business. High performance leaders recognize that the only lasting competitive advantage today is a skilled, engaged, and responsible workforce. In order to *Enable*, the leader must stop telling and start teaching by fulfilling four sequential leadership expectations.

The first part of *Enable* is simply to recognize that preparing others is your main responsibility. The products of high performance leaders are high performance employees. The key to long-term success is attracting, selecting, and developing the right people. The leader's eventual objectives are to be free from day-to-day performance issues, focused on strategic challenges, and able to move on to another position without any loss of momentum.

Through enabling others, true, high performance leaders learn that the greatest satisfaction comes from helping others succeed rather than from succeeding themselves. These leaders recognize that as those they lead become stronger, they also become stronger. High performance leaders do not fear those who are more talented. They seek out the most talented team and build from there. They recognize that continual improvement comes only from people and that people are the only lasting competitive advantage. Most importantly, they know that they cannot afford to frustrate and waste talented people by micro-managing them.

In sports, every coach recognizes the obvious, that he or she is not the one who makes the plays on the field. Success or failure lies in the hands of the frontline players. Success of the frontline players depends on the coach's direction and strategy. The coach's duty is to recruit or draft the right players, to develop players' skills, and to provide a sound game plan.

As a coach and teacher, the high performance leader recognizes his or her product is people. This sounds like common sense, but most leaders fail to make this leap of logic from thinking that they make steel, automobiles, or cement to understanding their role is to build people who make steel, automobiles, or cement.

The route of the problem is most coaches were once good players. Therefore, they are unable or unwilling to make the transition from doer to leader. Many leaders see themselves as the one who will step in to save the day, when in fact they are unable to be everywhere at once. The problem manifests when employees know the leader will step in; they learn and become more than willing to sound the alarm and sit back and watch the leader take over. Instead, effective leaders enable others and in a high performance organization, the Lone Ranger does not ride again.

The second part of *Enable* is: never miss an opportunity to train. It is true that most training happens on the field or on the job, not in the classroom. Most training takes only minutes occurring unexpectedly or spontaneously, as opposed to hours spent in a classroom.

In every industry and in every country where we have worked, we have observed employees coming to their leader with questions. The questions always resemble the following:

> Is this part good?
> Did I do this right?
> What tool should I use?
> Is this report OK to send?
> Will you approve this?

Unfortunately, many Supervisors unwittingly respond to the questions with an answer. The golden rule in the *Enable* phase is, "You never respond to a question from your employees about their job with an answer, you respond with a set of questions instead."

Examples of proper responses to an employee question would go as follows:

Employee:	Is this part good?
Leader:	What do you think?
Employee:	I do not know.
Leader:	Where would we find the specifications?
Employee:	They are in the quality specifications book.
Leader:	Good, we will get it together. What should we measure?
Employee:	Measure these five dimensions with a caliper and visually check the location of these two holes.
Leader:	Good, how would we measure the dimensions?
Employee:	We would measure dimensions with these calipers.
Leader:	How would we assure the visual requirements?
Employee:	We would compare it to the master and count holes.
Leader:	Great, now let me watch you do the inspection. Is the part good?
Employee:	Yes, we can ship the part.
Leader:	I agree. Now, can I count on you to make these decisions correctly on your own from now on?
Employee:	Yes, you can.
Leader:	Great. Call me only if you go through these steps and are still unsure about shipping a part. We will resolve it together. Congratulations on learning how to assure quality using the quality manual and master. I will update your records and verify you on assuring visual and dimensional quality.

This training approach may take a few more minutes once; however, it will save hours in the future. Failure to make this simple change in the way you provide direction is fatal to employee development. We have actually heard leaders saying, "I do not have time to train my people because I spend all my time making decisions and answering questions on the shop floor." What irony! Until you develop the patience to help others take action, rather than do it for them, you will never move beyond *Enable* to *Empower*. This approach applies to all levels. For example:

Supervisor:	Should I discipline the employee?
Leader:	What do you think?
Supervisor:	I do not know.
Leader:	What tool should we use to make the determination?
Supervisor:	The Human Performance Improvement Worksheet.
Leader:	Good, we will get it together. What should we do first?
Supervisor:	Describe the actual versus expected performance and the impact.
Leader:	Good? What is next?
Supervisor:	Describe whether the expectations were clear, training adequate, and opportunity to perform were in place
Leader:	What comes next?
Supervisor:	We would ask the employee questions to help us determine if the performance environment: expectations, training, and opportunity were in place.
Leader:	Great, what if they are not in place?
Supervisor:	I must fix the performance environment and document the improvements.
Leader:	I agree. What if the performance environment is in place and the employee chose not to perform?
Supervisor:	There must be clear, consistent, and appropriate consequences or discipline for this occurrence and any further occurrence.
Leader:	Great. Call me only if you go through the Human Performance Improvement Worksheet with the employee and you are still unsure of what to do. We will resolve it. Now can I count on you to use the worksheet whenever performance does not meet expectations before you come to me?
Supervisor:	Yes, you can.

I remember when I was showing my daughter Amanda how to play the piano. I started out at the keyboard, demonstrating and preaching. We made little progress.

She finally said, "Unless you move over and let me do it, I will never learn. I do not want to watch you anymore." I realized that I needed the patience to watch her struggle, make mistakes, and help her play, not play for her. It was time to move past *Example* and *Encourage* to *Enable*.

The third part of *Enable* is to expect continual learning, skill verification, and versatility, and then provide the time and resources for training and development. If you do not expect people to develop, like a self-fulfilling prophecy, they will not develop. If you expect employees to train, verify their skills, cross-train, learn to solve problems, and be involved in continuous improvement, then you must provide time for training and involvement during the workday.

While practicing law in the early 1980s I moved from a large, silk-stocking law firm and formed a small two-person firm. We hired a secretary who could type fast. I told her that I expected her to learn to use our new Apple computer. To my dismay, she continued to do her work on the typewriter and revisions were made with whiteout tape. Our new secretary was resisting the change to computerized typing, electronic pleadings, and electronic filing. Amy said, "I am too busy to spend time playing with the computer."

We were at a standstill until I scheduled Amy and myself to attend a three-day computer training class. Next, I insisted that Amy spend the first two hours of every day working on the computer. Amy's response was, "If you want to pay me to learn the computer, it's your money."

Four months later, all the work in the office was done on the computer and we retired the typewriter. As our firm grew to seven lawyers, by edict, all the attorneys were making their own revisions. Our business level grew and Amy's response was predictable, "I do not know how we ever survived without the computer."

In over twenty years of developing high performance workplaces, we have found a universal truism. For every hour of job-related training and development, the company gets at least one hundred hours back in improved employee productivity, as well as improved quality and safety performance. For every hour employees work on solving problems or implementing projects in pursuit of continuous improvement, the company gets back at least one hundred times the total cost of that hour in improved quality, productivity, and safety.

True high performance leaders recognize that the time spent on training, development, and involvement in continuous improvement is value-added time. The short-term cost cutters lose out on an inestimable contribution from their only long-term competitive advantage—a well-trained and engaged workforce—simply to save one hour of training time.

High performance leaders provide the resources to carry out the task. They seek agreement on the challenge, they ask what employees need to meet the challenge, they provide the resources, they offer their help, and then they insist on successful completion. Many false leaders point out the challenge, but do not provide the resources. Then, in order to protect themselves, they blame others for failure to meet the challenge.

The fourth part of *Enable* is to provide systems with clear boundaries. Everyone must have boundaries to work within. Effective boundaries are quantifiable and most often involve time, money, and procedures. Providing clear boundaries is a precondition before moving beyond *Enable* to successful empowerment.

I was involved in an initiative to remove Inspectors and move responsibility for quality to the operating workforce in the newly refurbished Cadillac Livonia Engine Plant. This change was part of a total change effort aimed at high performance called the Livonia Opportunity. Moving quality responsibility to the Operators sounded like the right thing to do. We started by training Operators on the quality specifications and gauges they would use to check the parts. Next, we told the Operators, now called "Quality Operators," to shut down any operation that was producing off-quality parts. Although we provided the skills, we did not provide the system with clear boundaries.

The result was unavoidable, and in retrospect, predictable. We suffered some serious and unnecessary production delays and came dangerously close to shutting down the Cadillac assembly plant on several occasions. It was a serious dilemma. We did not want to add Inspectors and take the product quality responsibility away from the Operators. We did not want to eat crow and tell Operators not to shut down the line for quality problems, as our credibility with them would evaporate.

The solution was to create a quality system with specified actions and clear boundaries. For example, our current quality system called for dimensional inspection for the first piece, last piece, and every tenth piece in between. Every time a defect occurred, the line shut down, idling 230 employees. The new quality system not only empowered the employees to control quality and shut down the line, but also gave them clear boundaries of when to shut it down. Examples of the boundaries we described are as follows:

- If you find a defect, measure the next ten pieces and if they are all OK then continue production.
- If you find another defect in the next ten pieces, check your running parameters and reset them to the prepared script for that product and again measure the next ten pieces.
- If you do not find another defect, continue production.
- If you find another defect, then shut down the line and call for help.

The result is a matter of record. The Livonia Engine Plant soon became the most productive and highest quality engine plant in the corporation. The lesson here is that leaders must assure that all systems, such as quality, upkeep, job placement, and capital expenditure, have specific quantifiable boundaries within which employees are empowered. These boundaries grow as employees gain skill and experience.

➲ High performance leaders build people and never pass up a training opportunity, trying to be the expert.

➲ High performance leaders have high expectations and provide the resources to achieve those expectations.

➲ High performance leaders recognize the need for clear systems and boundaries in preparation for successful empowerment.

10

Leadership Direction: Empower

Like the baton in a relay race, authority must be
passed to others to win the high performance race.

The fifth and final sequential "E" is **Empower**. For a leader, it means to let go and
give others the authority and ownership to manage their piece of the business. *Empower* has four steps.

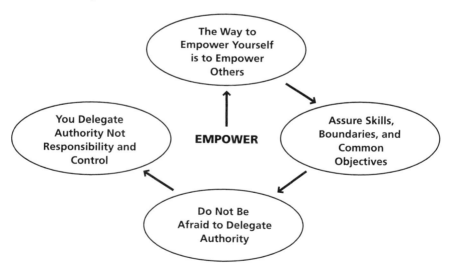

The first part of *Empower* is to recognize that the only way to free yourself to do
your job is to free others to do theirs. When we see corporate Vice Presidents calling
each of their manufacturing plants every day to get daily production numbers and
Production Plant Managers calling to see if a machine started up on the second
shift, what we are witnessing is "The Peter Principle."[1] The Peter Principle states

that everyone rises to their level of incompetence. This means that they still do work from their previous position instead of their new job. Laurence Peter, who created the principle, did not know about the five E's of leadership Direction so he thought the fate of incompetence was inescapable.

Leaders become incompetent only when they are unable to trust others to do their jobs, and end up doing some of it themselves. Such leaders have not succeeded in sequentially following the five E's of leadership from *Envision* through to *Empower.* Doing the work of those they lead takes away time from the leaders' own responsibilities for implementing high performance, developing people, pursuing strategic initiatives, and insuring future competitiveness. The result is that nobody is steering the ship, and just like the speeding Titanic, the organization will strike an iceberg and sink.

For example, a Paper Mill Manager left a critical new customer in a conference room for three hours while he ran down to oversee recovery from a paper break on a paper machine. The frustrated customer took their business elsewhere and said as he left the conference room, "If they cannot fix a paper break without the Mill Manager, we do not want them making our paper." The loss of this potential customer resulted in substantial layoffs. Later that day we asked the Mill Manager, "What did you do on the floor?" He said, "I watched them fix the machine." Then we asked him, "Why?" He said, "I had to make sure they were working on it and if my boss calls, I had better be there."

Some defensive, ineffective leaders say, "It is easier in the short-term, not to trust anyone and try to oversee all key activities yourself." However, this means you must do their job and as well as yours. This means you will be solely responsible. As operating issues have more immediacy than strategic issues, the leader's job is the one left undone. This means the leader will become the bottleneck, trying to do the job of several people on the team.

The answer is to set up clear expectations, train others, develop clear systems with quantifiable boundaries, and then *Empower* others and hold them accountable. Moving to an empowerment style of leadership is difficult; however, it is essential for high performance. There is no alternative.

This is in sharp contrast to most organizations where so-called leaders and workers come to work, do only what they are told to do, and go home. I remember the remarks of the late General Motors Chairperson, Richard C. Gerstenberg, at his 1974 retirement party. He confessed, "I remember when I became a Supervisor and I just reacted to the daily issues, confident the General Supervisor was guiding the ship. I remember when I became General Supervisor; again, I just reacted to daily issues, confident the Superintendent was guiding the ship. I remember when I became Plant Manager; again, I just reacted to daily issues, confident the Vice

President of Manufacturing was guiding the ship. Now that I am retiring as the Chairman of the Board, I am still looking for the person who is guiding the ship."

In today's rapidly changing, competitive world market, your company will not exist long without developing and empowering the people who work there. The front line workforce manages building the product or providing the service as well as the daily schedule and concerns. The first-level leadership develops the front-line workforce, and manages continuous improvement efforts. Mid-level leadership manages large operational issues and strategic changes in how things are done. Top leadership must be strategic and focus on what the organization does, where it is done, and for whom it is done.

The second part of *Empower* is assuring that three key elements are in place before empowering others. As a leader, you can reap all of the benefits of empowerment, namely ownership, responsibility, productivity, continuous improvement, and have time to fulfill your role without many growing pains. The key is to carefully assure that employees have the necessary skills, know the boundaries, and share common objectives with you before you *Empower* them.

Just recently, I learned again, the importance of common objectives. My former stockbroker convinced me to *Empower* him to make several trades to buy and sell stocks his company recommended. He would set a profit and loss price and when one stock would sell either making a profit or incurring a loss, he would buy another. After six months, I realized the total value of my portfolio had gone down fifteen percent but I had made thirty trades costing me one hundred dollars each.

Before you *Empower* another person or group, always ask the key questions. "Do they have the skills to do this? Do they have clear boundaries within which they can act alone? Do they have the same objectives as me?"

The third part of *Empower* is the ability to let go when the situation dictates. Some leaders are seemingly incapable of getting out of the way and letting others handle their job. They think that no one can do anything as well as they can or they just cannot trust others. This fatal fault is often ego related.

I remember my old Superintendent of Final Assembly. He slept in the Medical department because he was afraid to go home. He would brag about not taking a vacation in five years. He solved every problem. What he did not understand is that he had created the biggest problem of all by killing the initiative of many talented people. For six months after he retired, performance suffered, until out of necessity, others learned to do what they should have been doing all along. Soon we were performing at a higher level with the former Superintendent gone.

My favorite story to illustrate the fear some leaders have about empowering others is about a mountain climber who fell after a metal spike gave way. He clung to a branch while looking down a thousand feet. The man lifted his eyes up and shouted, "God, please help me!" A loud and deep voice answered, "Yes, I am here I will help you, but first I must know if you trust in me?" The mountain climber exclaimed, "Oh thank you, God. Yes, of course I trust in you." God said, "Well, then let go of the branch." The mountain climber then shouted, "Is there anyone else up there who can help me."

You will never get out from under the mountain of demands you face unless you let go. Once you have prepared your people, let go of the branch. You will be amazed at how high they will fly and how free you will feel to focus on strategic improvements.

When others are ready, the high performance leader insists that they act. At first, they will resist empowerment. They will come to you with their problems, fully expecting you to take them on your shoulders. You must make sure the problems they bring into your office leave with them. Give them guidance, not an escape, and make sure the ball stays in their court. The next step is theirs.

The fourth and final part of *Empower* is learning to delegate with control. *Empower* does not mean abdicate. You never *Empower* others without establishing a schedule of review to assure the person or group you empowered are moving toward success. Through scheduled reviews, you will discover if they need help or additional resources. Even though a leader can delegate authority, the leader still retains the ultimate responsibility.

Proper preparation and control are the keys to empowerment. This is where leadership Direction merges with using the proper leadership Style for different situations.

➲ Success demands that leaders share their authority with those they lead to fully utilize the talents of the workforce, and to free themselves to do their jobs.

➲ High performance leaders *Empower* others only when skills, boundaries, and common objectives are present.

➲ High performance leaders are not afraid to let go of authority because they stay in control of success.

Note

[1] Laurence J. Peter and Raymond Hull, *The Peter Principle* (London: Pan Books, 1970).

11

Leadership Styles: D1, D2, & D3

A leader must walk ahead of me and tell me what to do, walk next to me and ask for my input, and walk behind me and support what I decide to do.

To review, the first critical ingredient in effective leadership to assure success is **true** leadership. The second critical ingredient is **high performance** leadership. High performance leadership has two major parts: effectively leading people and managing systems in a disciplined manner. Effectively leading people is comprised of two major parts: **Direction** and **Style**. Leadership Direction incorporates the **five E's**. Leadership Style is utilizing **D1, D2,** and **D3**. Leadership Style complements leadership Direction in helping high performance leaders to effectively lead and engage high performance employees.

High performance leaders must use various leadership Styles depending on the situation. They consciously choose and correctly use the proper leadership Style.[1] Below, you will see the Styles described.

LEADERSHIP STYLES

D1—DIRECT: Command employees, decide and tell people what to do.

D2—DELEGATE ANALYSIS: Involve employees, decide after getting input from others.

D3—DELEGATE AUTHORITY: Empower employees, let others decide and support others.

Learning to use the correct leadership Style is a key to effectively directing people, involving them, and finally empowering them so the leadership Direction becomes theirs. This not only improves performance, but also develops a sense of pride and ownership in those empowered to fulfill their role. Like the five E's, the three D's are sequential and like all parts of an integrated system, one thing leads to another. The main leadership Style is D1 in *Envision* and *Example*. The main leadership Style is D2 in *Encourage* and *Enable*. The main leadership Style is D3 in *Empower*. The high performance leader's job is preparing people for D3 on as many aspects of their job as possible. Empowerment fully utilizes employees and frees the leaders to perform their leadership and strategic roles.

One of the most trying decisions we had to make as a family was where my oldest son should go to college. Joe was an excellent soccer player and had several scholarship offers. However, although he had a genius IQ, he was an average student at best. The proper choice of a university was integral to his long-term success.

Joe wanted to choose where he went to school, however, he was not ready to make this decision on his own. Joe knew soccer but had no idea how to select an academic environment where he could succeed. He was also stubborn. His mother and I knew he would not succeed if we forced our choice using a D1 Style. The answer for us was D2.

Joe visited several colleges with the understanding that we, his parents, would make the final decision after listening to his suggestions. We told him the reason was that we were in a better position to make a balanced choice and after all, we would be providing additional financial support.

Joe gave us his list of acceptable schools, including St. Bonaventure University in upstate New York. Although St. Bonaventure was not his first choice, the college had what Joe needed: Division 1 soccer, small campus, small student body, and personalized counseling. In addition, Coach Perry, the school's soccer coach, valued education first and athletics second. Unlike some parents, we did not allow Joe to decide on his own, as we felt he was not ready for D3 decision making on this matter. Joe's primary concern was where his high school friends were going to college.

We made the final choice, and to this day, feel we owe St. Bonaventure a debt of gratitude. This school was a major contributor to Joe's success. We have no doubt that if Joe had gone to his school of choice, he would not have graduated.

Understanding leadership Style is so important that it is a mainstay in leadership training and assessment. Detailed case study and participant demonstration is necessary to assure that each leader understands when and how to use each Style of leadership.

WHEN TO USE EACH STYLE OF LEADERSHIP

D1
Direct
- Unimportant
- No Input Needed
- No Alternative

Remember
Do not waste people's time by involving them in unimportant things.

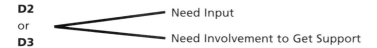

D2
or
D3
- Need Input
- Need Involvement to Get Support

Remember
Avoid making decisions without adequate information. Avoid answering questions without asking what the employee would do.

D2
Employee
Involvement
(Delegate Analysis)
- Boundaries Cannot be Identified
- Not Enough Skills
- Lack of Common Objectives

Remember
If you are in doubt about D2 or D3, use D2 or expand the group to get needed skills.

D3
Employee
Empowerment
(Delegate Authority)
- Boundaries Can be Identified
- Skills in Place or available
- Common Objectives

Remember
Use D3 when you are ready to fully utilize the workforce and free up your time to do your job. Use D3 with you present, when you and the group have different and needed information.

HOW TO USE EACH STYLE OF LEADERSHIP

What you must cover with those you lead when using each leadership style

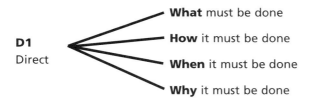

D1
Direct

What must be done

How it must be done

When it must be done

Why it must be done

Remember
You can use D1 on What, When, and Why and D2 on How to gain support, if necessary.

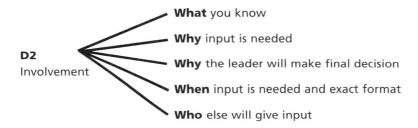

D2
Involvement

What you know

Why input is needed

Why the leader will make final decision

When input is needed and exact format

Who else will give input

Remember
Every D2 becomes a D1, once the decision is made. Tell those you involved, What, How, When, and Why.

D3
Empowerment

What you know

Why empowerment

Boundaries (time, money, procedures)

Statement of Support

Frequency of Review

Remember
You must stay in contact to assure success and support the delegated decision, even if those empowered make a mistake. You can use D3 with you present, when you and the group have different expertise.

Each Style of leadership has its own nuances. For D1, it starts with an understanding that D1 is a legitimate and proper leadership Style in a high performance organization. Involving and empowering employees does not mean that everything is participative, all decisions are consensus, or teams do everything. Safety rules, customer requirements, legal requirements, corporate requirements, and using high performance processes and tools are D1 decisions.

There are some hybrid situations. For example, many times issues arise and the leader knows exactly the course of action to follow. A D1 Style would be appropriate, except where the leader wishes to train someone else to act. In this case, always use a D2 so as not to miss a training opportunity.

The part of D1 that is most often violated is involving people in unimportant issues. This is not only a waste of time, but can make a mountain out of a molehill. I remember when we celebrated a huge achievement at Cadillac Motor Company and instead of selecting a suitable award for the workforce, the leader insisted on getting input from others. Two days were wasted gathering and compiling the input from three shifts. The employees' suggestions evenly split among five awards. When the leader finally made the final selection, eighty percent of the employees were disappointed. Do not involve employees in choices that have no importance to the business. Avoid demeaning employee involvement, wasting time, and creating unneeded dissension.

There is one hybrid D1 decision that is accomplished by changing how you use the D1 leadership style. There are times when the "what," "why," and "when" are given, yet the leader wishes to involve others to get needed support. In this case, use a D1 and tell others: "what will be done," "why it must be done," and "when it must be done," and involve others in "how to get it done in time," using a D2 Style to get their input on implementation.

D2 is the primary training Style and is safe to use because you the leader make the final decision. It is important when using D2 and involving people to specify exactly the time and format for their input. Recently, I made the mistake of asking several Internal Resources for a summary from their area on Operator certification progress for an important union presentation. I told them to e-mail the summaries to me by 3 P.M. Unfortunately, I forgot to specify the computer format I wanted. So I got one response in Microsoft Word, one in Excel, one in PowerPoint, and one in plain e-mail text. It took three hours to create a PowerPoint presentation. Whose fault was it? Mine, of course, for not specifying the exact format for the summaries.

Insisting on input is a vehicle used not only to get people thinking and to get their suggestions, but also to test whether they are ready for empowerment. It is important once you get the input and make the final decision, that you tell people what you decided and why, so they can see that you considered their input and learn from your final decision-making process. After the decision is made, every D2 becomes a D1.

D3 is the only Style that can assure full utilization of the workforce and free the leader from day-to-day issues. High performance leaders understand that moving to D3 on as many issues as possible is vital to success.

Some leaders are unsuccessful at D3, because they work in companies that treat mistakes as failure instead of opportunities for improvement. Other leaders are reluctant, as they work in an environment where their boss demands that they be involved in the details. In these work environments, leadership *Example* means the leader must work excessive hours and be personally involved with every decision, instead of properly delegating to team members. Finally, employees initially uncomfortable accepting delegation will try to reverse-delegate to the leader. If the leader succumbs and allows this pattern to dominate, accountability will be lost.

Too many leaders spend too much time on day-to-day issues that their team should handle and not enough time working on strategic issues. These leaders work more and more hours a day in a doomed attempt to do the job of those they lead, as well as their own. In this case, they perform poorly on both fronts. This is a time-management crisis. Such leaders become ineffective, overburdened bottlenecks, while their employees remain underdeveloped, unaccountable, and uninvolved. The good news is that using D3 appropriately and implementing the Continuous Improvement process, will make this dilemma disappear.

Leaders must move toward D3 for each member of their team and on as many issues as they can. Leaders must resist the fear of mistakes, manage their bosses' expectation that they be personally involved, and resist turning requests for help from team members into reverse delegation.

In their 1974 landmark article in the *Harvard Business Review*, "Management Time: Who's Got the Monkey?," authors William Oncken, Jr. and Donald L. Wass tell an important story.[2] They describe how employees overburden ineffective managers through reverse delegation. Employees take the monkey off their back and transfer it to the leaders' back by e-mail, memo, and personal requests for help. Effective leaders rarely accept monkeys from those they lead, they just "feed the monkey" (offer guidance) in a review session with the employee. The employee leaves the session with the monkey, instead of leaving it with the leader. The authors provide laws and rules that are useful in the D3 leadership Style. Some of their laws and rules, paraphrased to fit a high performance organization, are as follows:

- At no time while I am helping you with your problem, project, or human performance issue, will the problem, project, or issue become mine.
- Everyone is responsible as natural owners of problems and projects in pursuit of Continuous Improvement. You may ask for my help; however, you remain the natural owner.
- Do not accept problems, projects, or issues that team members try to delegate upward and instead, give them opportunities to meet with you to "feed the monkey," as this is the best choice for both the monkey and its keeper.
- The employee closest to the problem, project, or performance issue, usually has the knowledge and skill to solve the problem, implement the project, and resolve the performance issue. Employees must be empowered to take action within clear boundaries.
- Consultation with the leader is meant to help the employee understand the problem, project, or issue, as well as the timing of the next step they must take.
- As employees solve problems, implement projects, or resolve the human performance issues themselves, they learn valuable skills and accountability.
- Every monkey (problem or project) that can not be solved or completed quickly, is either fed or shot, but never left starving. This means the leader schedules efficient reviews with natural owners of problems and projects or else shoots the monkey.
- Every monkey should have an assigned owner and feeding time.
- The number of monkeys will be below the maximum number the leader has time to feed and natural owners have time to complete.
- Peers sometimes laterally steal time from the leader, so the leader must learn to help peers with their problems, projects, and human performance issues without taking ownership of their monkeys.

Three criteria govern the correct use of D3 with the people you lead. First, you must be able to give people the boundaries within which they can make independent decisions. Boundaries include time, money, or procedures. Second, you must believe they are capable of deciding prudently within the boundaries. Finally, they must share common objectives with the leader.

The final safety net is that empowerment is not abdication. You never delegate authority and give up control of the success of the person or group to which you delegated. You always schedule timely reviews to monitor progress and discover if you need to add resources. Coach Lombardi said, "The commander alone is responsible for everything his unit does or fails to do and must be given commensurate authority. He cannot delegate his responsibility or any part of it; he may delegate a portion of his authority."

These safety nets should provide more than enough protection to allow leaders to let go. Delegation is the only path the leader can follow to save time, to become strategic, and to sleep at night.

Occasionally, while a team or individuals may have some information, the leader can offer relevant information the others do not have. In this case, using D3 with you present as a part of the group is the correct Style. In this situation, always have someone else run the meeting so you remain a participant and the group, including you, can decide by consensus.

If a leader works for a boss that demands the leader's personal involvement in details, this is a training issue. The leader must slowly pick opportunities to start telling the boss that he or she does not know, but there is someone else intimately involved. Then, have that person update the boss. Training your boss to allow you to empower others is an important step for the high performance leader. Rather than fear it, effective leaders encourage team members to interact directly with their boss.

I remember becoming Quality Control Supervisor of the final chrome inspection area at Cadillac Motor Company. This was in the days when Cadillac had the industries only copper, nickel, and chrome-plated metal bumpers. The Superintendent of Plating was notorious for trying to ship substandard chrome to meet production quotas, saying that most customers would not know the difference. My boss wanted me to "personally oversee" the final chrome inspection line. He wanted me to be the Chief Inspector, not the Supervisor.

However, I knew nothing about chrome; it all looked shiny to me. I had a lead Inspector who was excellent. Carl knew chrome; he was concerned about quality, and he knew the boundaries of acceptable chrome. I empowered him to make the final decisions on what to send to Final Assembly and to call me only if the Plating Superintendent visited the line and tried to intimidate him.

Sure enough, two weeks later my boss got a call from the Plating Superintendent saying, "Your new Supervisor is rejecting good chrome and is going to shut down the final assembly line."

When my boss called, I said, "I was not inspecting the chrome on the line, but I had a good lead Inspector and I would follow up." After visiting the line, I set up a meeting on the line for my boss, the Plating Superintendent, my lead Inspector, and me. Carl reviewed all the defects and identified several repairable bumpers, that could be fixed in time to keep the line running. I told the Plating Superintendent, that if he dealt with me instead of calling my boss, we would have saved a day. I told my boss, if he has any questions on chrome, to feel free to call Carl directly.

The best outcome was that the meeting served to train my boss. He saw how talented Carl was and never again insisted that I be personally involved.

As a part of employee development, all employees require training on the three Styles of leadership. This gives the leader and employees a common language. Employees are encouraged to ask why a leader uses a particular Style and help the leader choose the correct Style. It is better for the employee to say, "My boss uses D1 too much," or "My boss is slow to use D3," instead of, "My boss is an arrogant dictator."

Leadership Direction and Style are powerful and integrated tools. They are the keys to engaging the workforce and allowing leaders the time and freedom to perform their jobs.

➲ High performance leaders recognize when to use each Style of leadership.

➲ High performance leaders know how to use each Style of leadership by covering all of the necessary information.

➲ High performance leaders develop accountability and resist reverse delegation.

Notes

[1] D1, D2, and D3: created by *Workplace Transformation, Inc.* in 1985, derived from the "Ultimate Theory of Leadership" as presented in *One Way*, by John J. Nora, Plymouth Proclamation Press, 1990. An extension and refinement of "Situational Leadership," developed by other behavioral scientists, most notably, Rensis Likert, Fred E. Fiedler, Victor H. Vroom, Philip W. Yetton, and Kepner Tregoe, Inc.

[2] William Oncken Jr. and Donald L. Wass, "*Management Time: Who's Got the Monkey?,*" (*Harvard Business Review*, November–December 1974), 75–80.

12

The Disciplined Management of Systems

The best way to get something done is not to do it yourself or to tell others to do it; you must assure that others do it.

In review: the first ingredient in effective leadership is *true* leadership. The second ingredient is *high performance* leadership. High performance leadership is effectively leading people through Direction (the *five E's*), Style (*D1, D2, D3*), and also managing the implementation of systems in a disciplined manner. Although leading people and managing systems are seemingly different issues, they need the same skills. Leadership Direction and Style are foolproof implementation tactics for any system or tool. They assure leadership development, ownership, accountability, responsibility, and implementation through others.

Companies spend hundreds of millions of dollars partially completing one program after another. The leaders who start these programs have no idea the program is doomed before it begins. These leaders become frustrated instead of recognizing the underlying reason for the failed implementation. Meanwhile, the workforce becomes more and more resistant to change. You can almost hear employees say, "The next leader will bring new programs. We'll just play along and wait for the next leader."

What is the answer? Again, the answer is effective leadership. The leader who starts a program either assures its success or dooms it to failure. In a high performance organization, effective leaders assure full implementation of what they choose to deploy.

Effective leaders avoid the loss of credibility that comes from implementation failures. Ineffective leaders grab program after program, which partially address one or two parts of a high performance organization, yet they tout them as overall, cure-all programs. There being no shortcut to success, the program naturally fails to meet expectations.

Ineffective leaders change programs with each new gimmick or at the requests of auditors or customers. Every new program has duplication as well as different emphasis, terminology, and tools. With each passing program that fails, people become more confused and gradually lose confidence in the leader's direction. These leaders never commit to the unchanging key, adaptive, and integrated systems comprising a high performance organization. They do not realize that the systems and proven complementary tools of a high performance organization will satisfy any customer, any certification audit, and respond to any threat.

Ineffective leaders do not have the skills, energy, or courage needed in disciplined implementation. They would rather complain about the lack of implementation than fix it. Effective leaders use the skills of leadership Direction and Style in a particular order to assure implementation. The steps of disciplined implementation are as follows:

HIGH PERFORMANCE LEADERS IMPLEMENT SYSTEMS IN A DISCIPLINED MANNER

Disciplined implementation flows back and forth from *Envision*, to *Example*, to *Encourage*, to *Enable*, and to *Empower*. Paralleling this pattern, a leader involved in the disciplined implementation of systems also flows between D1, direct; D2, employee involvement; and D3, employee empowerment.

Following "understanding and commitment" (see chart), implementation starts with *Envision* and the D1 leadership Style. Sharing the direction and clearly specifying the systems and tools needed in the move to a high performance organization, the leader sets the expectation for implementation. This creates the understanding that following the Direction and using the systems and tools, is a D1 decision.

The leader must then assure implementation of the Direction and the use of the tools. This means following all the steps of disciplined implementation. Usually, the leader must make it more painful to resist than to comply, until others see the results.

The same is true when the leader decides to add a tool to augment an existing Direction or move to high performance. Once effective leaders decide a new tool is essential, timely, and not duplicative, they make it a sequential improvement of their Direction, not a change or new Direction. The key systems never change!

For some reason, leaders want to get input, have consensus, a vote, or let others decide whether to follow the path to high performance. These are not correct styles at the beginning of a change process. Yes, a leader should explain, sell, convince, and listen to dissent. However, the leader makes the decision to move to high performance for everyone. Hence, the leader does lead the way. Still, the leader can involve others in developing the implementation plan and timetable to gain support, as needed.

Ninety percent of all people need a push into high performance before they recognize that the benefits far outweigh the effort. Left to their own choice, most will not expend the energy to change, as they are too comfortable with the status quo. The only choice an effective leader gives others about learning and using the systems and tools of a high performance organization is a career choice.

Before beginning implementation of any system or tool, the effective leader is honestly able to say the following:

- I understand the process and tools.
- I agree to implement the process and utilize the tools.
- I believe in the process and tools.
- I am excited about the process and tools and those I am responsible for will feel that excitement.
- I will set the example in using the process and tools.
- I will teach others to use the process and tools.
- I will demand implementation of the process and use of the tools by others.
- I will handle those who do not choose to follow the path to high performance using the process and tools.

- I will not add new processes or tools without first assuring they are essential, there is no duplication, and the timing is right.
- I will delegate authority to others when they are ready to spread the process, and I will follow up to assure they are being successful.

The leader is among the first trained, the first to understand how a particular process or tool will strengthen the move to high performance, and the first to commit. The leader is the first to implement and the first champion of the process or tool. You cannot delegate this responsibility. If the leader does not use the process or tool, eventually no one will.

AN ORGANIZATION IS A REFLECTION OF ITS LEADERSHIP!

The steps of disciplined implementation never fail and never change. However, if you do not follow them sequentially, you will not succeed as a high performance leader. Your organization will not become high performance. Learn, commit, demonstrate, teach, involve, discipline, and delegate at the right time, and the new system becomes part of the way you do business.

➲ High performance leaders recognize that disciplined implementation does not just happen; it is led.

➲ To implement, leaders must learn, commit, demonstrate, teach, delegate, and hold people accountable, or else the implementation will fail.

➲ If something is not important enough to take to the mat, do not do it.

13

Strategic Leadership

To escape the arrows of the competitive world market, you must become a moving target.

Effective leaders develop, engage, and empower the people reporting to them. This fully utilizes the workforce and allows the leader to have the time to become **Strategic**.

Most leaders think they are strategic, when they clearly are not. Some are just copycats, trying everything others are doing. Others start duplicative or overlapping initiatives hoping something will stick. Some try to do everything at once and wonder why basic performance suffers. To be strategic, a leader must understand the strategic process and follow it step-by-step.

High performance organizations require true, high performance, and *Strategic* leadership. All top and mid-level leaders have a strategic role to fulfill. Effective leaders develop their people so the leader can spend eighty percent of their time in pursuit of strategic improvements. Remember: "The Peter Principle" explains that leaders who are over involved in the work of their employees and fail to build time for the strategic components of their job, have reached their level of incompetence.

Top or corporate leadership must focus on large strategic issues. Examples include new markets, new customers, new products, new services, new facilities, new locations, and new acquisitions that fundamentally change *what* we do, *who* we do it for, or *where* we do it. Middle or plant management must focus on smaller strategic projects. Examples include new technology, new systems, and new processes that fundamentally change *how* we do business, with the exception of the mandatory high performance pillar systems. By contrast, the role of first-level leadership is continually improving what we do today.

Behavioral expectations associated with becoming an effective leader should be clear. A leader must be a true leader to win the hearts and minds of the workforce. A leader seeking high performance must effectively lead people by providing Direction and using the proper leadership Style. A leader must assure disciplined implementation of systems, processes, and tools to assure continual improvement. A leader must be strategic to anticipate and make fundamental changes before the competition, so their group and company can compete into the future.

The strategic role is essential because you can have the best leadership, workforce, products, processes, and performance today, yet fail tomorrow. You will fail tomorrow if you are:

- making the wrong products
- providing the wrong services
- producing in the wrong country
- serving the wrong markets
- selling to the wrong customers
- using the wrong materials
- using the wrong equipment or technology
- buying from others what you should be doing yourself
- doing what you should be purchasing from others
- growing too fast
- growing too slowly
- carrying too much debt

Top, middle, and first-level leadership must all perform their roles in the organization. An example of a strategic subject, as opposed to a continuous improvement subject, comes from the world of sports. If you are the world's best pole-vaulter and go to the Olympic Games with a bamboo pole, you will lose. In terms of continuous improvement, no matter how hard you try, how much you work, or how much you improve, you will lose. However in a strategic effort, if you switch to a fiberglass pole, like all of the other athletes use, you will win the gold metal. A strategic leader never brings their team into competition with bamboo poles.

Continuous Improvement (CI), covered in Part Three of *Lead the Way,* is a process to involve all employees in ongoing incremental improvement. CI slowly improves upon what we do today, where we do it today, whom we do it for today, and how we do it today. The Strategic Planning process fundamentally changes what we do, where we do it, whom we do it for, and how we do it.

For example, in the early 1970s, we worked for a high performance carburetor manufacturer. Blinded by past success, the top leadership believed that internal combustion engines would always use carburetors and that fuel injection was a passing fad. This one strategic error led to complete company failure. The same was true for the leading maker of persimmon woods for the golf equipment industry, who did not develop metal wood technology. The same fate awaited the North American precision machining company that believed it could manually match computer controls for accuracy and flexibility; and for the basic jewelry manufacturer who believed it could compete, making standard products, on standard equipment in the United States while the competition moved basic production offshore.

A strategic leader manages the Strategic Planning process in a disciplined manner. The industrial landscape is full of the skeletons of once vibrant companies that did not understand the need for disciplined strategic planning.

The main reasons for failure in strategic planning are as follows:

- Failure to empower others so top and middle management are fatally immersed in daily performance issues, leaving leaders too little time or energy for strategic planning and strategic project implementation
- Failure to prioritize strategic initiatives and trying to do everything at once, resulting in incomplete and untimely implementation
- Failure to separate top-level strategic projects from mid-level strategic projects, resulting in the failure to empower mid-level management
- Failure to assure accountability from natural owners or review progress in completion of strategic projects
- Failure to be flexible enough to admit mistakes and modify strategic projects in the face of sudden changes in the product, customer, market, industry, or world

HIGH PERFORMANCE STRATEGIC PLANNING PROCESS

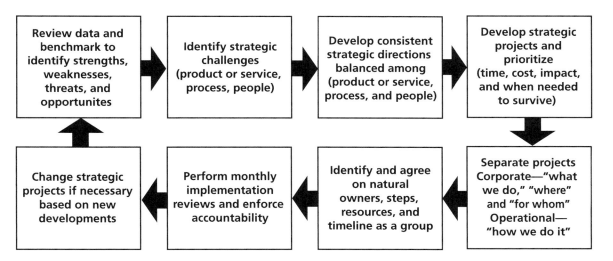

The Strategic Planning process has eight fundamental steps. The first step of strategic planning is essentially ongoing self-education. Strategic leaders recognize the need to study their products or services, the customers, the competition, the market, the industry, and the world, to identify external threats or opportunities and internal strengths or weaknesses.

Too many companies go on "benchmarking trips" without understanding the underlying reason for the trip and without a dynamic, disciplined Strategic Planning process to capitalize on information gained. The main reason for benchmarking is to provide input into the Strategic Planning process, not to copy specific approaches of those benchmarked. If you find yourself trying to do what others did in half the time, you usually cannot, and even if you could, when you get there it would be obsolete. The purpose of benchmarking is only to identify internal strengths or weaknesses and external opportunities or threats, not to be a copycat of systems and processes.

A recent industry trend portrays a painful example. Some companies have spent millions of dollars on black belts, green belts, Six Sigma, and lean manufacturing without any analysis to know if the specific tools are appropriate for their company, product, process, or their stage of development. Blindly copying General Electric or a GE clone, these companies are trying to universalize specific tools because they have reportedly worked elsewhere. Dollars are wasted, workflows are disrupted, and improvements are disappointing or temporary. The problem is not with the systems or tools, the problems occur because of a lack of integration with the five Pillars of High Performance, improper timing, mistakenly believing these sophisticated tools by themselves lead to high performance, and a mismatch with the level of sophistication of the company. The people involved in these purportedly stand-alone, yet incomplete, systems often exaggerate improvements and understate costs in order to perpetuate the process.

The second step of strategic planning is to review strengths, weaknesses, threats, and opportunities for strategic challenges. A strategic challenge identifies major changes demanded by the customer, the market, the industry, the environment, the community, the business plan, or the world.

Today, strategic challenges come from a truly global perspective. To be globally strategic, you must recognize that customers, technologies, and trends are different throughout the world. Strategic leaders must learn about products, services, competitors, markets, and industry, from sources throughout the world. Today, no Strategic Planning process should begin without information on the trends, technology, and customer needs from every corner of the world. For example, a client in Mexico recently responded to a forecasted shortage in aluminum, because of increased demand in China. Leaders need to learn from the examples of companies that were not globally strategic, like those in the U.S. telecommunications industry thinking they were being globally strategic in moving production offshore. The companies tried to sell the same mobile phones in both the United States and the European market, but their European sales crumbled. The Americans did not understand the sophistication or desires of the European cell phone user.

In the third step of strategic planning, challenges are restated as broad directions the company should follow. For example, our client in Mexico established a strategic direction to buy controlling interest in its major aluminum bar supplier, to lock in supply and price in response to the challenge of a shortage in aluminum.

The leader must also assure consistency and balance in the third step of strategic planning. Consistency means removal or change of strategic directions that violate agreed upon principles. For example, an automotive supply company had a strategic initiative to build a facility in Hungary to support Ford Motor Company simply because it was "Ford," even though it violated the company's debt principle. Moving forward with the initiative had a tragic result. Volumes fell, debt outstripped profits, and the company eventually failed.

In addition to the principles and values of High Performance, core strategic principles usually include margin, growth, and debt. Others that may be relevant include cash flow, geographic boundaries, market or customer boundaries, and core competency product, service, material, or machinery boundaries. Yearly reviews of strategic principles assure that they still make sense in our rapidly changing world.

For example, a recent client had a "core product" boundary in the steel industry that would exclude making coke and a "geographic" boundary preventing movement into the Far Eastern market. Following the recent explosive growth in China and China's huge consumption of coke, these two principles had to change.

Without this change, the price of coke and market limitation could have caused closure of some mills. Admitting a mistake and changing accordingly is far less painful than taking your mistake to the grave.

Balanced strategic directions assure all flanks are covered. Balance means addressing all of the following areas:

- products including materials, services, markets, and customers
- processes including equipment, locations, methods, and environment
- people including the move to high performance and developing or attracting the talent needed for success

The fourth step of strategic planning involves setting priorities. Many companies make a huge mistake by trying to do everything instead of doing only what is most important and doing it extremely well. Each company must identify the time and money they can devote to implementation of strategic projects. As a rule, top management and mid-management groups should have no more than three strategic projects each.

Every strategic project receives a priority number, with one being the highest priority and nine the lowest. Projects requiring little time, low cost, and having a high return, are obviously a high priority and given a one, two, or three. However, projects that determine survival may be ranked number one, even if they will take a long time to implement and cost dearly.

Prioritization continues by determining which of the high priority projects must start today to assure success. Just because a strategic project is a high priority, does not mean it has to start this year. A recent client simultaneously tried implementation of a high performance organization, entering the Asian market, acquiring capacity in Eastern Europe, implementing SAP, and going through target reductions at the behest of a large consulting firm. The results were inevitable; millions of dollars were wasted, implementation was incomplete, and performance suffered. Regrettably, many of the "high priority strategic initiatives" did not need to happen at one time to assure success.

Prioritization ends as strategic projects are timed with relativity to each other to assure serendipity, rather than having one project blocking the implementation of another. For example, a recent client in the paper industry had three high priority strategic projects: to reduce energy rates for energy purchased from the municipal utility, to add a new machine to serve a new market, and to secure work rule changes in the collective bargaining agreement to assure competitiveness with the new equipment in the new market. Obviously, getting the municipality to agree to an energy rate decrease and ratification of a modification in the labor agreement to correct unproductive work practices had to occur first. The investment in a new machine and resulting employment increase were the leverage needed to gain the support of the municipality and the union. Had the purchase of the new paper machine come first or occurred simultaneously with starting the projects to reduce energy costs and secure productive work rules, the advantage would have been lost and the government and union would not have agreed.

In the fifth step of strategic planning, the leader or team selects **natural owners** for the prioritized strategic projects selected. A *natural owner* oversees the implementation of each prioritized strategic project. Strategic projects that will fundamentally change what we do, where we do it, or whom we do it for, will have a natural owner from the top leadership group. Strategic projects that will change how we do what we are doing today receive natural owners from the mid-level or operational leadership group.

In the sixth step of strategic planning, the natural owners of strategic projects develop the major steps, timetable, and responsibilities. The top leadership team reviews the steps, timeline, responsibilities, and needed resources for input and agreement. Implementation now begins. Agreement and team commitment are essential in assuring that all top leaders are in the strategic loop. Our clients track implementation by using the same project management tool and software used in the Continuous Improvement process, as outlined in Part Three of *Lead the Way*.

In step seven, a monthly review meeting assures timely implementation of strategic projects and assures accountability from natural owners. Lack of progress because of inaction is a performance issue. Leaders only extend timelines because of new information gained during implementation.

The eighth and last step in the Strategic Planning process is to discuss current events at the monthly review meeting, to see if there is a need to change strategic projects. Changes in products, customers, competition, markets, industries, and in the world happen so fast now, that flexibility is essential.

We started in chapter one with the question, "What is the answer?" Our simple answer was: effective leadership. As Paul Harvey, the famous and seemingly ageless radio announcer says, "Now you know the rest of the story." Effective leadership is *True, High Performance*, and *Strategic* leadership. Now you know how to be a true, high performance, strategic leader! The next chapter explains how to develop the needed leadership at each level to implement the other key systems of a high performance organization.

⇨ Effective leaders recognize that they must be ready to make strategic changes to allow their strong and improving workforce to compete in the market.

⇨ Top leaders change: what we are doing, for whom we are doing it, and where we are doing it. Mid-level leaders change: how we do what we are doing today.

⇨ Strategic leadership means implementing the Strategic Planning process in a disciplined manner.

14

Effective Leadership at Every Level

When it comes to people, you get what you expect.

Now that you know how to be an effective leader yourself, you must understand and commit to the process of developing effective leaders at every level of your organization. Developing effective leaders is a long-term, never-ending, incremental improvement process that is absolutely crucial for success.

Developing leaders at all levels is a system made up of six sequential steps. There is no other way to develop the leadership that you need at every level in your organization.

Development of effective leadership at all levels occurs on two fronts; you must enhance the skills of existing leaders and turn as many as possible into effective leaders, as well as assure that exceptional leadership skills are present when hiring leaders from outside the company or promoting internal candidates into leadership positions. Over time, the result is effective leadership at all levels that is stronger than the competition.

Leadership development, like every other pillar in high performance, is a proven system. Leadership development consists of six sequential steps that cannot fail, if implemented in a disciplined manner. There is no other way to develop the leadership you need at every level of your organization.

DEVELOPING EFFECTIVE LEADERS AT EVERY LEVEL

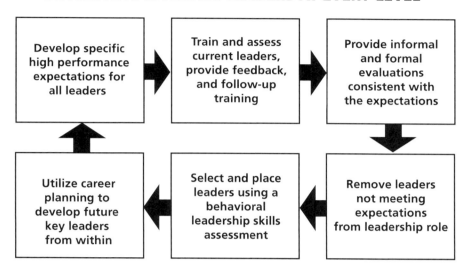

The first step is to develop specific leadership expectations for effective leaders at all levels. These typically include expectations for all leaders and specific leadership expectations for top leadership, mid-level leadership, and first-level leadership. Following are some examples.

GENERAL LEADERSHIP EXPECTATIONS

- High performance leaders will learn the skills to manage high performance processes and systems as well as the skills to lead high performance employees.

- Leaders will provide clear Direction for the group they lead using the five E's.

- Leaders will know when and how to direct, involve, and empower those they lead.

- Leaders will systematically and fairly deal with people who do not perform as expected and have the courage to do so without exception.

- Leaders will achieve a positive trend of Continuous Improvement (CI) in all key measures, and use the prescribed process and tools to achieve those results.

- Leaders will focus on Safety by: supporting the housekeeping and orderliness system, doing daily audits to find and correct unsafe conditions before injury occurs, and reducing injuries utilizing the CI process.

TOP LEADERSHIP

- Leaders will make strategic changes in what we do, who we do it for, and where we do it before the competition using a disciplined Strategic Planning process.

MID-LEVEL LEADERSHIP

- Leaders will make strategic changes in how we do things in order to meet the business plan and outperform the competition using a disciplined Strategic Planning process within the boundaries of the five pillar high performance system.

FIRST-LEVEL LEADERSHIP

- Leaders will involve the operating workforce in performance improvement and the skill verification and versatility-enhancement process.

Every high performance company develops a complete list of expectations for effective leaders. This list should come together easily now that you understand all of the components of true, high performance, and strategic leadership. Again, the expectations include results; however, the emphasis is on how the results are achieved.

The next step is to develop training for leaders to teach them how to fulfill these leadership expectations. This is not just training for training's sake. Rather, it is the basic training required for you to lead your organization into the battle to become high performance. Mandatory training modules include the following:

Initial Leadership Training
- True Leadership
- High Performance Leadership
- Effectively Leading People
    › Leadership Direction—Envisioning
    › Effective oral communication skills
    › Running efficient business meetings
    › Leadership role model—setting the example
    › Leadership Maturity Quotient
    › Getting others engaged—Encouraging
    › Recognizing exceptional performance
    › Improving performance problems
    › Preparing others and giving them responsibility—*Enable* and *Empower*
    › When and how to use the correct leadership styles
- Disciplined implementation of systems and processes

- The Strategic Planning process
- The formal, data-driven, Continuous Improvement process and tools
  - › Major performance areas and key measures
  - › Measuring performance
  - › Using diagnostic data to define specific problem patterns and needed projects
  - › Problem-solving
  - › Resolving human performance problems
  - › Project management
  - › Decision-making
  - › Using the CI portion of the Transformation Software to assure implementation and to facilitate effective CI meetings
- The JOBS skill verification and versatility system and software

A behavioral skills assessment follows the training to determine if the leader has understood enough to utilize these essential skills in the workplace. The assessment will identify whether or not a leader will need more training in some areas. In the assessment, leaders demonstrate the skills they have just learned in work related situations. Behavioral assessments are the only accurate way to assure that there has been an acceptable level of skills attainment.

Performance areas for a typical skills assessment are:

- Oral communication skills
- Written communication skills
- Problem-solving skills
- Ability to grasp and apply critical concepts
- Working effectively in a team
- Decision-making skills
- Human performance improvement skills
- Leadership skills
- Planning, prioritizing, and organizing skills

A team of trained assessors observes and numerically scores each leader's performance by consensus. Following individual feedback, those leaders who do not score well enough in a skill area to predict success, receive follow-up training. We call our follow-up leadership training LEAD, which stands for Leadership Enhancement And Development. LEAD training gives each leader a more thorough, more personalized, more experiential exposure to skills in their areas of deficiency.

Many of our most effective leaders initially had several areas where they needed LEAD training. The time it takes to develop a leader varies from individual to individual. LEAD training gives every leader a fair opportunity to develop. Leaders receive clear expectations, training, feedback, re-training as necessary, and informal and formal feedback as they apply learned skills to meet expectations in the workplace. Those who do not respond are performance problems.

The assessment process is not only a development tool for existing leaders, it is a selection tool for hiring leaders from outside the company or promoting internal candidates into leadership positions. Our findings over twenty years indicate that an interview is about sixty percent accurate, while a behavioral skills assessment is well over ninety percent accurate in predicting whether the candidate has the skills necessary for the job of leadership.

While a sound leadership skills assessment is well over ninety percent accurate in determining skill level, it does not measure character, nor does it guarantee that leaders will utilize their skills in furtherance of the high performance organization. This is why informal and formal leadership evaluations are necessary.

Ongoing informal leadership evaluations assist a company and its leaders progress to high performance. The purpose of informal evaluation is for feedback only. The only time informal evaluations become a matter of record is when an individual leader is not improving their skills in an area of identified weakness.

Informal evaluations review all expectations. For example, leaders are reviewed on: their use of the scientific, three-step Continuous Improvement process, using correct leadership Styles, consistently handling and documenting performance issues, disciplined implementation of systems, and use of the CI portion of the software.

Furthermore, an annual formal evaluation is performed in order to assure that these are leaders who can lead the way. The formal evaluation reinforces the high performance leadership expectations. Emphasis is balanced between results and how the results were achieved.

Another difference in a high performance leadership evaluation is that it provides a 360-degree viewpoint, taking the input of customers, peers, those reporting to the leader, the leader's boss, and a trained Internal Resource. As a part of the 360-degree process, the leader and Internal Resource present the formal evaluation together, without forcing employees to confront their leaders.

Almost anyone can learn the needed leadership skills. Leaders who do not develop to meet expectations following training, assessments, feedback, re-training, informal feedback, and formal evaluations, effectively make the choice not to perform. For the overall good of the company, and those working for leaders who choose not to develop, the only recourse is removal from leadership roles or from the organization. Remember the principle: in a high performance organization there is no room for ineffective leaders.

The last step in leadership development is to institute a simple but effective career planning process and form. Career development plans allow an organization to identify leaders with potential and systematically prepare them for a future key leadership position. High performance organizations evaluate future leadership needs, including replacement and growth. Then, they assess internal or external candidates for development to fill future key leadership positions. The career plan assures that each year the candidates receive training and experience necessary to prepare them for a future key leadership position.

Career planning is not just reserved for high level positions. In a high performance organization, front-line leaders have significant responsibility to implement CI and employee development. As a result, they need significantly greater skills. In many organizations, management trainee candidates with a technical degree are assessed for leadership skills. The successful candidates become familiar with the company and then spend approximately three to four years as a front-line leader.

⮑ Leadership development is a system that develops existing leaders and assures that the leadership skill level improves whenever new leaders are hired or promoted.

⮑ Developing leaders begins with specific expectations and the training to assure that leaders can fulfill the expectations.

⮑ Informal and formal evaluations on meeting high performance expectations may lead to replacement, as there is no room for ineffective leaders.

PART THREE

Engaging the Workforce in Continuous Improvement

15

Understanding Continuous Improvement

To win the race, you must progress faster
than your competitor's pace.

The formal **Continuous Improvement process** (CI) is the second pillar and the second key, adaptive, and integrated system in a high performance organization. The matching principle is: everyone must be in at least one natural workgroup pursuing CI with aligned key measures and objectives. The corresponding value is: CI comes only from people.

The term *Continuous Improvement*, is popular, although, if you ask five people to define it, you will get five different answers. Continuous Improvement has many definitions as it denotes different things to different people. Continuous Improvement is both a philosophy of "getting better every day," and an attitude of "never good enough." However, you cannot implement a philosophy or an attitude. Continuous Improvement is a scientific, three-step process. Unless you know this definition, you will not be able to implement CI, let alone intimately engage your workforce in ongoing performance improvement.

You cannot threaten people or pay people to adopt the Continuous Improvement philosophy and attitude. The philosophy and the attitude of Continuous Improvement only become the philosophy and attitude of your workforce *after* they are successfully engaged in the scientific, three-step Continuous Improvement process. When leaders implement CI in a disciplined manner and successfully involve their employees, Continuous Improvement in performance is guaranteed. Concurrently, almost like magic, the philosophy of CI, "getting better every day" and the attitude of CI, "never good enough" permeates the workforce. This phenomenon is a natural result of successfully involving your workforce in CI.

CI is a proven, fail-safe, data-driven, disciplined, motivational, and incremental improvement process that is essential to engage the workforce in ongoing performance improvement. To fully understand the Continuous Improvement process, it is helpful to understand its many characteristics.

Several of the characteristics of the CI become clear from the origins of the process. I believe that I have spent more time researching the origins of CI, as well as refining the process for business, than any other living human being. Continuous Improvement did not originate in the United States or Japan. The change that put in motion the development of CI occurred in 760 BC. This is before Christ, not before consultants!

Before 776 BC, the Greek Olympic Games were amateur events held yearly in small towns all over the Greek Empire. In 776 BC, the Games were held at Olympia for the first time. Olympia, a sanctuary built to honor their god Zeus, subsequently became a huge sports complex where Greek athletes lived and trained for months before the Olympics, held every four years.

Early Olympics at Olympia with paid athletes consisted of only the footrace. As the years passed, the pentathlon became the major Olympic event. The pentathlon developed not only fast athletes, but also those who were strong, accurate, and agile. It consisted of five events: running for speed, discus throwing for strength, javelin throwing for accuracy, long jumping for agility, and wrestling for endurance. Winners of the Pentathlon, like a god, wore a crown of wild olive branches and received significant financial reward.

The **discipline** of Continuous Improvement began at these early Olympic Games in Olympia. To enter the games at Olympia, ancient Greek athletes had to submit their bodies to the Olympic coaches for three months of rigorous training. It was intended to weed out the weaker athletes and develop the strong. Hundreds of athletes from all over the known world, worked under the watchful eyes of the strict Olympic coaches. The number of athletes decreased during the training and through competition to one pentathlon winner. Rigorous exercise, practice, strict diet, punishment for poor performance, and elimination rounds made up the extremely disciplined approach.

The **data-driven** nature of CI came from the Greek Olympic coaches. They forced the athletes to work on their weakest event, rather than practice what they were good at and enjoyed. Similarly, in CI, like early Olympic training, employees focus on their biggest problem in their worst area, not on what they are good at or want to work on. As it was for the Greek Olympic coaches, data will point to the areas needing improvement.

Centuries of success prove that CI is **fail-safe**. Greeks were the first to associate diet, exercise, practice, and consequences for poor performance, to improved athletic performance. As long as athletes followed the discipline of diet and exercise and worked on weak areas identified by coaches, their performance improved. This is also the case in CI. As long as you follow the three steps in a disciplined manner, you will sustain ongoing improvement.

This is why the length of long jumps and the speed of runners continue to improve today, well over two-thousand years later, and why it will continue to improve, forever. In business, as in sports, and in life, everything that keeps you from higher performance is either a problem to solve, a project to implement, or a human performance issue to resolve. As long as you solve the correct problems, complete the right projects, and resolve human performance issues, it is guaranteed that you will improve.

Olympic coaches and athletes unknowingly began to implement the last two steps of the scientific three-step Continuous Improvement process first. Second in the three-steps of CI is **Focused Improvement**. *Focused Improvement* means using diagnostic data to identify your biggest improvement areas, where they are, specifically what they are, and the patterns of when they occur. The Olympic coaches focused the Olympic pent-athletes to improve in the worst area of their worst event.

Step three of CI is to solve problems, improve human performance, and implement projects. Athletes that worked to resolve identified problems in their weakest event and followed the recommended diet and exercise program continued to improve.

Before they wrestled in the center arena at Olympia, the two chosen athletes in ancient Greece had survived many elimination rounds and performed well in four events. This led to the need to score and measure an athlete's total performance, to see who won. Similarly, CI is a tool with key measures in all eight major performance areas or business drivers.

As Olympic coaches began to measure the performances of each athlete, the natural next step was to begin to set up specific targets for each athlete in each event. Soon, coaches visibly posted the specific targets for all to see. Pride naturally motivated the Greek athletes to achieve their objectives.

The actions of selecting the right key measures, setting proper objectives, and visibly measuring performance toward objectives comprise the first step of CI. The thrill of achieving objectives, being in control of your performance, and understanding that you can make a difference create the **motivational force** of CI that changes the philosophy and attitude of the workforce.

While the proven, fail-safe, disciplined, data-driven, motivational, three steps of Continuous Improvement started centuries ago, coaches today use these steps to train and improve the performance of athletes throughout the world. For example, every excellent long jumper measures each jump, plots each jump on a chart to show the performance trend, and visibly tracks progress toward an established objective. The jumper's coach points out the biggest opportunities for improvement. If the coach points out the right areas to improve and the athlete has the discipline to do what is necessary to resolve the issues, performance improves—guaranteed.

Learning CI is like learning how to golf. First, you learn the major steps, like grip, stance, and swing. Next, you learn the parts of each major step. For "grip," you would learn the position of the left hand, position of the right hand, and proper grip pressure. Finally, you learn the sections of each part of each major step. Continuing with the grip example: learning the proper position of the left hand, consists of several sections, such as position of the club in the left hand, position of the fingers of the left hand, and where the V in between your left thumb and forefinger points in the left-hand grip. To assist in learning CI, we have divided it into major steps, the parts of each step, and the sections of each part. The three major steps of CI in the proper sequence are as follows:

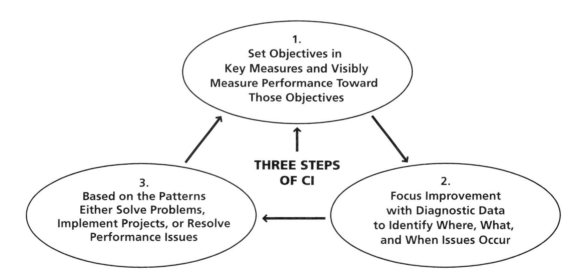

The first recorded implementation of CI to engage an entire industrial workforce occurred in 1980 in Cadillac Motor Car Division's Livonia Engine Plant. The Livonia Plant Planning Team, which I had the privilege to lead, was given the responsibility to create the "Livonia Opportunity."[1] The Livonia Opportunity was a comprehensive change plan to transform a very traditional work environment into a world class and high performance work environment.

Part of the Livonia Opportunity was to create a system to engage all employees in ongoing improvement. The Livonia plant leadership and employees implemented a crude, but effective, five-step process. The process at the Livonia Engine Plant combined learning from sports training, several plant tours, management by objectives, the theory of motivation, problem-solving techniques, project management techniques, and performance management principles.

At Workplace Transformation, Inc., following the Livonia Engine Plant experience and for over two decades, we have perfected this scientific method for fail-safe implementation in business. We improved the original five-step process countless times and have recently refined the process to three steps for ease of understanding and implementation. This proven process has and will work in any company, industry, or nation of the world.

The Continuous Improvement process builds a strong organization and yields **incremental** improvement. It is like trying to build up your body by lifting weights. As you get stronger, you slowly add weight to the bar. The incremental nature of CI is in contrast to strategic changes or short-term directed improvement efforts that quickly and dramatically change what you do or how you do it. Dramatic one-time changes will not make you strong—they just keep you in the game. Only the discipline of incrementally getting better at what you do every day, will make you strong. Recall the differentiation between a strategic effort and CI. Just as CI alone will assist but not ensure victory, providing fiberglass poles instead of bamboo poles to pole-vault jumpers will dramatically improve their performance, but not make them stronger pole-vaulters.

Accordingly, if you need a fifty percent increase in productivity in just six months to satisfy your biggest customer, CI alone will not suffice. You will need to implement a short-term, directed improvement effort. Likewise, if you need to expand your customer base to stabilize your volumes in the next three years, you will need a major strategic change to survive. Still, every day of every year you need to engage your workforce in CI. Continually improving faster than the competition is what will secure the future for you and everyone in your organization.

Greek storywriters tell of the weight lifter who was the strongest athlete in ancient Greece. He could lift a fully-grown bull on his shoulders and then up over his head. His Greek coaches had him lift the bull in front of other athletes to inspire them to pursue incremental improvement, even if they probably could never match his feat. As the coaches explained, "This bull was born when this weight lifter was twelve years old. Every day he lifted the bull over his head. As the bull slowly got bigger, the weight lifter slowly got stronger."

Continuous Improvement is the second pillar of high performance because effective leadership is a precondition to successful implementation. In the first pillar, leadership development, leaders learn the skills necessary to implement CI in a disciplined manner. CI flows to all levels in a company and requires effective leadership at every level.

When effective leaders successfully engage an entire workforce in CI, and the philosophy and attitude of CI spreads throughout a company, month after month, and year after year, all of the company's performance key measures will improve. Although CI is a long-term and never-ending process, it yields quick, visible, and endless improvement. The more skilled you and other company leaders become at disciplined implementation of CI, and the more employees that are intimately involved, the more improvement you will get!

➲ Continuous Improvement is an attitude, a philosophy, and most importantly, a scientific, three-step process.

➲ The three-step Continuous Improvement process is a proven, fail-safe, data-driven, disciplined, motivational, and incremental improvement process.

➲ CI builds a strong organization by engaging all employees in the daily pursuit of performance improvement.

Note

[1] John J. Nora, Robert Stramy and Ray Rogers, *Transforming the Workplace*, (Princeton, NJ: Princeton Research Press, 1985).

16

Setting Objectives in Key Measures

If you measure the right things, the right things will improve.

The first step in the formal, three-step Continuous Improvement process is to set proper objectives in the correct key measures and visibly measure performance toward those objectives. To do this successfully, it is important to implement the following five sequential parts of step one.

STEP ONE OF CI HAS FIVE PARTS

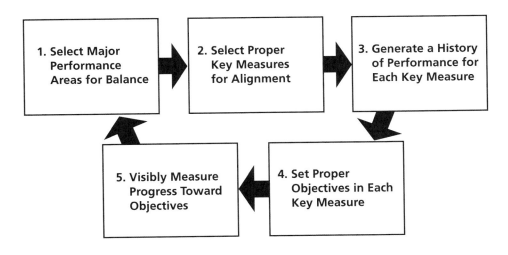

1. Select Major Performance Areas for Balance

2. Select Proper Key Measures for Alignment

3. Generate a History of Performance for Each Key Measure

4. Set Proper Objectives in Each Key Measure

5. Visibly Measure Progress Toward Objectives

Before learning to carry out step one of CI, it is important to understand the motivational power of the first step more fully. Additionally, comprehending the limitation of only setting objectives and visibly measuring performance, without fulfilling steps two and three of CI is also imperative.

When we set an objective, or others set one for us, our first and natural response is to endeavor to achieve or exceed that objective. This is especially true, if visible measures track our progress toward meeting the objective. The need for accomplishment, to make a difference, and to prove to others that we can do it, are engines that power the motivation behind CI.

In the 1940s, American psychologist Abraham Maslow developed his famous "Hierarchy of Needs" model of human motivation. It appeared in his groundbreaking book, *A Theory of Human Motivation.*[1]

According to Maslow:

> Human life will never be understood unless its highest aspirations are taken into account. Growth, self-actualization, the striving toward health, the quest for identity and autonomy, the yearning for excellence (and other ways of phrasing the striving "upward") must by now be accepted beyond question as a widespread and perhaps universal human tendency.[2]

Maslow's original "Hierarchy of Needs" is still valid today. In recent years, it has expanded from his original five levels of needs to the eight summarized here.

UPDATED HIERARCHY OF NEEDS

Transcendence Needs— helping others succeed

Self-Actualization Needs— realizing potential, self-fulfillment

Aesthetic Needs— beauty, balance, form

Esteem Needs— achievement, status, responsibility

Belonging Needs— work-group, family, relationships

Safety Needs— protection, security, order

Biological Needs— food, drink, sex, sleep

According to Maslow, a person must satisfy lower-level survival needs before motivation and satisfaction can flow from satisfying higher-level needs. Starving people are not interested in knowledge or beauty until they eat. Maslow claimed:

> Any motivated behavior . . . must be understood to be a channel through which many basic needs may be simultaneously expressed or satisfied. Typically an act has more than one motivation. . . .

> Human needs arrange themselves in hierarchies of pre-potency. That is to say, the appearance of one need usually rests on the prior satisfaction of another, more pre-potent need. Man is a perpetually wanting animal. Also no need or drive can be treated as if it were isolated or discrete; every drive is related to the state of satisfaction or dissatisfaction of other drives.

In other words, once people satisfy their biological, safety, and belonging needs (the de-motivators or dis-satisfiers), they will move to the motivators or satisfiers. Achieving CI objectives with a team, celebrating success, and then setting new objectives is a channel that promotes the simultaneous satisfaction of belonging and esteem as well as satisfying cognitive and self-actualization needs.

Thus, experiencing success with CI is a powerful motivator; it changes the philosophy and attitude of entire companies. Note that satisfying transcendence needs, the highest form of motivation and satisfaction, is only for true leaders, as their motivation is to foster the success of those they lead.

Because of the motivating power of meeting objectives, an entire management theory developed called "Management by Objectives," or MBO. Peter Drucker introduced the phrase in his 1954 book, *The Practice of Management*.[3]

During the 1960s and 1970s, MBO became the most popular of all management practices. Most companies adopted some form of MBO, which, as Drucker proposed, allows management to focus on achievable goals and to get the best possible results from available resources. The principle behind MBO is making sure that everyone in an organization has an understanding of its aims or objectives, as well as an awareness of their own responsibilities in achieving them. In this manner, MBO provided focus and alignment for organizations.

While remnants of MBO exist in nearly all business organizations, this once pervasive process has fallen into disrepute. The reason is two failures in design and two failures in application. First, in design, MBO focuses on and rewards achieving targets, rather than achieving trends of improvement. Thus, the target, whether arbitrary or not, becomes gospel and determines success or failure, despite the progress made toward that objective. As a result, leaders end up spending their energy in manipulation of the target and making excuses instead of actually improving.

Secondly, MBO focuses solely on achieving results, rather than on achieving results in the right manner. Short-term actions to meet current objectives rob a company of long-term improvement opportunities. False and self-centered leaders make shortsighted decisions to meet short-term objectives to enhance their bonus and move up before the consequences of their actions come to bear.

In application, MBO failed as organizations abandoned Drucker's advice to keep the number of objectives small and the objective amounts realistic. Companies set scores of unrealistic "stretch" objectives. This frustrates people as they continually experience failure. Eventually, they will ignore the objectives. Unrealistic objectives are actually de-motivating, because they prevent esteem, meaning, and most basically, that they are impossible to achieve.

There is a corresponding philosophy among some weight-training practitioners that you should always stop after the last complete repetition you can fully accomplish before failure. If you always lift until you stop in the middle of a repetition, realizing that you cannot do it to completion, you are teaching your muscles to fail. You are setting an unrealistic target and telling your body over and over again that most likely you won't succeed, and that it's okay to stop midsteam and abandon the goal number of repetitions or sets. Over time, your objectives of weight and number of repetitions become obsolete. The objectives lose all power because you don't expect to reach them and it has become habitual for you to fail in the middle of your attempt. You are essentially practicing how to quit and fail.

On the other hand, if you usually set realistic goals (as Drucker advised) in weight training and follow through on your sets and repetitions to completion, you are teaching your muscles to succeed. The effects of this physical attitude are amazing. Should you by some chance set a goal that is actually a bit too high—your body will rise to the occasion and power up to succeed, because this is the trend. You are practicing how to succeed, complete, and accomplish.

Similarly in business, suppose your company faces an unrealistic survival challenge. Your company is more likely to power up and meet that challenge if the people are conditioned to succeed, rather than being used to and comfortable with failing to meet objectives.

Drucker also proposed MBO to be a five-step process, but unfortunately, most companies stop short at merely setting targets. Just like with MBO, implementing one or two steps of the three-step Continuous Improvement process may produce early results but fail to produce the ongoing improvement needed. Setting objectives in key measures and visibly measuring performance toward objectives is powerful, but it is just step one.

CI removes the failures in design inherent in MBO. We treat objectives as mere targets and achieving an objective as an excuse to celebrate. Achieving a positive **trend** in all of your measures simultaneously is success. The three-step Continuous Improvement process removes failures in application, as the first step of setting objectives is tightly linked to the two remaining steps. CI is not only setting objectives, it is creating an endless trend of improvement by using data to identify patterns of improvement opportunities and then applying specific tools to resolve issues adversely affecting performance.

STEP ONE OF CI HAS FIVE PARTS

Akin to every new pursuit, implementing CI demands that you learn some new terminology. The first new term is **major performance areas**. Understanding them is the first part of correctly setting up Step One of CI. The major performance areas in business never change. They are like the events in the Olympics' pentathlon.

Instead of the race, long jump, discus throw, hammer throw, and wrestling that were necessary to win the pentathlon, the events that win the battle for security and growth in business are:

- Safety
- Productivity
- Internal quality
- External quality
- Cost
- Environment
- Training
- Housekeeping and orderliness

In business, with the possible exceptions of strategic changes or short-term directed improvements quickly addressing competitive weaknesses, you are doing your job as a leader if you can simultaneously and incrementally:

- reduce the number of injuries to employees
- improve productivity
- reduce mistakes that are caught and fixed before they get to your customer
- reduce the mistakes that get to your customer
- reduce the cost of building your product or providing your service
- improve environmental sensitivity and compliance
- increase the skills of your workforce
- improve the housekeeping, orderliness, ergonomics, and safety of your facility and equipment

Success with CI happens as leaders realize that CI is their everyday job, lock—stock, and barrel—and not something they must do besides their job.

The major performance areas never change regardless of the country, industry, or company. All you have to do is memorize them and then assign the correct performance areas to each group and each level in your organization.

For example, a top-level production team will typically use seven major performance areas with the exception of environment. Maintenance leadership teams do not use productivity. Human Resources and Purchasing Teams each usually use four major performance areas, however, the areas they use are different. In addition, lower-level production teams typically use five performance areas compared to seven for the top-level production leadership team.

The key to selecting the proper major performance areas for each group is to ask three questions.

- What does the group manage?
- What do their customers need?
- What areas will keep the group in **balance**?

Just as you take your car to have the wheels balanced for a smooth ride, the performance areas must keep a group in balance for smooth performance improvement. *Balance* means the group seeks improvement in all of its required performance areas. For example, in terms of maintenance, if the only performance area tackled was cost, the team's continual reductions in the cost of maintenance would put the company out of business.

Just like the pent-athlete who must excel and improve in many events simultaneously to win the Olympics, so must the successful leader and team improve several major performance areas at the same time in order to keep in balance. Therefore, besides reducing maintenance costs, this group must properly seek improvement in:

- external quality (downtime on the equipment serviced)
- internal quality (percentage of preventive vs. reactive maintenance)
- training (number of fully verified maintenance resources)
- safety (injuries per 2000 hours)
- housekeeping, orderliness, ergonomics, and safety of maintenance areas (4-S score)

You are doing your job as a maintenance leader if you simultaneously improve all of these five performance areas at once. In part two, each performance area is assigned a key measure.

STEP ONE OF CI HAS FIVE PARTS

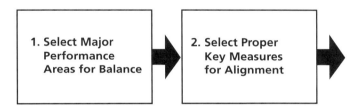

The second term to learn is **key measure**. A *key measure* is the broadest measure of whether a group is improving or getting worse in a performance area. A key measure *does not* tell a group where to work for improvement, what to work on to improve, or when the patterns of issues occur. A key measure is also the only measure for which the group will set an objective in a major performance area. All other measures related to a performance area are diagnostic and applicable to the second major step of CI.

For example, the top purchasing and material management group must manage the cost of materials. Of the following three choices (A, B, or C), which is the correct overall cost key measure?

A. Inventory cost per dollar sales
B. Percent of certified suppliers
C. Material cost per dollar sales

The only correct answer from these three choices is (C), material cost per dollar sales. This is the broadest cost measure for the group, yet does not tell the group what to work on to improve. Inventory cost is not the broadest cost measure so it is not the key measure. Selecting a key measure that is not the broadest measure allows the team to sub-optimize. The purchasing and material management group could reduce inventory to the point of increasing cost or putting the company out of business. While the team will always strive to reduce material cost per dollar sales, it may not always need to reduce inventory. Success for the top purchasing and material management group is reducing the total cost of material. Diagnostic data in Step Two, not the key measure in Step One, will tell whether the group should focus on inventory cost, transportation cost, or other purchasing and material cost areas. Percent of certified suppliers is an internal quality measure for this group, not a cost measure.

Not only does every group have different key measures depending on what it manages and who its customers are, measures also differ based on the group's level in the organization. For example, the productivity measure for an engine Plant Manager and the top leadership team might be plant-wide average machine efficiency. However, for the Supervisor and Operators on Line 1, the measure might be average pieces produced per shift on Line 1.

Selecting key measures for operating areas is easier than in service areas. However, both have customers, both have products or services, both have employees, and both have processes and equipment. Therefore, key measures must be set in the proper major performance areas, to better serve customers, develop and fully utilize people, and efficiently utilize and maintain managed assets.

Some key measures are a given. All facilities should have a key measure for housekeeping, orderliness, ergonomics, and safety. This measure is part of a process, or system, we call 4-S. The 4-S system recognizes that a clean and orderly workplace is a safe, productive, and quality workplace. The origin of 4-S dates to 1980 in the Cadillac Livonia Engine Plant.

4-S: Plant cleanliness, orderliness, safety, and ergonomic system
1. **S**elect area and audit team
2. **S**ort out, clean, and straighten out the area
3. **S**afety and ergonomics reviewed
4. **S**ustaining the process with Continuous Improvement

Many plants achieve outstanding and ongoing results in housekeeping, safety, and ergonomics with the 4-S system. It not only achieves quick results, but ongoing improvement, as it is integrated as a key measure in CI. The physical appearance improvements and orderliness provide visible evidence of change. As employees participate, they gain pride in their work area. That leads to greater pride in their work, and taking greater pride in themselves.

It is important to start with a well-designed 4-S audit form and a strict standard for the audit. The stricter you are with 4-S initially, the better you can become. As with all CI key measures, it does not matter where you are at the start, only that your trend is in the proper direction and you engage your workforce to out-improve the competition.

Not only must a group be in balance with the proper major improvement areas to avoid sub-optimization, each group must use the proper key measures to be in **vertical** and **horizontal alignment**. *Horizontal alignment* means that the key measures of each group support the key measures of the overall company or operation, and all contribute to reduced cost. For example, a human resource group that works to reduce employee turnover, absenteeism, workers compensation cost, and repetitive injuries, is in alignment with improving productivity, quality, safety, and cost of operations.

Vertical alignment means that the measures at each level in the organization support improvement in the measures of the group in the level above. Thus, if the Supervisor improves the number of pieces produced per shift, this is in alignment with the Plant Manager's measure of plant-wide average efficiency.

When a group begins to set up CI, it is better to begin with two or three performance areas and matching key measures, and grow from there into a full complement. This allows time to perfect leadership skills while team members learn accountability as natural owners.

For first-level operating teams, good areas to start with are productivity, internal quality, and housekeeping, orderliness, and safety. These major performance areas have huge impact on an organization, and 4-S yields quick, visible improvement. The quick improvements will serve to bolster the confidence of group members as they advance their skills. Top-level production teams initially focus on quality, productivity, the 4-S measure for housekeeping orderliness, and safety. Service groups start in the performance areas where they most need to improve service to their customers or expect to have the most impact on the bottom line.

An example of the adaptive nature of the key high performance systems emanates from an engine plant in Mexico. Workplace Transformation, Inc. helped the plant implement CI in the late 1980s. The plant showed strong improvement trends in all measures and won the Mexican national quality award. As a result of a record drought, the engine plant was running out of water and the wells were running dry. There was no time to dig new wells and the cost of digging existing wells to the depth necessary would have significantly threatened the plant's competitive position. The plant exported engines to the United States, Canada, and Japan. Maintaining the cost advantage was essential to complement the engine plant's quality advantage.

Leadership created a new, interim, plant-wide key measure and integrated the new measure into the plant's mature Continuous Improvement process. The key measure was gallons of water per engine. Because this was a new key measure, the plant had no diagnostic data about the location of improvement opportunities, what specific improvement opportunities existed, and the patterns of occurrence. A new diagnostic data path identified several significant improvement opportunities. Based on the data, teams completed projects and solved problems related to water usage. To make a long story short, gallons per engine fell over sixty percent in five months, the company did not have to invest in new wells, the drought ended, and the engine plant continues to grow today.

In response to a new threat, the adaptive CI process provided short-term performance improvement and improved the long-term future of the organization. As shown by the Mexican plant, once the leader sets up the five Pillars of High Performance, there is no need to change systems or adopt any new programs to respond to new challenges.

STEP ONE OF CI HAS FIVE PARTS

A history of performance for each key measure helps establish a realistic objective. For example, long jumpers look at the distance of their last one hundred jumps before setting up a realistic objective for the future. A **Continuous Improvement Form**, one of the five tools necessary to implement CI in the correct manner, displays performance history as well as all steps of CI for each major performance area and key measure.

STEP ONE OF CI HAS FIVE PARTS

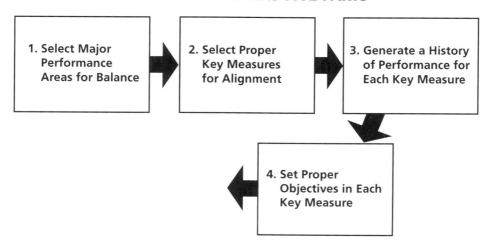

A proper objective for CI has three sections. Section one is amount, defined as the quantifiable target the team wants to achieve. For example if you were setting a target for weight loss you would quantify the number of pounds to lose.

A proper objective amount is realistic to provide motivation to the team and not deflate the members' spirit. Section two is **completion date**. The date helps determine if the amount is realistic. For example, to decide if losing twenty pounds is realistic, you would have to know how much time you have to lose the weight. Factors to evaluate when setting a realistic amount and completion date are as follows:

- history of performance
- performance variability
- past record performance
- process capability
- anticipated changes in product, process, or people

The third section, **duration,** measures how long performance should be "at" or "better than" the objective amount before celebrating and setting a new objective. Duration prevents setting a new objective the first time a team meets the objective amount. The result may be a fluke and setting a new objective amount would be unrealistic. Variability in past results is the key factor to consider when setting duration.

STEP ONE OF CI HAS FIVE PARTS

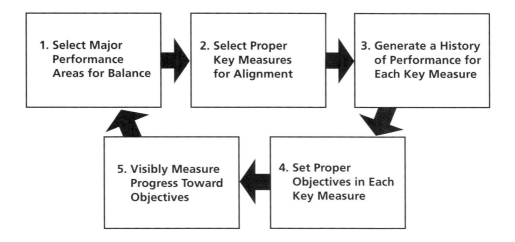

Posting a team's key measures and objectives on the CI form in a visible place completes the first step of CI. Visibly posting proper key measures and objectives in the correct performance areas for each natural work group is a big step forward. Improvement will occur from Step One alone. However, doing all three steps of CI is necessary to ensure continued success at a pace faster than the competition.

An example will help you picture Step One of CI. A leadership team working in an engine plant wanted to improve the productivity major performance area. The key measure chosen was average monthly efficiency. In 2006, the engine plant achieved an average monthly efficiency of 72 percent. The result reached was 75 percent in January 2007, 74 percent in February 2007, and 76 percent in March 2007. The top section of the blue CI form, showing Step One with a proper objective set, would look as follows:

CONTINUOUS IMPROVEMENT FORM

Team: Engine Plant Leadership Team
Major Performance Area: Productivity   Objective ⎯⎢ Target Amount: 78 Percent
Key Measure: Average Overall Efficiency   Time to Hit Target: 6 Months Sept. 5, 2007
                                                          Duration to Hold: 3 Months

STEP 1 -- SET OBJECTIVE AND VISIBLY MEASURE PERFORMANCE TOWARD OBJECTIVE

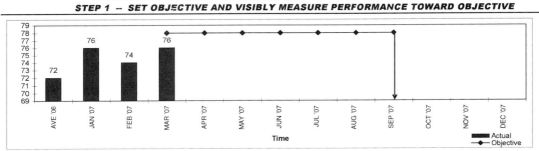

To complete the explanation and comprehension of Step One, it is important to answer several questions. First, why celebrate after a team meets an objective and holds performance at or better than the objective amount for the duration period? The answer is that CI is not only important to get results, but also to allow the workforce to change its attitude from apathetic to never good enough.

Through CI, engaged employees see that they make a difference. They can influence results, and therefore influence their own future. Celebrating as a team to recognize meeting or exceeding objectives hastens this essential attitude change necessary to become a high performance organization.

What if the engine team's results did not meet or exceed 78 percent within the six-month period? What if it stayed at 76 percent for two months, rose to 77 percent for two months, and then stayed at 77.5 percent for the last two months of the objective time allotment? If you answer, "The team failed," you are dead wrong. The trend is what is important in CI, not the target. Instead, the target serves as an excuse to celebrate and set a new objective. The Continuous Improvement process and the need for a positive trend, never end. The Team Leader should congratulate the team on its trend, extend the target date two months, and then express confidence that members will meet the target.

On the other hand, what if the team's performance does not show a trend of improvement? What if performance is static or decreasing and there are no significant external changes? Then something is wrong either with the leadership or the team's Continuous Improvement process. Again, when properly implemented, CI always works.

Sometimes external changes occur that cause a slip in performance. For example, shutting down a blast furnace to meet environmental standards will reduce output in a steel mill. What happens then? The leader resets the target after obtaining enough performance history with one less furnace. The team continues to seek improvement from the new baseline performance.

If there are no external changes, either the leader or the team's Continuous Improvement process needs correction. You are born, you die, you pay taxes, and if you implement the three-steps of CI correctly, you will continually improve!

If a leader is uncertain if 78 percent or 80 percent is the most realistic target amount for the engine plant, which one should be chosen? The answer is simple: 78 percent. The only downside to setting an objective too low is that the team celebrates one more time on their Continuous Improvement journey. If the team is at 79 percent and goes higher for the first three months of a six-month duration, celebrate immediately and set a new objective. CI is a journey, not a destination.

The final lesson about CI, before we move to Step Two, is that the reward for Continuous Improvement cannot be negative. This is the reason growth is essential in a high performance organization, so it can use the increased capacity created by CI and avoid reducing the employees who made it possible. Along the difficult journey to high performance in a competitive world market, there most likely will be decreases in the workforce. Reasons include attrition, loss of sales, introduction of new technology, and unavoidable cost reductions demanded by the customer or forced by the competition.

A true leader recognizes there must be positive rewards for incremental performance improvement, from CI and from development of increased workforce skills. The result of employees engaging themselves in the long-term incremental journey of CI and engaging themselves in the long-term incremental process of developing their individual skills and versatility cannot be that they directly lose their jobs.

Only the true rival, the competition, should cause a company to reduce its competitive advantage—its people—and then only as a last resort. The aim is always to save as many jobs as possible.

- Major performance areas assure balance and proper key measures assure vertical and horizontal alignment as you pursue Continuous Improvement.

- Specific, realistic objectives are necessary so the team can feel accomplishment and celebrate on the never-ending journey of Continuous Improvement.

- Success means achieving a positive performance trend in all key measures simultaneously.

Notes

[1] Maslow, "A Theory of Human Motivation," *Psychological Review* (1943): 50, 370–396.

[2] Abraham H. Maslow, *Motivation and Personality. 2nd ed.*, (New York: Harper & Row, 1970)

[3] Peter F. Drucker, *The Practice of Management* (New York: Harper & Row, 1954; repr., New York: Harper Business, 1993).

17

Focused Improvement

Continuous Improvement is a rifle, not a shotgun.

The second major step in the formal three-step Continuous Improvement process is Focused Improvement. Focused Improvement uses diagnostic data to determine where, what, and when performance issues occur that affect performance in a key measure established in Step One. To do this correctly, it is important to implement the following three sequential parts in Step Two.

STEP TWO OF C.I. HAS THREE PARTS

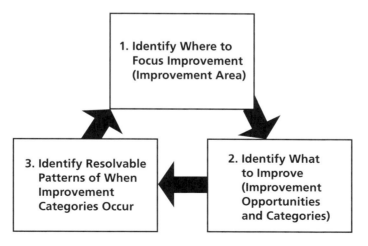

1. Identify Where to Focus Improvement (Improvement Area)

2. Identify What to Improve (Improvement Opportunities and Categories)

3. Identify Resolvable Patterns of When Improvement Categories Occur

Focused Improvement is the key to steady performance improvement. Like rolling ten beach balls up a steep hill, the only way to do it successfully, is one at a time. Focused Improvement causes you to select and roll the most important beach ball up the hill first. If you switch back and forth among the ten, you will never get any of them up the hill.

To see graphic evidence of the power of Focused Improvement, have a friend hold an ordinary 8.5-by-11-inch sheet of paper tightly in the horizontal position. Now try to push your open hand through the paper. You will fail. Now try with one finger . . . *Voilà*, you push right through.

Full understanding of the data-driven nature of CI comes from applying step two of CI. The Focused Improvement process uses several levels of diagnostic data to perform the role of the ancient Greek Olympic coaches. Diagnostic data focuses improvement efforts to identify issues the workforce can resolve. The major reason organizations cannot successfully involve their workforces in resolving issues to improve performance is lack of the right data in the right format to identify and refine issues into resolvable patterns.

Using data to focus improvement efforts is the heart of CI. Unfortunately, this is the step where most companies fail and the major reason they do not improve consistently or faster than their competition. They struggle every day, unsuccessfully trying to push their entire hand through the paper at once and constantly juggling their time attempting to push ten beach balls uphill simultaneously, with each ball sliding backwards when they jump to catch another ball.

One reason for this tragic malaise preventing improvement is an information crisis in industry. On one hand, there is too much information. Unfortunately, most of the information feeds duplicative reports that show results in several ways to different people. On the other hand, almost no data exists in a proper format to drive focused performance improvement.

Ask leaders what their biggest quality defect is, or biggest equipment downtime issue, and most likely they will be able to tell you the answer. Ask them how often it happens and the pieces or minutes lost and they will likely guess. Ask them if it happens mostly on one shift, tool, day of the week, time of the day, or when one operator is working and they will look at you with a blank stare. This "deer in the headlights" look means that the data they have is inadequate to drive CI in their organization.

The information crisis is like an athlete without a coach. When athletes guess at what is wrong, performance remains stagnant regardless of the athlete's effort. They work on the wrong issues and repeat flawed movements making them even harder to correct. Likewise, organizations without good diagnostic data to drive CI go around in circles. These companies work on many inappropriate and costly projects aimed at everything they can think of that could possibly cause a performance issue. The issue may disappear for a while; however, as they never find the actual cause, the same problems will occur again.

The data needed to drive CI is diagnostic data, not reporting data. Several levels of diagnostic data are necessary to drive CI. Rather than using simplistic methods like cause and effect diagrams or asking "why" five times, a diagnostic data path focuses improvement and narrows improvement opportunities into patterns so that the correct tool can be applied in Step Three of CI.

The first of three parts of Focused Improvement are as follows:

STEP TWO OF CI HAS THREE PARTS

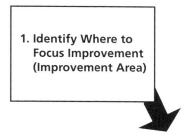

An important term to learn in the first part of Focused Improvement is **improvement area**. Improvement area denotes **where** to focus improvement efforts. Depending on the level of the team in the organization, several levels of diagnostic data help identify an improvement area.

Most companies do a miserable job with Step Two of Continuous Improvement and we must teach clients all about diagnostic data. We teach what data to gather, how front-line Operators or service providers gather data, provide data gathering check sheets, and develop data paths for each key measure. The **Focused Improvement Worksheet** is the second of five tools that are used in CI. Recall the first tool is the Continuous Improvement Form which shows a key measure and objective and tracks all activities to improve that key measure. The *Focused Improvement Worksheet* sequentially leads people through the data-driven, scientific part of Continuous Improvement. The worksheet becomes the coach and points out specifically where, what, and when performance issues occur so the workforce can resolve them.

Like unpeeling an onion all the way to its core, you have to look at several layers of skin or diagnostic data to focus improvement efforts. It's the best way to get at the heart of a problem, and see a pattern that can be resolved. Once the data path is in place and automated, employees use the *Focused Improvement Worksheet* sequentially and replace the reporting data crisis with a diagnostic data advantage.

Continuing with the engine plant example will aid understanding of diagnostic data and a proper data path. As you will recall, for Step One of CI, the engine plant's leadership Team Leader chose the key measure of average monthly machine efficiency in the productivity major performance area. The objective amount was set at 78 percent, with a completion date of September 30, 2007, and an objective duration of three months. The team plotted and posted its CI form for all to see. Now the team members are ready for Step Two, focusing their improvement efforts.

To begin, assume the engine plant has two business units: Machining and Assembly. The plant knows that Machining is the bottleneck. This means that Assembly can produce more quality parts than the plant can machine. The first level of diagnostic data begins to uncover the improvement area.

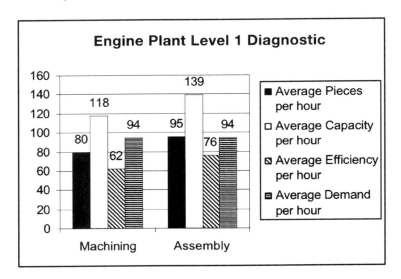

Based on the data, the engine plant team should focus improvement efforts in the worst area: Machining. After viewing the first-level diagnostics, Machining becomes the first part of the improvement area. As the diagnostic chart shows, Machining produces fewer pieces than Assembly produces, runs at lower efficiency, and cannot meet hourly demand. This leads to costly overtime and unused capacity.

In Machining, there are four lines: Line 1, Line 2, Line 3, and Line 4. We will begin to see the drill-down effect of diagnostic data as we unpeel each layer of diagnostic data. The engine plant team knows demand for products on each line is the same; all parts assemble into an engine.

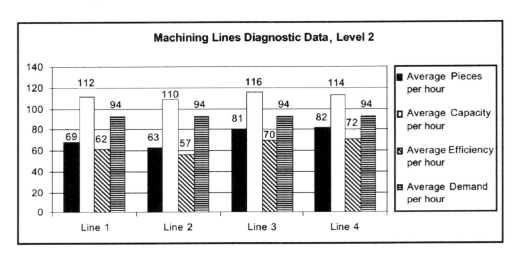

The worst line is clearly Line 2 because it is the least efficient and produces the least average number of pieces per hour. It has fallen the furthest behind its demand per hour. So Line 2 becomes part of the improvement area. This is how CI helps prioritize and focus resources to fix the worst area first. If the next worst line is close in performance, like Line 1 in our example, it will replace Line 2 as the improvement area as soon as the performance of Line 2 surpasses the performance of Line 1. Resist the temptation of working on both lines simultaneously. You must roll one ball all the way up the hill before you start pushing the second ball. All the way to the top means that the performance on Line 2 should surpass that of Line 1 before switching the improvement focus.

In this example, the only reason to pick a line other than Line 2 would be because of a difference in demand. If the demand for products from Line 1 is much higher than on Line 2, we may focus on Line 1 first, even though it is more efficient than Line 2. This is especially true if the higher demand is causing employee overtime or putting customer shipments in jeopardy.

The next level of diagnostic data used to uncover the improvement area is tracking the machine or process. Line 2 in Machining has four machines or operations called Operation 10, 20, 30, and 40. Their performance is as follows:

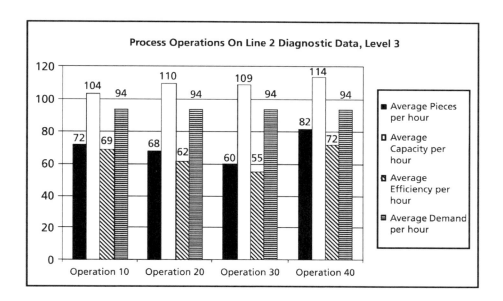

The improvement area now becomes clearer; it is our worst operation, Operation 30, in our worst line, Line 2, and in our worst unit, Machining. The final section of the improvement area comes from the diagnostic data from Operation 30, which produces two products: Product A and Product B. The results are as follows:

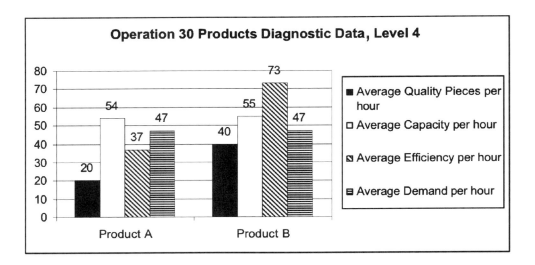

The issues with Operation 30 occur fundamentally when it produces Product A, not Product B. Therefore, the improvement area, where to focus improvement efforts, is: Machining, Line 2, Operation 30, and Product A. If the performance for both products were similar, the improvement area would be All Products on Operation 30.

We are now ready for the second part of focusing improvement.

STEP TWO OF C.I. HAS THREE PARTS

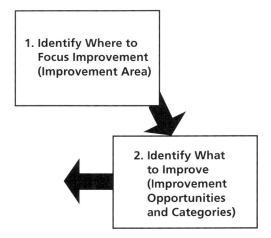

Part Two of Focused Improvement moves from **where** to work, to **what** to work on in the improvement area. After identifying the improvement area, the engine plant team naturally will ask itself, "What is occurring when we machine Product A, on Operation 30, on Line 2?"

Two sections, opportunities and categories, comprise Part Two of the Focused Improvement process. The next term to learn is **improvement opportunity**. *Improvement opportunities* are the major issues occurring at the improvement area that adversely affect performance. For productivity performance, the culprit is downtime or delays. Continuing the example, the downtime experienced on Line 2, Operation 30, when producing Product A, is mechanical downtime, tool change downtime, and staffing downtime. These are improvement opportunities. Notice the drill-down effect of the diagnostic data path and the Focused Improvement process. It is important to look only at downtime occurring in the improvement area. In this way, we will work on the biggest opportunity, in the worst area of the plant.

Check sheets from Machining, Line 2, Operation 30, when producing Product A provide the following data:

Mechanical Downtime	20 total occurrences	182 total minutes downtime
Tool Change Downtime	23 total occurrences	102 total minutes downtime
Staffing Downtime	12 total occurrences	32 total minutes downtime

Improvement opportunities are prioritized looking first at impact. If the impact of two opportunity areas is about the same, use frequency. The more frequently something happens, the easier it is to resolve. The *Focused Improvement Worksheet* prioritizes improvement opportunities on a scale of 1 to 9. It is important to prioritize areas relative to one another. For example, if there is a Priority 1 and also a Priority 2 opportunity, you would look for patterns to resolve in each. If there is a Priority 1 and the next is a Priority 5, you would probably resolve several patterns in the Priority 1 improvement opportunity before even looking at the Priority 5 improvement opportunity.

The number 1 Priority improvement opportunity in our example is mechanical downtime because it has the greatest impact. Based on the data, tool change downtime would be Priority 3 and staffing downtime is Priority 7.

The next section is **category**. *Categories* are specific types of an improvement opportunity. For example, in the improvement opportunity of mechanical downtime, the categories of mechanical downtime might be top drill breakage, bottom drill breakage, and coolant system failure.

The diagnostic data for improvement opportunities and categories usually comes from the front-line operator and is then tabulated to drive CI. This is where the workforce begins to become engaged in Continuous Improvement. The workforce accurately codes the downtime effecting productivity and defects affecting internal quality on a check sheet.

Proper downtime and defect codes require two fields to drive CI. The first alpha field of the code is the improvement opportunity and the second numeric field is the category of that improvement opportunity. For example, if an Operator encountered 20 minutes of downtime in the first hour of production because of top drill tip breakage, the worker would enter "20 minutes" on the check sheet and code it "ME 03." "ME" stands for mechanical downtime and "03" stands for top drill failure.

The categories of mechanical downtime when machining Product A, on Operation 30 of Line 2, in order of priority as identified by the compilation of checksheet data, are as follows on the chart:

Top Drill Tip Breaks	9 total occurrences	70 minutes of downtime
Bottom Drill Tip Breaks	8 total occurrences	90 minutes of downtime
Coolant System Failure	2 total occurrences	22 minutes of downtime

The *Focused Improvement Worksheet* facilitates prioritization of categories. Unlike improvement opportunities, where impact is first and frequency is second, for categories, frequency comes first and impact is second. Use impact only if the frequencies are approximately the same. The reason for this is that we already focused on the worst area, the worst line, the worst operation, the worst product, and the biggest opportunity. Now the premium is on frequency. The more frequently something happens, the easier it is to find a solvable pattern to resolve. Solvable patterns help to pick the right tool to use in Step Three of CI, to involve the workforce in resolving the issue.

The priority 1 category is top drill tip breakage, priority 2 is bottom drill tip breakage, and priority 7 is coolant system failure. We are now ready to move to part three of Focused Improvement.

STEP TWO OF CI HAS THREE PARTS

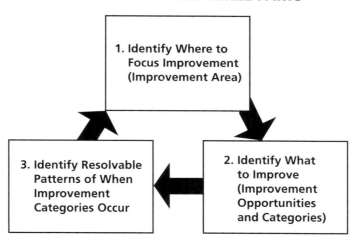

Part Three of Focused Improvement has two sections: finding patterns and selecting the proper tool in preparation for Step Three of CI. Patterns come from observing when categories of improvement opportunities occur. In our engine plant example, we find the following solvable patterns from our categories.

1. 7 of the 9 top drill tip breakages happen in the first hour on Monday mornings.
2. 7 of the 8 lower drill tip breakages occur on second shift when Operator 112 runs Operation 30.
3. Both coolant failures occur on Fridays during second shift.

Once patterns are established for when categories of improvement opportunities occur, we can decide which tool is the proper one to use to resolve the pattern. For example, we know that seven times the top drill tip broke during the first hour on Monday. Obviously, something is different when running Product A on Operation 30 in the first hour on Monday. We are not sure yet what is causing the drill tips to break. In step three of CI we would use the proven, five-step Problem-Solving process and worksheet to solve this problem through to prevention.

Seven times the lower drill tip broke when Operator 112 was running Operation 30. Most likely, Operator 112 is doing something different, which contributes to the breaks. In step three of CI we would use the proven, three-step Human Performance Improvement process and worksheet to resolve the problem and prevent reoccurrence.

We also know that the coolant system has failed twice on the second shift on Fridays. If, for example, we looked at the pattern and suddenly remembered that filters on the coolant system are changed on Sundays, we could realize that the filters become contaminated after five days at our new higher volumes. Because we are sure we know how to resolve the pattern, in step three of CI we would use the proven three-step Project Management process and worksheet to implement the correction in a timely fashion.

Once resolvable patterns are identified and the proper process and tool is selected, we are ready to move on to the last step in Continuous Improvement.

- ◗ Every performance area and key measure needs a diagnostic data path to focus improvement.

- ◗ The data path flows from "where" *(Improvement Area)*, to "what" *(Improvement Opportunities* and *Categories)*, to "when" *(Patterns)*.

- ◗ The *Focused Improvement Worksheet* is a guide through Step Two of CI, using diagnostic data to identify resolvable patterns of performance issues.

18

Resolving Patterns of Performance Issues

Nothing makes a job easier than having
and using the right tool.

The third and final step of Continuous Improvement is effectively using one of three tools at the proper time. Each part of Step Three represents the use of a different tool as shown below.

STEP THREE OF CI HAS THREE PARTS

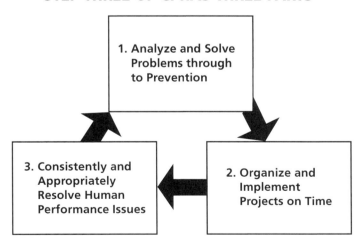

1. Analyze and Solve Problems through to Prevention

2. Organize and Implement Projects on Time

3. Consistently and Appropriately Resolve Human Performance Issues

The disciplined nature of CI and the high level of accountability needed become clear in Step Three. Natural owners are accountable for the disciplined and consistent use of the three tools necessary to resolve patterns of when categories of improvement opportunities occur.

The three tools in Step Three of CI are thorough enough to resolve every pattern identified on the *Focused Improvement Worksheet*. The tools are also simple enough so that everyone in the organization can become expert in their use. Remember, everything that stands between you and achieving your objective is either a problem to solve, a project to implement, or a human performance issue to resolve.

Problem-solving applies whenever the cause of a performance issue is not clear. Only when the cause and solution for a pattern is certain or when the pattern strongly suggests the solution lies in correcting human performance, are the other two tools used prior to problem-solving. If there is any doubt, you cannot go wrong by starting with the proven problem-solving tool. You can move to project implementation or human performance improvement, when the actual cause becomes clear. Therefore, our focus begins with the Problem-Solving process and worksheet.

STEP THREE OF CI HAS THREE PARTS

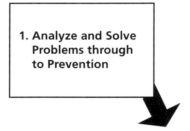

Many people have had some training in problem-solving, and there are many problem-solving techniques. Some techniques are complex and suited for scientific problem-solving. Some are simple and suited for brainstorming sessions. Some are just plain bad. They are poorly designed with too many or too few steps sequenced in the wrong order. The only answer is a problem-solving tool designed for business, with enough complexity to solve the vast majority of problem patterns, yet simple enough for everyone in the organization to use.

Problem-solving is a linear thought process. Each step is dependent on the previous step and a prerequisite for the next step. A correct and straightforward problem-solving tool helps you gather the information necessary to solve problems you face.

Workplace Transformation Inc. has enhanced the Problem-Solving process and corresponding worksheet countless times in the last twenty years.[1] Experience shows that our five-step *Problem-Solving Worksheet* (sometimes called an "Analyze and Implement Worksheet") will solve about 95 percent of all product, service, material, machine, and method problems in business. Resolving human performance problems needs a different logic, format, and the *Human Performance Improvement Worksheet*.

Solving rare, complex problems with simultaneously interacting variables needs sophisticated tools, like design of experiments. Solving rare, complex, variation problems needs sophisticated techniques, like Taguchi Analysis and Six Sigma. A high performance organization usually has a few people trained in such advanced techniques, so these tools are available when needed. These difficult to use, rarely needed, and sophisticated tools do not suit the vast majority of employees, including the operating workforce in their daily pursuit of Continuous Improvement. To engage the entire workforce, a vital action for the success of CI, the tool of preference is the proven five-step Problem-Solving process found on our **Problem-Solving Worksheet**.

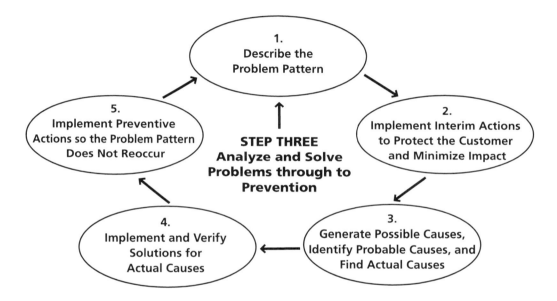

A problem well-defined is three-quarters solved. That is why the first of the five steps of effective problem-solving is: **describe the problem pattern**.

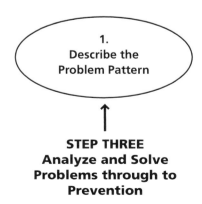

A problem definition should be complete, but not too complex. To describe a problem pattern correctly, simply answer as many of the following questions as you or others familiar with the problem can answer.

What?
- What is the problem or defect?
- On what product, machine, material, or process does it occur?
- Are there any physical characteristics, specific dimensions, or descriptions of the problem or defect?

Where?
- Where is the problem defect found?
- Where does it originate, if known?
- Where on the product, machine, material, or process is the problem or defect?

How much?
- How many problems or defects do you have?
- What is the impact or potential impact of the problem or defect in terms of pieces, cost, customers?

When?
- When did the problem or defect first occur?
- When does it reoccur?
- Is there any pattern to its recurrence?

Before moving to Step Two in problem-solving, there is one last question to ask: "Are you working on one problem likely to come from one or a single set of causes, or are you working on more than one problem pattern?" If the answer is, "More than one," then choose one problem or pattern to solve for that particular worksheet. Start additional *Problem-Solving Worksheets* for each of the other problems or patterns that need solutions.

Some poorly designed, yet widely used problem-solving tools do not begin with problem definition. They begin with steps like, forming a team! Imagine forming a team before describing the problem. For example, we might find in the description that the problem only occurs on the second shift. Yet when we formed our team, we did not include anyone working on the second shift. More importantly, such flawed techniques also assume that forming a team is the best way to solve a problem. While CI is a team endeavor, problem-solving is not. Only complex problems that need multi-disciplined input, need a team. Individuals using a proper problem-solving tool can solve most problems simply by getting information from others in person or by e-mail.

It is impossible to specify interim actions until after the problem definition. In business today, customers do not get mad. They just do not come back! Problems that get to the customer carry a heavy cost, not only in money, but also in potential loss of business. This is why the proper second step in business problem-solving is **interim actions**.

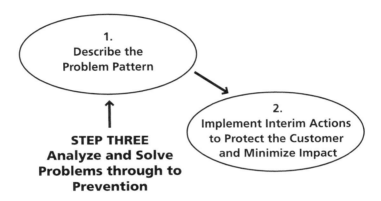

The purpose of an *interim action* is to reduce the impact of the problem and protect the customer while the problem gets solved. Any problem-solving tool that does not have interim action as the second step does not fit in the business world.

It is important to understand that an interim action does not solve or even try to solve a problem. An interim action will reduce the impact and protect the customer *no matter what caused the problem.*

Imagine you are a steelmaker. You find that slivers are sporadically occurring, but only on 48-inch-wide sheets found in the mill and at customer locations. Examples of potential interim actions for this defect include:

- Increased or 100% inspection
- Inspection of inventory at the mill, in transit, and in customer locations
- Replacement of defective material
- Stop making 48-inch-wide steel if quantities of acceptable inventory and customer orders allow
- Substitute steel from a sister mill or increase schedules to offset defects to meet customer delivery
- Substitute a different sheet customers can use, at no extra cost

Notice how none of the interim actions described here solve the problem. They are intended to reduce the impact of the problem and protect the customer, no matter what the cause of the slivers turns out to be. If an interim action *could* solve the problem, for example changing a roll, it would not be a proper interim action.

Another example relates to making paper. Imagine you are a papermaker and Re-winder No. 3 continually stops because its spindle bolts fail, causing loss of production. Proper interim actions include:

- Order enough spare bolts
- Have a Maintenance Technician on each crew or teach Operators to replace the bolts
- Stop using Re-winder No. 3 if schedules permit
- Rewind paper at a sister mill with excess capacity while you solve the problem
- Increase inventories in front of Re-winder No. 3, so it never runs out of paper to rewind when it is running
- Increase the run schedule of Re-winder No. 3 to meet delivery requirements

Both of the examples given list interim actions that do not solve the problems. Instead, these are interim actions that reduce the impact of the slivers or broken bolts and protect the customer. Now, we can move to the third step of the Problem-Solving process.

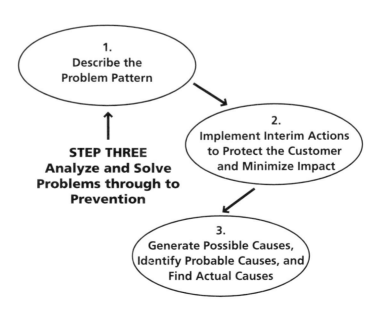

The third step is almost magical if done correctly. Unfortunately, few other problem-solving tools provide the right steps or sequence of steps to lead an individual or team systematically from possible, to probable, to actual cause.

Begin by listing all possible causes for the problem. Generating possible causes is the only place in CI that allows brainstorming in place of facts or data. This is the creative part of problem-solving. Just as a good problem solver involves others in defining the problem and identifying interim actions, this is the time to involve as many people as needed who have knowledge of possible causes of the problem. Ask the Operator, ask the Engineer, ask the Supervisor, ask the Maintenance Technician, ask the Equipment Manufacturer, ask anyone else who might have information you need to answer the following question, "What do you think is causing the problem, be it machine, material, method, or people?"

A common mistake many make at this point in problem-solving is to rush out and fix anything that could possibly be causing a problem. This is expensive and though the problem might go away for a while, it will come back. Prevention can occur only after the actual cause is found. Our *Problem-Solving Worksheet* leads problem solvers to the next step, toward uncovering the actual cause of problems. Problem solvers classify each possible cause as a "no," "yes," or "?"moving from the possible causes to probable causes.

To move from possible to probable causes, mechanically compare each possible cause to each part of the problem description created in Step One. Remember, a problem well-defined is three-quarters solved. A probable cause is one that logically explains what the problem is, where the problem is, how much of the problem is present, when the problem started, and when the problem reoccurs.

For example, assume your auto parts plant that die casts and machines aluminum water pumps is experiencing mounting surface porosity across the entire mounting surface. The porosity appears in machining on every piece for two to three hours and then disappears. The porosity occurs on pieces cast at the beginning of the shift on Monday mornings and then disappears. It then reoccurs for two or three hours on pieces cast on the next Monday morning and then disappears. The problem started three weeks ago.

A list of possible causes for mounting surface porosity might be:

- Operator error
- Bad aluminum alloy
- Mold deterioration
- Improper pressure at the die-casting machine
- Aluminum temperature coming out of the furnace on the first load after the weekend
- Broken hoses on the die-casting machine

By systematically comparing each cause against the definition, "operator error" could explain porosity on the entire mounting surface, but operator error would not logically explain why the porosity appears for two or three hours and then disappears. Operator error does not logically explain why the porosity occurs only on pieces cast during the first two hours on Monday mornings, so operator error as the problem's cause is a "no." The same would be true of "bad aluminum alloy." "Mold deterioration" would not explain porosity across the entire mounting surface or that the problem disappears. "Improper pressure" and "broken hoses" would not explain why porosity occurs only on pieces cast during the first two hours on Monday mornings and why the problem comes and goes in a predictable fashion. The only option on the list that is a "yes" and graduating to a probable cause is "aluminum temperature coming out of the furnace on the first load after the weekend."

Our *Problem-Solving Worksheet* explains that if there is only one probable cause (a possible cause marked "yes"), test the probable cause and see if it explains all or part of the problem. If the test is controlling the temperature of the first load of aluminum from the furnaces on Monday morning and the problem disappears, then this is the actual cause. Move to the next step of problem-solving.

If more than one cause is marked "yes," problem solvers must test each probable cause independently to find out whether each probable cause actually caused all or part of the problem. Independent testing is preferable to avoid changing multiple variables at once, which complicates identifying actual causes. Sometimes, it is just not practical to test probable causes independently. For example, if die cast furnaces have to be shut down to make adjustments to test probable causes; the cost of the downtime is so significant, that the only choice might be to make all adjustments at once. Never test possible causes that do not rise to the level of probable causes.

If no possible causes in the brainstormed list are marked "yes," then there are no probable causes. The *Problem-Solving Worksheet* teaches problem solvers to go back to the problem definition and ask what is changed or different about each part of the problem definition. Sometimes causes are elusive and they do not appear on the first list of possible causes. The problem solver will have to dig a little deeper and do some research. Go to the furnaces and die-casting machines on a Monday morning, watch the process and the Operators. Then list everything that has either changed in the last three weeks or is different during the first two hours on that Monday morning.

To your surprise, you may learn that for the last three weeks, a new employee has been training on the casting job for two hours every Monday morning. Up jumps a probable cause. The problem's answer has to do with what is different during the first two hours on Monday morning when heating the alloy or casting the water pump, or in what has changed in the last three weeks.

If all possible causes are marked "yes," the *Problem-Solving Worksheet* teaches problem solvers to redefine the problem pattern to work on one pattern at a time. If every brainstormed cause matches each part of a problem description, redefine the problem to one solvable problem pattern likely to come from one cause or a common set of causes.

Entering a "?" on the worksheet for possible causes allows groups to get beyond causes that they cannot say without a doubt are a "no." In other words, causes that are marked with a "?" could explain the problem definition, but only if several coincidental factors occurred at once or several assumptions are made. You cannot eliminate the possible cause as it could potentially match the definition of the problem, but it is not a probable cause. Rather than bog down the group, write the question mark symbol on the worksheet and move on. On rare occasions, a problem is so baffling that even causes marked with a "?" will be tested.

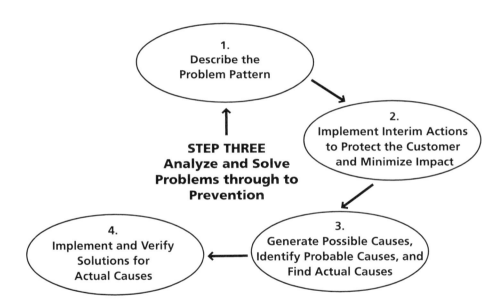

Step four in the Problem-Solving process is implementing and verifying solutions for actual causes. There are two major parts to step four. The first is quick implementation of solutions for an actual cause and corroborating that the solution works. The second part is to determine if there are any other places the same problem might occur. If so, the same verified solution can be implemented before the problem occurs. Think about how many problems could be avoided if your workforce looked beyond the primary fix to see where else a solution could be applied to fix problems before they occur.

The best example showing the importance of thinking beyond the primary fix involved an elevator repair company located in downtown New York City. A worker repaired a recurring problem of frayed elevator cables by placing a plastic spacer between the cables and a switch box. He verified the fix after three weeks of use without any wear on the cables. Then using the *Problem-Solving Worksheet*, he thought beyond the fix and called a colleague who maintained the same model of elevators in a large hotel. When this person examined the cables at his hotel, he found a cable worn to the brink of failure. The repairman installed plastic spacers on all of the cables and a potentially life-threatening incident was prevented.

The final step in problem-solving is prevention. In business, it is normal to confront problems every day, what is unacceptable is to confront the same problems every day. Prevention means changing the machine, method, or material, so that the problem can never happen again.

The actual cause of a serious bearing failure was a missing translucent plastic bearing race. The solution was to load the machine with the exact number of the small plastic races needed for the bearings being produced. If parts were left after the production run, all the bearings would be inspected. The translucent plastic races were so small and hard to see that there seemed to be no way to alter the machine to prevent reoccurrence.

While brainstorming ways to prevent the problem and to fill out the last part of the Problem-Solving Worksheet, a new employee suggested, "If a bearing has all the parts, it will weigh the same, and if parts are missing, it will weigh less." The maintenance team put a sensitive programmable electronic scale at the end of the line. If a bearing weighed more or less than the target weight, the scale automatically rejected the bearing. The line never had another defect again because of missing or extra parts. Using the *Problem-Solving Worksheet,* the Lead Operator asked, "Where else will this preventive action prevent similar problems?"

Another employee said, "All the other lines in this plant and in our sister plants." This plant went on to set new records for the fewest defects per million for the industry after installing scales in every line. The change led to increased sales and for the first time in years, the plant grew. The same happened at the sister plants. The final positive outcome of using the *Problem-Solving Worksheet* came when the bearing company added a new high-profit line of products. The new sensitive, electronic, programmable scales were a big hit in the marketplace.

A high performance organization uses the *Problem-Solving Worksheet* for patterns identified by diagnostic data in CI and any time a problem occurs. A problem occurs whenever there are undesirable results and it is not clear exactly why or how to fix it. If a customer calls with a problem, instinctively reach for a *Problem-Solving Worksheet.* If a quality or downtime problem occurs on your shift and the cause is not known, reach for a *Problem-Solving Worksheet.* If an injury occurs while an employee uses the proper safety equipment and follows safety procedures, reach again for a *Problem-Solving Worksheet.*

STEP THREE OF CI HAS THREE PARTS

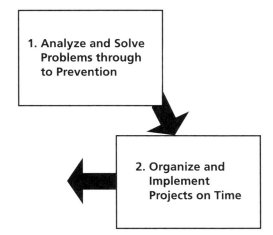

A project management tool is used when the Focused Improvement data path describes a pattern, the solution is immediately recognized, and it is not a human performance issue. Solutions or preventions coming from the *Problem-Solving Worksheet* often need project management to assure timely implementation.

Project management tools and software have become so complex, that sometimes managing the project management tool and software is more difficult than implementing the project itself. This becomes overwhelming given the number of projects facing the typical businessperson or team.

The answer is using the simple, yet effective, three-step *Project Implementation Worksheet* (sometimes called an "Organize and Implement Worksheet"). There is no project too big for this project management tool; for larger projects, each major step of the implementation can be organized as a project unto itself.

Whenever you have a project to manage, a task that will take several steps, several days, or several people, use the *Project Implementation Worksheet*. Projects come from everywhere, CI, implementing problem solutions and preventive actions, from the boss, and from the customer . . . now you can keep it all straight!

The three major parts of the *Project Implementation Worksheet* are thorough enough to guide implementation and enforce accountability, while still simple enough for everyone in the organization to master. See the diagram depicted here.

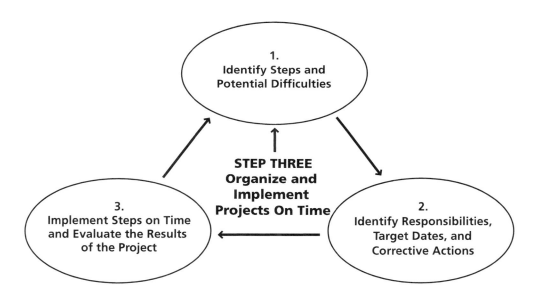

The *Project Implementation Worksheet* manages projects, not activities. An activity occurs when completion is almost immediate, does not involve several people, does not have several steps, or already has a detailed procedure to follow. When it comes to an activity, as the Nike commercial says, "Just do it." When considering a project, the first action is to decide if it should be implemented in light of other projects.

Projects are prioritized on a scale of from 1 to 9 on the *Focused Improvement Worksheet*. Priority determines whether and when to start implementation. Expected time, cost, and benefit determine the priority. Projects are high priority (ranked as 1, 2, or 3) if they require little time and cost, and yield a large impact. Once a team decides to implement a priority project, the three-step management process starts. The first part of project management starts once a natural owner is assigned to oversee a priority project.

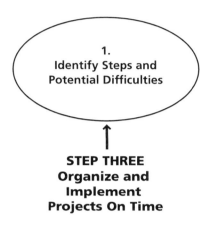

When there is a project to complete, the owners' first action is to identify the major steps needed and potential difficulties. As with gathering input in problem-solving, it is advisable to involve others in contributing this information. However, while CI is a team sport, project implementation is not. Only complex projects, needing multi-disciplined input, require a team. Forming teams is expensive, time consuming, and usually unnecessary for completing projects. Individuals using the project management tool can manage most projects simply by getting others' input in person or by e-mail.

Lazy project leaders create a barrier to the timely and successful completion of projects when they neglect their responsibility to identify potential problems. The first part of our project management tool helps with this process.

The experience of a stamping plant in Kentucky shows the importance of identifying potential problems. Its project encompassed the installation of a large new transfer press line. Using the project management tool, the project leader identified the needed steps and asked his team, "What difficulties could we face with any of the project steps?" A young tradesperson said, "What if the large presses on the trucks do not fit under the highway underpasses?" Everyone laughed, but she persisted and volunteered to check it out. Sure enough, if the presses had come as planned from Germany to Chicago, there would have been no way to deliver the presses on time for a major new product start-up. Seventeen overpasses were too low for the loaded presses. Instead, thanks to spending ten minutes on a discussion of potential problems, the presses traveled by barge up the Mississippi River and were delivered on time.

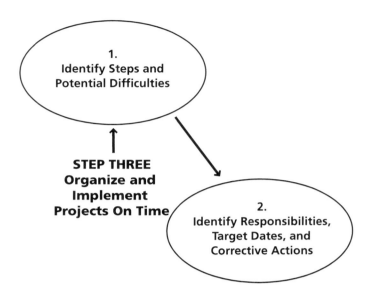

After identifying the steps and potential difficulties of implementing a project, the second step of project management is to identify the natural owners, target dates for each step, and corrective actions for each potential problem. Every project has an overall natural owner who is responsible for timely implementation of the overall project. Others are responsible for timely implementation of their step of the project. A rule of thumb is that natural owners and responsible parties should commit to the target dates before their names are formally assigned and written on the *Project Implementation Worksheet.*

The natural owner and the target completion dates for every step are listed in sequential order of implementation. Our computerized *Project Implementation Worksheet* automatically orders the steps and creates a Gantt Chart to help the natural owner manage the project. To help all responsible parties, our software develops a list of responsibilities for every person and signals employees when target dates are approaching.

The last part of Step Two of project management is to identify corrective actions, so as to avoid the potential problems identified in Step One. Delivering the large transfer presses by barge on the Mississippi instead of to the Port of Chicago is an example of a corrective action for a potential problem.

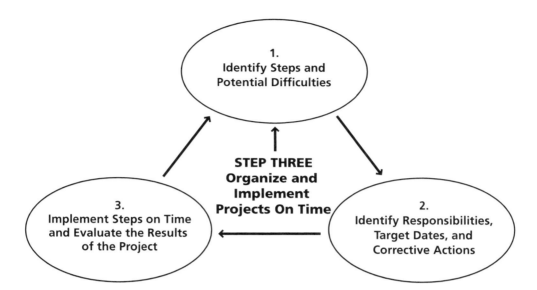

The last part of project management includes the timely implementation of the project followed by an evaluation of project results. Timely implementation depends upon accountability. Regularly scheduled CI meetings monitor progress and assure accountability for problem-solving and project implementation. The golden rule of project implementation is, "Target dates will not extend because of inaction." On the other hand, if a natural owner or responsible party learns that a project or step will take more time because of taking action, the dates change. For example, the person responsible for the step of tearing down a wall to accommodate the new large transfer press line added steps and extended the completion date because as he started demolition, he discovered asbestos in the insulation.

Project evaluation concludes the Project Management process. An analysis of the results of completed projects provides information on how to improve project management for future projects. The natural owner asks three questions. The first question is "Did the project meet expectations for time, cost, and impact? The second question is "Should this project be implemented elsewhere to prevent similar performance issues? The final question is "If we were to do this project again, what would we do differently?" Answers to these questions are particularly valuable when using our CI software, which stores details of every project. For example, if we need to install another transfer press line, we start with the previous *Project Implementation Worksheet*, updated with our experience and lessons learned from the last time we installed a press line.

STEP THREE OF CI HAS THREE PARTS

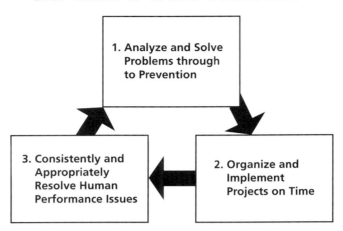

The third and final part in Step Three of CI is consistently resolving human performance issues through the Human Performance Improvement process. Our **Human Performance Improvement Worksheet** addresses every facet of human performance in a high performance work environment. It provides positive reinforcement for exceptional performance as well as assuring that all parts of a high performance work environment are in place. Occasionally, when the performance environment is in place and an employee still chooses not to perform, leaders will apply consequences for poor performance.

The *Human Performance Improvement Worksheet* assures that leaders sequentially: describe and discuss performance issues, decide the cause of the issue, and document appropriate action. The leader will either fix the performance environment or administer consistent and appropriate consequences, depending on whether the lack of performance is a "can't do" or "won't do" issue.

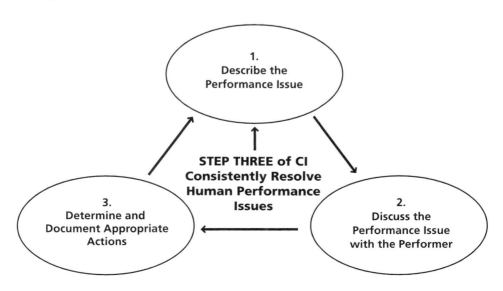

The *Human Performance Improvement Worksheet* is the problem-solving tool to resolve patterns of performance issues uncovered by diagnostic data in CI. The worksheet guides leaders through the three parts of consistently resolving human performance issues.

My son Patrick, although he has since proven to be an outstanding student, had two small problems in grade school. When he entered first grade, he had difficulty reading and with learning the multiplication tables. This was ironic because he could remember and recite the lyrics to every popular song. His mother and I clarified our expectations. We let him know we thought he was capable, and gave him plenty of time to improve. Yet for some reason, he still would not perform. We believed we were dealing with a "won't do" motivational issue.

Our last activity before applying consequences was to investigate the training Patrick received at school. As it turned out, Patrick went to kindergarten in a public school that had abandoned teaching phonics. Patrick needed phonics training. Once we discovered the training deficiency and his new first-grade teacher worked with Patrick as well as two other transferees from the same public school on phonics, the first problem disappeared. Patrick became an avid reader.

The trouble with learning the multiplication tables was different. Patrick had received enough training at school and at home, but simply refused to learn the tables. We clarified how important learning multiplication is and how essential it is to progressing in math in the next grade. We developed flash cards and constantly reviewed them with Patrick. He still would not learn the multiplication tables. Finally, on a summer vacation to Rhode Island, after hours of unsuccessfully reviewing the multiplication tables in the car, we decided that Patrick was choosing not to perform. The time had come to apply negative consequences.

After unloading the car at the beach house in Narragansett, Rhode Island, our three children were chomping at the bit to go to the ocean. Painfully, we told Patrick that he could not go to the beach until he completed the multiplication tables without a mistake. Patrick held out for one day to see if we were serious. Then, almost like magic, he completed the multiplication tables without a mistake in five minutes. He never had a problem again. To this day, Patrick says he does not know why he refused to learn the multiplication tables in the first place. Sometimes, only the proper consequences will inspire the needed performance.

**STEP THREE of CI
Consistently Resolve
Human Performance
Issues**

Human performance problem-solving, like all effective problem-solving, begins with problem description. To describe a performance issue, leaders must do their homework and answer the following questions:

What?
- What was the actual performance?
- What is the desired performance?
- What is the impact or potential impact of the performance problem?
- What documentation indicates that the performer:
  › knew what was expected?
  › was adequately trained?
  › had ample opportunity (including time, information, tools, material, machines and/or resources) to perform?

How?
- How was the performance problem identified?

When?
- When did the performance problem occur?

Have?
- Have there been prior discussions about the performance?

Has?
- Has the performer performed as desired in the past?

The last two questions are particularly important. If there have been prior discussions, this would have a bearing on appropriate consequences as well as whether the lack of performance was *defendable* or *bad faith*. For example, if a lack of performance occurs for the first time and the employee contends that he or she did not know how to do the job correctly, this is far more believable than if this were the second instance for the same employee, and we have retrained and documented that the person knows the duties of the job. In addition, if a lack of performance occurs again and again for the same employee, consequences must become more and more severe because the employee is not getting the message.

If performance has been acceptable in the past, then expectations and training are not causing the performance problem. This information is important in deciding what questions to ask during the performance discussion to find out if the lack of performance is *defendable* or *bad faith*.

A proper description of a performance issue takes only minutes to complete. Just like with problem-solving, a complete description of the problem must be developed in order to solve it through to prevention.

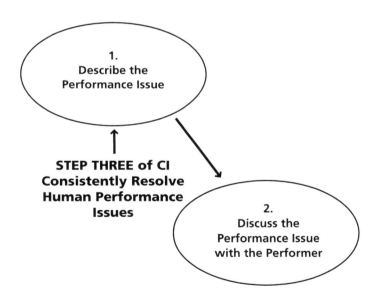

The performance discussion is essential in resolving human performance problems. Even when the problem description clearly points to the need for consequences, it is not known for certain, until a discussion is had with the employee.

A good example of this occurred in a sheet metal stamping plant. The Supervisor saw an employee neglect using a gauge to check the diameter of a part. This lack of performance could lead to serious quality defects and costly scrap. A clear job description, training, and verification using the gauge, and correct performance in the past pointed to a *bad faith* mistake. Even though this was a good employee, the situation seemingly called for consequences.

During the performance discussion we asked, "Has anything changed that caused you to fail to use the gauge?" The employee, to our surprise, answered "Yes." She said the new Superintendent of production visited the job and said, "We are behind shipment, so stop measuring the parts and ship them." Thank goodness we asked her before acting. We had a performance issue, but it was not with the employee; it was with the new Superintendent.

Most leaders need training, skill assessment, and retraining, before they can conduct an effective performance discussion. The performance discussion begins with the leader explaining the problem by methodically reviewing the problem description on the *Human Performance Improvement Worksheet*. Following a review of the problem description, the leader must ask the correct questions at the proper time to decide whether the lack of performance is *defendable* or *bad faith*. Some guidelines for a proper performance discussion are as follows:

- Schedule participants for the discussion at an appropriate time and location.
- Explain the purpose for the discussion, which is to improve performance, and review the problem description word for word from the worksheet.
- Remain in calm control and listen attentively to the answers to your questions.
- If performance was acceptable in the past, ask if anything has changed (expectations, skills required, opportunity) to prevent desired performance.
- If performance was never as desired, ask if the performer knew what was expected and what was unclear.
- If performance was never as desired, ask if the performer knew how to perform and what skills are missing.
- If performance was never as desired, ask if the performer had the opportunity and what was missing (such as, time, information, tools, materials, machines, resources, or extraordinary circumstances).

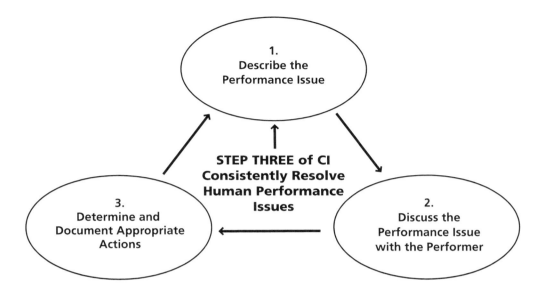

After hearing the performer answer, determine and document the appropriate actions.

- Decide whether help is needed to fix the performance environment and work for a positive conclusion.
- Decide whether the lack of performance is *defendable* or *bad faith*.
- Do not compromise requirements or make exceptions.
- Recognize when the discussion should end and take a stand with specific consequences for this and any future occurrences if the lack of performance is in *bad faith*.

If you determine that the lack of performance is *defendable*, as is usually the case, the leader must fix the performance environment for all performers and document the actions taken. If the lack of performance is found to be *bad faith*, then clear negative consequences for this and any future reoccurrence of the performance issue are in order. A high performance leader's use of consequences is consistent, appropriate, and timely. "Consistent" means that there will be consequences every time a *bad faith* mistake occurs, regardless of the performer. "Appropriate" means that the consequences match the issue and the performance history of the performer. "Timely" means that the *Human Performance Improvement Worksheet* and discussion are completed soon after the performance issue has occurred. If the performer is a represented employee, the form of discipline must be as specified in the collective bargaining agreement.

In high performance organizations, leaders and the workforce consistently follow the best practices and use high performance tools. The three tools comprising the third step of Continuous Improvement are prime examples. High performance organizations use all three tools in Step Three of CI whenever there is a problem to solve, a project to complete, or a human performance issue to resolve. In this way the tools not only support Continuous Improvement, they become a way of doing business every day.

➲ Everything standing between you and your objective is either a problem to solve, a project to implement, or a human performance issue to resolve.

➲ Five-step problem-solving will solve 95% of the problems you face and three-step project management will complete all projects on time.

➲ Three steps of human performance improvement will resolve all performance issues consistently, fairly, appropriately, and in a timely fashion.

Note

[1] Workplace Transformation's "Problem-Solving process" is a refinement and extension of the five-step "Problem-Solving Process" we developed for use by General Motors Ramos Arizpe Complex in the mid-1980s. The Ramos Arizpe Problem-Solving process is a simplification, reordering, and refinement of a Problem-Solving process developed by Kepner Tregoe Inc. of Princeton, New Jersey.

19

Leadership and the CI Process

> Continuous Improvement . . . the buck
> stops with leadership.

Remember, high performance leadership is effectively leading people and managing systems and processes in a disciplined manner. All high performance systems must be managed in a disciplined manner. Nowhere are these leadership skills more important than in implementing the Continuous Improvement process.

CI is the second key pillar system in a high performance organization. To out-improve the competition, your Continuous Improvement process must be stronger than that of the competition. Disciplined implementation is essential. An example and a review are in order to assure complete understanding of the disciplined management of systems previously presented in Part Two and to clarify leaderships' role in implementing CI.

HIGH PERFORMANCE LEADERS
IMPLEMENT SYSTEMS IN A DISCIPLINED MANNER

Successful implementation of CI starts with training and awareness for the top leadership team. The leader must understand CI tools and software. Beyond awareness, the leader must fully understand the critical role of CI in creating a high performance organization. Following this understanding, the leader must make a personal commitment to assure implementation of CI. Without leadership commitment, no system or tool—not even CI—will succeed.

Having all employees involved, accountable, and using CI becomes part of the leader's direction during the *Envision* stage. The use of the process, software, and tools is a D1 decision. A true, effective leader will establish the direction, the expectations, and be the first to implement and direct Continuous Improvement using data.

The leader's personal commitment is revealed when starting CI with the team. This means that the leader will select performance areas, establish key measures and data paths, and publicly display the key measures and objectives. Diagnostic data is used to focus improvement and identify patterns of problems. Setting an example starts with using the proper tools to resolve the problem patterns identified. The leader will adopt the three tools of Step Three in CI, whenever there is a problem to solve, a project to implement, or a human performance issue to resolve. The leader must be positive about the process and its guaranteed success as part of the *Example* stage.

One tool the leader uses and teaches others is how to use the CI software. The Web-based software we have developed:

- guides users through the process and tools
- automatically fills out the worksheets
- links the worksheets together and to the overall CI form for display
- links diagnostic data to key measures
- simplifies conducting CI meetings
- provides reports to help the leader enforce accountability
- stores problem-solving and project management worksheets for future use
- allows access outside the plant and communication through e-mail
- allows leaders in one plant to see if there have been similar problems or projects in other plants
- tracks assignments and due dates for all natural owners of projects, project steps, interim actions, solutions, and preventions

Leaders involve others in CI as they teach their team to use the process, tools, and software. The leader must get everyone on the team involved in the process, by making them a natural owner of a problem or project. One way to get early involvement is to assign a caretaker for each measure. The caretaker will update the results as well as develop a diagnostic data path for their measure.

Following training, the leader must insist on the use of the Continuous Improvement process, data, tools, and software. Using tools and being accountable are learned from and reinforced by the example of the leader. The leader shows accountability by being a responsible natural owner, solving problems, completing projects, and resolving human performance problems in a timely manner.

Whenever an employee reports an identified problem solved, the leader's first response is, "Show me the *Problem-Solving Worksheet.*" If no worksheet was completed, the leader's response is, "You have not finished solving the problem yet." The leader provides clear expectations that employees use the CI tools without exception.

At a regular CI meeting, each natural owner reports to the leader on progress made with problems and projects using the software. The leader does not tolerate lack of progress based on inaction, as accountability is essential to CI.

Some Managers at Hewlett Packard started a process in the 1970s called "Management by Wandering Around." Bob Waterman and Tom Peters, who wrote the introduction to *Transforming the Workplace*, a case study of the Cadillac Livonia Engine Plant, made the phrase popular in their book, *In Search of Excellence.*[1]

When CI is in place, you can make your wanderings or daily walks ten times more meaningful. High performance leaders schedule a walk to each team's CI board every week, briefly reviewing the CI forms and progress of the team. The Team Leader may use the face-to-face opportunity to request any needed support.

The performance of those who do an exceptional job is recognized and documented on the *Human Performance Improvement Worksheet*. The leader also handles those who do not perform consistently, during the *Encourage* stage. If an employee persists and fails to use the process or tools, or fails to be accountable, this is a performance issue to be addressed on the *Human Performance Improvement Worksheet*. If the expectations are clear, the training adequate, and the opportunity sufficient, there must be negative consequences. If the lack of performance continues, the consequences continue to increase in severity up to removal of the employee.

You might ask, "Is it necessary to take it to the mat?" Although it should not be, the answer is "Yes," In a high performance organization, the leader must be willing to deal with performance deficiencies up to removal, or the system fails. Sometimes one or two white rabbits will have to leave the leadership ranks; however, immediately after this occurs, the rest change color.

Once leaders complete the training of those on their team they prepare to empower them to lead the process. Using D2, the leader gets input from the team in establishing objectives and interpreting the diagnostic data. The leader sets boundaries for the process and prepares the next generation of leaders to lead the process during the *Enable* stage.

When boundaries are clear, skills are present, and team members support the Continuous Improvement process, the leader allows members of the team to go forward and run their own CI process with their own key measures. The leader turns over the day-to-day business and key measures during the *Empower* stage. As a result, employees gain ownership and become responsible. This frees the leader to focus on chronic problems, large projects, and strategic changes. The leader will stay involved and monitor the Continuous Improvement process, use of tools, and meetings, to assure consistent and disciplined implementation.

CI is a large part of leadership development. Many expectations for leaders come from implementation of the process. As leaders are trained, assessed, re-trained, evaluated, and empowered, CI becomes the way you do business.

⮑ Disciplined implementation depends on effective leadership.

⮑ Continuous Improvement, one of the key systems of high performance, has tools and software to implement in a disciplined manner.

⮑ Sequentially following the pyramid of disciplined implementation assures successful implementation of any system and tool.

Note

[1] Thomas J. Peters and Robert H. Waterman, *In Search of Excellence* (New York: Harper & Row, 1982).

PART FOUR

Developing the Workforce

20

High Performance Employees

Your only lasting competitive advantage
is the right people.

In today's rapidly changing world, new equipment and processes are obsolete three days after installation. Competitive advantages based on product differentiation usually last a matter of months, compared to a matter of years back in the 1960s. Therefore, only a more skilled, versatile, and engaged workforce will separate your business from the competition for years to come. This is why employee development is the third pillar and the third key, adaptive, and integrated system of a high performance organization. The matching principle is: the workforce must gain a broader range of skills, be more versatile, and more engaged in CI than the competition. The corresponding value is: all employees must enhance their skill and pursue performance improvement to secure their future.

It takes a matter of years not months to build a high performance workforce. The quicker you start, the better you become, and the more difficult it will be for the competition to catch up. How do you get the right people? You develop them.

The employee development system must be strong enough to overcome the mistakes of the last thirty-five years, of what I call "the age of the axe." Employee development stops disenfranchising employees, starts developing employees, and engaging them in the move to high performance to secure their future through securing the future of the organization.

I remember in the late 1960s, when a job with General Motors was a job for life. New employees fully expected to retire from the company 30 years later. Competitive wages and steady employment were enough to engender loyalty and performance from those born in the depression era and the baby boomers. In the good old days, the company was like another family.

As worldwide competition began to take its toll on North American industry, employees became expendable. They were treated as short-term costs instead of life-long family members. Cutbacks and constant threats to job security eroded loyalty and the company families dissipated. What was once a career became only a job. What was once a trusted company became another heartless employer. Loyalty and performance suffered greatly.

Unfortunately, in far too many companies, low expectations, flawed systems, and lack of values, fostered an apathetic and stagnant workforce. And what's even worse, the workforce stopped learning long ago. What happens when the learning stops? The workforce begins to lose both its desire and capacity to learn.

Experience working in Eastern Europe, in formerly communist countries, clearly shows how low performance expectations can kill initiative in complete generations. Experience in Western European countries with liberal entitlement programs clearly shows how rewarding those who work and those who do not, equally, destroys the performance as well as the competitiveness of entire countries.

When the concepts of performance and Continuous Improvement become foreign, employees avoid responsibility, cover mistakes, and do as little as possible to get through the day. Employees become disengaged and their overall attitude is one of quiet desperation. This desperation not only permeates their job, it also invades the workers' entire life. The iconic, historic Helen Keller once said, "Science may have found a cure for most evils; but it has found no remedy for the worst of them all—the apathy of human beings."[1]

Competitiveness demands a transformation! This is why employee development is a key system in a high performance organization. In business, effective leaders, CI, and employee development are the only remedies for employee apathy.

I believe that the "age of the axe" will end. Heartless companies will cut training budgets and resources, including staff, to the point that they could not develop their workforce even if they wanted to. At that point, the die will be cast; they will be on their way out of business.

Whether you are in a developing country with over staffing and unengaged employees or in a developed country that must compete with developing countries and lower wage rates, the answer is the same. To compete, you need to become a high performance organization. A high performance organization must have an engaged high performance workforce that out-performs and out-improves the competition. This is true from the Nurse to the Teacher, to the Purchasing Buyer, to the Accounting Analyst, to the Quality Inspector, to the Maintenance Technician, to the Machine Operator.

Before describing the employee development system, it is important to understand the exact meaning of a high performance workforce. Just as leadership Direction results from sequential implementation of the five E's, so will adopting the five V's develop high performance employees.

HIGH PERFORMANCE EMPLOYEES

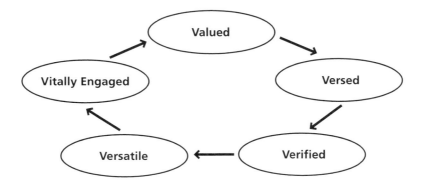

The five V's of high performance employees are sequential. First and foremost, you must **Value** your employees. After thirty years of cuts and reductions in business, employees will give their commitment only to organizations that make them feel genuinely valued. Companies must develop employees for the future, and stop treating them as a cost to reduce in the short-term. It is self-defeating to say, "We do not have the resources or money to train our workforce." Investment in people, your only lasting competitive advantage, is not discretionary.

Mindless, across-the-board cuts do not occur in a high performance organization. Unavoidable workforce reductions follow careful analysis of where overstaffing exists, a restucturing of the work to remove waste, and retraining for those who remain. In high performance companies, executives do not take bonuses while the workforce makes consessions. To lessen the number of direct reductions, a high performance company uses as many "rings of defense" as possible, including redeployment, attrition, early retirement, or having employees do work currently outsourced to contrators. Employees know that reduction of the workforce is a last resort and only done if needed for survival and to position the company for future growth. Sometimes you must get smaller to position yourself to compete and then grow.

Versed means that your employees have the broadest range of skills in the industry. Your high performance employees can do more on the job than the employees of your competitors. Versed machine Operators, for example, have a broader range of skills. They are not an extension, but the master of their job or machine. At a minimum, they do machine set-ups, programming, tool or product changes, machine parameter control, preventive maintenance, workplace upkeep, product inspection, information gathering, and data entering.

Not only does your versed high performance workforce perform a broader range of skills, each individual employee verifies on their job. **Verified** employees have demonstrated that they consistently follow the current best practice in doing each aspect of their job. More importantly, they re-verify every time a best practice is improved.

High performance employees verify on more than one job. Gone are the days when accounts receivable people were different from accounts payable people, who were different from billing people, who were different from analysts. Gone are the days when employees operate just one machine. Now they must learn and willingly operate many machines, showing the **Versatility** to produce the proper product mix. They must also be productive throughout the day, and they fill in for colleague vacancies.

The fifth V is **Vitally Engaged**. This begs the question, "Vitally engaged in what?" The answer, of course, is vitally engaged in the process of Continuous Improvement. It is not enough to employ skilled manual workers. They must also be engaged, knowledgeable workers.

Peter Drucker, the famous management consultant, broadly defined a "knowledge" worker many years ago as, "Someone who knows more about his or her job than anyone else in the organization." Similarly, B.F. Skinner asserted that, "The real problem is not if machines think, but if men do."[2] Clearly, Drucker and Skinner understood the need to utilize the minds and knowledge of the operating workforce. In a high performance organization, knowledge employees are intimately involved in CI: gathering data, setting objectives, solving problems, implementing projects, and improving performance.

Employee development is the system used to build high performance employees. True, high performance leaders not only value employees, they believe in employee development, they invest in employee development, and they implement the employee development system in a disciplined manner. Just like CI, it starts as a part of the leader's direction in the *Envision* stage. True leaders believe what we have seen all over the world, that every dollar and every hour spent on employee development or CI pays back at least one hundred dollars and one hundred hours.

Fortunately, people are resilient. Leaders can win back the minds and hearts of the workforce even after years of improper treatment and entitlement philosophy. Employee development, like leadership development, is a long-term sequential system that simultaneously builds the skills of the current workforce to the extent possible, while assuring that when the company hires new employees, it hires only those with the demonstrated skills and ability to become high performance, knowledge employees. There is no alternative way to build high performance employees. The five steps of the employee development system are shown in sequence below:

EMPLOYEE DEVELOPMENT SYSTEM

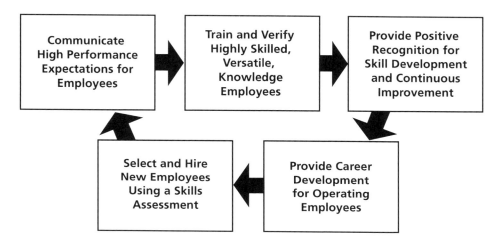

● To succeed, leaders must win back the hearts and minds of the workforce, and the first step is to value workers and treat them accordingly.

● To build a high performance workforce, develop as many existing employees as possible and hire people whose skills and abilities strengthen the company.

● Effective leaders implement the employee development system in a disciplined manner.

Notes

[1] Helen Keller, *My Religion* (Swedenborg Foundation, 1964), 127.
[2] B.F. Skinner, *Beyond Freedom and Dignity* (New York: Knopf, 1971).

21

The Power of Expectations

When you lead people, you get what you expect.

The "**Self-fulfilling Prophecy**" and the **"Pygmalion Effect"** predict that if you expect something to happen, chances are it will. Employee development, like leadership development, begins with specific and observable expectations. If you expect leaders to be true, high performance, strategic leaders and expect employees to be high performance employees, you are well on the way to making it a reality.

The term "Pygmalion Effect" comes from an ancient myth about the sculptor Pygmalion, who sought to create an ivory statue of the perfect woman. Pygmalion fell in love with the statue and prayed it would come to life. He fully expected the statue to come to life and sure enough, it did.

A modern portrayal of the "Pygmalion Effect" took place in *My Fair Lady, the* film portrayal of George Bernard Shaw's play *Pygmalion*.[1] In the movie and play, Professor Higgins bets that he can train a Cockney flower girl and pass her off as a duchess. Professor Higgins wins his bet, but it is the Cockney girl, Eliza Doolittle, who makes the main point of the play: "You see, really and truly, apart from the things anyone can pick up, the difference between a lady and a flower girl is not how she behaves, but how she's treated."

The truth behind the "Self-fulfilling Prophecy" and the "Pygmalion Effect" is that we tip people off about our expectations for them. We form expectations for people and communicate them with various cues. People respond to these cues and adjust their behavior to match our expectations.

Scientific experiments have proven the power of both the "Self-fulfilling Prophecy"' and the "Pygmalion Effect." Harvard University Professor Robert Rosenthal led a most convincing experiment. In the study, Rosenthal randomly selected twenty percent of the students in each room of an elementary school. He lied to the teachers telling them, "The selected students are intellectually gifted and will show remarkable gains during the school year." Sure enough, the randomly selected students progressed on average significantly faster than their counterparts. The randomly selected students improved greatly in verbal ability, reasoning, and overall IQ.

Why did the randomly selected students bloom? They bloomed because their teachers had high expectations for them and unknowingly had treated them differently. Rosenthal also found that people who perform well in response to high expectations are liked more, while those who perform poorly in response to low expectations are liked less.

Effective leaders communicate with employees in a way that suggests the leader values them as the only lasting competitive advantage and believes success depends on their development. When leaders communicate specific, observable, high expectations they believe employees can achieve, the result is that the leaders' expectations are met by high performing employees.

EMPLOYEE DEVELOPMENT SYSTEM

Communicating high performance expectations is the first step in implementing the employee development system. Expectations for high performance employees are clustered around two areas. The first area of expectations focuses on being versed, verified, and versatile. Examples of these high performance employee expectations include:

- Learn a broader range of skills on the job you perform.
- Verify and consistently follow the best practices in doing a job to assure safety, quality, and productivity.
- Be versatile and learn the tasks necessary to fill in for others and increase productivity.
- Rotate on the jobs you perform to stay current and re-verify whenever the best practice for a task changes, assuring that you are following the latest best practice for safety, quality, and productivity.
- Become less dependent on support resources and supervision.

The second area of high performance expectations focuses on developing vitally engaged, knowledge employees responsible for performance and Continuous Improvement in their area. Examples of employee expectations include:

- Gather and enter diagnostic data to drive CI in productivity and internal quality.
- Learn to use the *Problem-Solving Worksheet* and the *Problem Implementation Worksheet.*
- Be an accountable, natural owner of problems and projects in your team's CI process.
- Take part in the 4-S Process to improve housekeeping, orderliness, safety, and ergonomics.
- Join in setting objectives and managing the day-to-day performance of your group.

To paraphrase Chester L. Karrass[2] who wrote, "In business you don't get what you deserve, you get what you negotiate," when it comes to employee development, you don't get what you deserve, you get what you *expect.*

- ➲ The major difference between employees and high performance employees is how leaders treat them.

- ➲ Specific and observable expectations are the first part of employee development.

- ➲ If companies value employees and expect versed, versatile, and vitally engaged knowledge employees, chances are they will have high performance employees.

Notes

[1] *My Fair Lady* (1964), George Cukor's film adaptation of George Bernard Shaw's 1912 play, *Pygmalion,* that played on Broadway from 1956 to 1962.

[2] Charles L. Karrass, Ph.D., *The Negotiating Game* (New York: HarperCollins Publishers, Inc., 1970).

22

The Employee Development System

The only two ways to get the right people is to build them or hire them.

With clear expectations in place, the focus of employee development is to prepare the workforce to meet those expectations.

Clear expectations not only guide employee behavior, they also establish training requirements. In a high performance work environment, each high performance expectation leads to on-the-job or business skills training. For me, it is hard not to laugh when companies do a training-needs analysis. Clearly, in order to remove waste in any training curriculum, you should train people on what they will use. All you have to do is answer the question, "What do we expect of our employees?," and your training analysis is complete. However, with unclear expectations in low performance companies, training needs are obscure. Such companies wastefully provide the same training for everyone, whether they will use it or not.

EMPLOYEE DEVELOPMENT SYSTEM

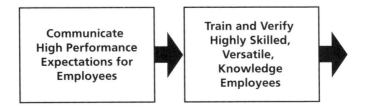

If you expect versed, verified, versatile, and vitally engaged employees, your training system should reflect that. For example, our on-the-job skills training, verification, and versatility system for operating employees, first level administrative employees, and first-level supervisory employees is **JOBS**. The acronym JOBS stands for: Job identification, Operator guidelines, Basic training, and Skills verification.

The JOBS system ensures that employees learn a broad range of skills through operator guidelines. Operator guidelines include safety, quality, tools and equipment, upkeep and maintenance, performance sequences, and classroom training needed to do the complete job. Operators help develop guidelines by documenting how they perform the job today and identifying problems with the existing method. A rough draft becomes a finished guideline by removing waste, adjoining value-added activities, and adding the detail, pictures, references, and information needed to effectively teach a new employee to do the job.

The JOBS system has four levels of verification: **learning, able, fully trained,** and **expert**. The *Learning* level means the employee is not yet skilled enough to work on the job alone. *Able* means the employee can do the basic job in a safe manner while meeting productivity and quality requirements. *Fully trained* means the employee can do the full range of tasks in the broadened operating guideline. *Expert* means the employee can handle unusual and emergency situations without needing supervision or help from support or indirect resources.

A training checklist contains every task from an operator guideline. Operators verify on every task through demonstration, explanation, or observation. The training checklist assures each employee performs each task correctly. This verification process promotes consistency among employees and shifts. Every time any part of a job changes, every employee doing that particular job as either their primary job or a versatility job, re-verifies to the latest best practice.

Versatility is not like money, you can actually have too much versatility. Too much versatility causes over-rotation, waste of training resources and time, and excessive retraining when a job changes. Many companies create waste, safety issues, productivity problems, and quality concerns by over-rotation and insisting that Operators learn too many jobs.

A mathematical formula calculates ideal versatility. The versatility formula is as follows:

> (Minimum number of Operators required for a job per shift) times (one plus the average absenteeism percentage) times (one plus the percentage of average vacation days in a year) times (one plus the average annual turnover percentage) times (1.20 safety factor for training, meetings, injuries, and unpaid leaves) = # of verified employees, per shift, per job for ideal versatility.

For example, if the minimum number of Crane Operators needed per shift is 4, the average daily absenteeism percentage is 4 percent, the vacation and time off is 7 percent, and the average turnover is 4 percent, ideal versatility would require that 6 people per shift verify as crane Operators.

$$4 \times 1.04 \times 1.07 \times 1.04 \times 1.20 \text{ (safety factor)} = 5.55 \text{ rounded up to 6 employees}$$

The number of employees on each shift and the number of employees needed to learn each job will indicate the ideal number of jobs each employee should learn.

The JOBS module of our Web-based high performance Transformation Software supports the JOBS process. The software:

- controls the training documents
- tracks verification level
- identifies the jobs each employee needs to learn
- lists employees needing re-verification when a job changes
- prints the job change to simplify re-verification
- tracks employee training
- stores documents for each employee including *Human Performance Improvement Worksheets*
- records progression history
- provides a history of job changes
- identifies trained replacements when Operators are missing
- specifies the needed job rotation to stay current
- develops reports and data about employee training

The JOBS module of the Web-based Transformation Software also measures the percentage of fully verified employees and provides a data path to focus improvement, as this is a key measure in the training major performance area for CI.

TECS is our on-the-job training system to develop and verify maintenance and first-level technical employees. The acronym TECS stands for: Tasks and skills needed, Establish levels of skills, Create operating guidelines, and Skills verification. The TECS training system is similar to JOBS. The difference is that technical employees learn skills used only when needed across the company, while operating employees learn a job done almost every day in the same place. The JOBS and TECS systems assure that front-line employees learn and verify on a broad range of skills for their job.

To develop knowledge employees, business-skills training complements skills learned in on-the-job training. In a high performance organization, employees learn how to gather diagnostic data and how to become effective natural owners in

CI. This means every employee understands CI and is trained to solve problems and implement projects. On-the-job training coupled with business training prepares employees to fulfill high performance expectations.

EMPLOYEE DEVELOPMENT SYSTEM

Recognition systems accelerate individual employee skill development and encourage involvement in Continuous Improvement. Like any other behavior, skill development and involvement are more likely to reoccur, if reinforced with immediate positive consequences.

High performance recognitions systems, as discussed in Chapter Twenty-Seven: Pillar Support Systems, reinforces two types of behavior. Informal team recognition and gain sharing promote achieving CI objectives and "Pay-for-Skills" encourages individual development.

EMPLOYEE DEVELOPMENT SYSTEM

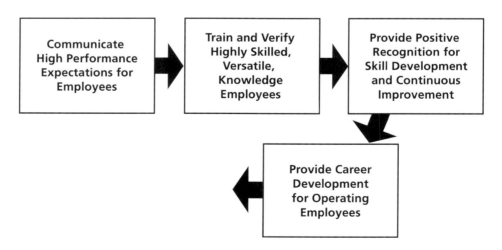

Providing career development opportunities is a form of rewarding skill development. While it is true that a great worker can become a terrible Supervisor, it is also true that some workers become excellent Supervisors. This is no different than the fact that some Engineers become terrible Managers, while some Engineers become excellent Managers.

The solution is not to bar workers from joining the management ranks or becoming operating Team Leaders, but to select only those skilled workers who also have leadership skills. The same is true for engineers becoming leaders. The most accurate method of predicting the presence of leadership skills is a behavioral leadership skills assessment. In a high performance organization, hiring or promotion into a leadership position requires that candidates score well enough on a leadership skills assessment to predict success. This is true even for a first-level Operating Leader who remains a member of a bargaining unit or operating workforce.

To move into a leadership position, an Operator must be able to perform many tasks. These tasks include resolving performance issues, running meetings, leading CI, using the high performance software, solving problems, managing projects, and training and verifying others. A behavioral leadership assessment accurately measures these abilities.

By using a well-designed leadership skills assessment, a high performance company can offer employees that move to the top of their pay levels an opportunity to progress into a new career and become a high performance leader. Ensuring leadership skills before promotion helps to prevent employees from the stigma that comes from failing in a job assignment.

EMPLOYEE DEVELOPMENT SYSTEM

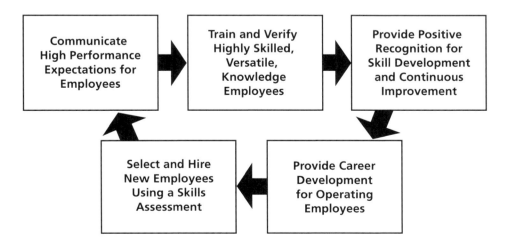

A behavioral skills assessment is also the tool used for new employee selection. The assessment activities are different from those used in a leadership assessment, but the process is the same.

High performance companies never hire an employee unless they score well on a new-hire behavioral assessment process. Potential employees need the ability to learn a broad range of skills in an operating guideline as well as participate in the Continuous Improvement process. They must do the calculations to set up machines and program their equipment. They must gather data accurately on a check sheet to drive CI. They must learn how to solve problems and complete projects. They must be able to communicate and work effectively in a team environment. A behavioral skills assessment accurately measures the prospective employee's potential to fill these needs. A good score means the candidate is capable of gaining the skills and verifying to the top level of high performance employees.

Some of our clients say, "The biggest difference we find when we implement the high performance systems is the difference in employees hired and those selected for leadership positions using a behavioral skills assessment." Our experience indicates that an assessment tailored to each company and job is more than 90% accurate in selection compared with 65% for written tests and 55% for interviews.

Like leadership development, the only way to develop a high performance workforce is to develop as many of the current workers as possible. At the same time, when hiring, make sure the new employee has the potential to become a high performance employee.

Developing high performance employees, the third pillar of a high performance organization, is not optional in today's competitive world market. Your company's employee development system is the key to survival and success today and into the future. As the need for technological skills expands and the expectations, training, and operating guidelines change to reflect the latest best practices, the employee development system will adapt accordingly.

➲ Employee skill development depends on a well-designed employee training and verification system.

➲ Positive rewards will promote employee skill development and involvement in CI.

➲ Use a behavioral skills assessment when hiring employees or promoting them into leadership positions to assure needed skills.

PART FIVE

**Short-Term
Directed Improvement**

23

Understanding Short-Term Directed Improvement

Necessity is the mother of invention.[1]

Our rapidly changing world catches every company with their proverbial pants down. Sudden changes with a customer, in a market, in an industry, or in the world can pose a new and immediate survival threat. When this happens, there is not enough time to respond with a strategic change or through incremental Continuous Improvement. Facing such a survival threat, leaders must react quickly with a short-term directed improvement process.

For example, modern-day changes caught one paper mill flat-footed and in need of an effective, short-term directed improvement system. The company's survival was challenged when its biggest customer suddenly demanded daily, just-in-time delivery. Unfortunately, it took the mill 3.3 working days to process orders, schedule production, and produce the paper. Moreover, the customer expected next day delivery for orders placed before 10 A.M. on the previous day and that the just-in-time delivery system be in place within thirty days. If just-in-time delivery was not offered within thirty days, the customer, a large printing house, threatened to find another supplier of paper.

The mill did not have time to buy new computers and scheduling software, or add production capacity. Incremental improvement from CI would not meet this challenge in time. The mill faced losing its main customer unless it quickly and fundamentally changed how it received and processed orders, scheduled production, and produced coated, ground wood paper, or lose the business. The only answer was short-term directed improvement.

There are only two choices in an immediate survival threat: quickly change or lose the business. In a high performance organization, a key, integrated, and adaptive short-term directed improvement system quickly responds to emergencies

The fourth pillar of a high performance organization, is a key system because of its ability to help a company respond to immediate survival threats. Short-term directed improvements integrate with the other pillar systems. Short-term directed improvements rely on employee development to achieve consistency and reduce the impact of difficult changes on employees. Integrated, short-term directed improvements also rely on CI to assure that ongoing improvement follows the one-time, immediate improvements.

The short-term directed improvement process reacts to survival threats and also has a proactive side. Proactive use of a short-term directed improvement analysis removes waste from operator guidelines in the JOBS process, finds bottlenecks to help teams prioritize in CI, helps design the work areas of new front-line operating teams, and helps combine jobs or levels when spreading a high performance structure.

The power of a short-term directed improvement comes from having many people focused on one product family or administrative service for a significant and uninterrupted block of time. This is similar to sunlight. Though the sun shines every day, it is only when focused with a magnifying glass, that the sun can start a fire. Short-term directed improvement is the magnifying glass to focus the company talent that is there every day. The intensity of effort causes a fire to quickly change the way business is done, and results in beating back the survival threat.

The proper time to use a reactive short-term directed improvement is only when needed as a last resort. Reactive applications of short-term directed improvement typically involve large and disruptive changes. The existing way of doing business is turned upside down, torn apart, and put back together again with all the associated risks. Planned strategic changes and incremental Continuous Improvement also dramatically change results, but with far less trauma. Evolution happens successfully every day in a high performance organization; revolution only succeeds at the proper time. The necessity must occur before the invention.

Many times, reactive short-term directed improvement becomes necessary to repair damage done when companies repeatedly and arbitrarily reduce the workforce without first removing waste or changing the way the work is performed. Short-sighted leaders often dictate repeated, across-the-board workforce reductions until the company is on the brink of failure, and the workforce is totally overwhelmed and alienated. Out of desperation, some companies finally see the light and implement a well-designed, integrated short-term directed improvement process to re-move waste and provide the skills and versatility that the already reduced workforce needs to succeed. These efforts buy time to allow the company to begin a move to high performance.

The early improvement from a large reactive short-term directed improvement effort can be enormous. On the positive side: cost, lead-time, inventory, flow, and bottlenecks improve. On the negative side, as is always the case with drastic changes in how business is done, quality and output may vary, injuries may increase, and the security of employees may decrease.

Many companies and leaders make the serious mistake of using reactive short-term directed improvement tools as part of their ongoing process instead of only using them when needed. They do not realize that reactive short-term directed improvement is like penicillin. It is great when you are sick, but used on a daily basis it can kill you. The result of using short-term directed improvement as an ongoing improvement process is a constant state of flux. Downtime crashes, injuries, and quality escapes increase and worst of all, the workforce becomes threatened, detached, and alienated.

It's like playing with fire to routinely use Kaizen events, black belt projects, and process or value-stream mapping. The measure of success then becomes how many and how often events occur instead of simply doing them when needed. An aerospace industry operator in a manufacturing cell, told us, "We did Kaizen events, 5-S, Six Sigma, green belt projects, black belt projects, and a process map . . . man, everyone is confused and upset. The worst part is our efficiency is down and we have just as many scrapped parts as before." Inconsistency in performance and a threatened workforce will destroy a company's chances of evolving into a high performance organization.

We have heard leaders say, "We need to create a compelling need to convince the workforce and union to cooperate." You never create a compelling need, it either exists or not. Like the little boy in Aesop's fable, "The Boy Who Cried Wolf," if you make up a crisis too many times, when a real wolf appears, no one will lift a finger to help. "No one believes a liar . . . even when he is telling the truth!"[2] A true leader creates awareness of a compelling need, not the need itself.

Proactive, short-term directed improvements are small, localized initiatives done to help spread high performance systems across the company. The improvement analysis usually affects one job, one role, or one team. Proactive short-term directed improvement helps:

- natural work groups identify their bottleneck to focus improvement as they begin implementation of CI.
- remove wasted time, material, and effort from a job in developing an operating guideline in the JOBS process.
- a natural work group organize an efficient work area by eliminating process bottlenecks.
- in consolidating groups or jobs in structure design as a high performance structure evolves.
- in the removal of a level of leadership or teams in structure design as a high performance structure evolves.
- launch new products, teams, or new work areas.

High performance organizations do not make reactive short-term directed improvements very often. They rely on strategic leadership, disciplined strategic planning, and a vibrant Continuous Improvement process. The organizations frequently schedule proactive, short-term directed improvements to help spread high performance systems and structure throughout the company. Reactive short-term directed improvement is never allowed to become a numbers game or a regular routine.

Ineffective leaders abandon the people they lead when faced with a survival threat. Yet, these are the people who possess the information and innovation to develop the needed changes and the people who must support the changes for the company to succeed. Instead, these ineffective leaders rely on uninformed outside consultants and black belts, or mindless across-the-board workforce cuts. The results are a detached and disillusioned workforce, flawed changes, and the loss of the high performance organization. The reaction of most employees is typically, "They did it to us, not with us."

When employees understand the threat to the company, join in the analysis, witness efforts to minimize adverse affects, and receive training and recognition for performing effectively in the new way of doing business, you are doing it with the workforce, not to them.

When the going gets rough, a true leader turns to the workforce and engages them in the fight against a common enemy and in pursuit of a common objective. The workforce responds because they know the leader has their best interests at heart. A high performance leader who correctly engages the workforce in a short-term directed system will make the high performance organization stronger. As a team, a high performance leader and a workforce correctly engaged in a short-term directed improvement develop pride in the fact that together they have averted a survival threat.

The success of quick directed improvement depends upon leadership development, CI, and employee development. If these key, prerequisite systems are in place, short-term directed improvement is effective, ongoing, and positive, rather than destructive, fleeting, and divisive.

There are many forms of short-term directed improvement. For example, when we did the plan for the Livonia Engine Plant in 1979, we used a socio-technical change model to match our new technology and the human work environment. Some companies use Kaizen events, reengineering, redesigns, and lean manufacturing, including Six Sigma tools led by black and green belts. Still others hire large consulting companies, who send in a bevy of young MBAs to benchmark your processes against what they believe to be the best. Regardless of differences in industries and culture, their challenge is, "If they can do it, why can't you?"

While these tools have value when used properly, none of them fit naturally in a high performance organization. Leaders must understand when and how to make short-term directed changes. All of the approaches mentioned above aggravate the dangers associated with short-term directed improvement, as they invariably strive to become permanent. Soon they push the company and the workforce beyond the real need to change. The result is an abrupt crash, often putting the company on life support.

Not one of these short-term directed improvement tools include minimizing the adverse effects on the workforce through techniques like redeployment, in-sourcing, early retirement, and attrition. The tools fail to supply a method for properly selecting those who should remain, or an employee development system to teach them the skills, or recognition systems to provide the motivation they will need to succeed in the new environment.

Our short-term directed improvement process is called **PRIDE,** discussed further in the next chapter. PRIDE naturally works with the other integrated systems of a high performance organization to minimize the danger associated with reactive short-term directed improvement and to maximize the gain. PRIDE is the only short-term directed improvement tool that assures, as a part of its method, that the changes made are consistent with the values, principles, and systems of the high performance organization.

- ◯ The dynamic global market causes immediate survival threats; effective short-term directed improvement efforts react to the threats in a timely fashion.

- ◯ Proactive short-term directed improvement efforts help the spread of high performance systems and structure across the organization.

- ◯ Involve the workforce in short-term directed improvement efforts and integrate them with the employee development and CI systems.

Notes

[1] Plato, *Plato: The Republic*, 387–361 BC. Ed. G.R.F. Ferrari. Trans. Tom Griffith, (New York: Cambridge University Press, 2000).

[2] Aesop, "The Boy Who Cried Wolf," *Aesop's Fables*, (Greece: Sixth Century BC).

24

The PRIDE Process

When the going gets tough, the tough get PRIDE.

The name PRIDE is fitting because PRIDE is done *with* the workforce, not *to* them. Making short-term directed improvement to fend off a survival threat is something the workforce can take pride in, not fear. Doing an analysis to improve a team's work area, CI process, or an individual's job is something in which the workforce takes pride. PRIDE is also an acronym for the sequential steps necessary when performing a high performance, short-term directed improvement initiative.

PRIDE

Pre-Select the job, team, process, product family, or administrative service.

Pick and **P**repare the PRIDE team.

Picture the flow, steps, and processes in the way business is done today.

Review the picture for waste and bottlenecks.

Identify actions to reduce waste, break bottlenecks, add value-added activities, and balance the flow.

Implement quick changes and **I**nitiate projects for longer-term improvements.

Develop the picture of steps, process, and flow in the new way of doing business.

Develop new procedures to match the new way of doing business.

Establish efficient staffing levels, ways to minimize impact on the workforce, and effective selection systems to choose those who remain.

Establish JOBS or TECS to train and verify employees.

Evaluate Pay-for-Skills to reward those remaining and needing enhanced versatility.

Establish key measures and diagnostics to drive CI and **E**valuate results.

The first three steps of PRIDE start with the letter P and are as follows:

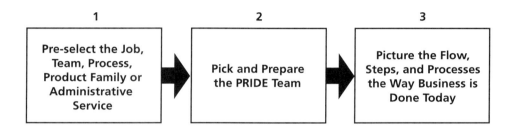

As seen above, the first step is to select and describe the exact job, team, or process for proactive initiatives or the product family or administrative service that is causing the survival threat calling for a reactive initiative. Proactive PRIDE has a narrow focus, while reactive PRIDE has a broad focus.

In reactive PRIDE, it is advisable to examine a product family or service from beginning to end and evaluate the entire flow, instead of just one or a few processes within the product or service flow. Survival threats demand that many processes get changed at once. Concentrating on the entire flow will avoid optimizing individual processes to the detriment of the entire flow. For example, for a product family, a reactive PRIDE analysis usually would begin from receipt of an order to delivery to the customer. A reactive administrative service PRIDE analysis usually would begin with the generation of a need for the service until the service is complete and payment made.

With a description of the job, team, process, product family, or administrative service from beginning to end, selection of the proper PRIDE team is easy. A reactive PRIDE team usually has twelve to fifteen people responsible for performing the PRIDE analysis. PRIDE team members include the top leader of the affected area, those performing the job, and those needed to change or automate steps in the product or service flow. A proactive PRIDE team usually includes five to six people. Members include those doing the job, their leader, their internal customer, and service employees.

PRIDE teams are ad hoc and cross-functional. Each team forms, does the PRIDE analysis, and disbands. The top leader of the area most impacted is a member of the team and champion of the process. Like all other high performance systems, PRIDE needs effective leadership, disciplined implementation, and accountability.

In a production PRIDE, members usually include representatives from production, maintenance, material management, quality, information technology, and shipping. In an administrative service PRIDE, representatives can come from the groups related to the service. For example, representatives from purchasing, accounting, warehousing, information technologies, suppliers, and production would make up a PRIDE team charged to improve the service of purchasing production materials.

An outside resource is in the best position to point out waste in the existing process. Those directly involved are too close. The outside resource can also facilitate the PRIDE meetings and process. Selection criteria for a PRIDE team include knowledge of the existing job, influence with others, ability to question the current practices, creativity, and willingness to suggest painful changes in the face of a survival threat.

There are several components to preparing the PRIDE team. In a reactive PRIDE, the first part is to assure the team understands the survival threat and the need to change. The participants must realize that having to change quickly can save the business, even if it involves some sacrifices. Besides the economic benefit, they will support change for the long-term security and growth that come with meeting the competitive challenge. In a proactive PRIDE, the first step is to assure the team understands how the analysis helps implement JOBS, CI, or a high performance structure.

The second part of preparing the PRIDE team is team-building. Every team must progress through several stages to become productive. PRIDE teams are usually uninformed and unprepared when they first come together. All effective team building centers on carrying out a mission, task, or achieving an objective. We use several team-building techniques to help the PRIDE team move quickly from a position of incomplete understanding, misgivings, and parochial thinking to a productive group focused on a common objective.

During the last step in preparation, the PRIDE team learns a technique to picture the current product or service processes in a flow from beginning to end. Creating a simple picture of how the job is done today takes two or three days to complete. Picturing the process is nothing more than developing a flowchart comprised of each process in a reactive PRIDE, or activity in a proactive PRIDE. A process occurs every time there is an input, an activity, and an output. The flowchart for the current order processing and scheduling service from the threatened paper mill needing just-in-time delivery to save its biggest customer is shown below.[1]

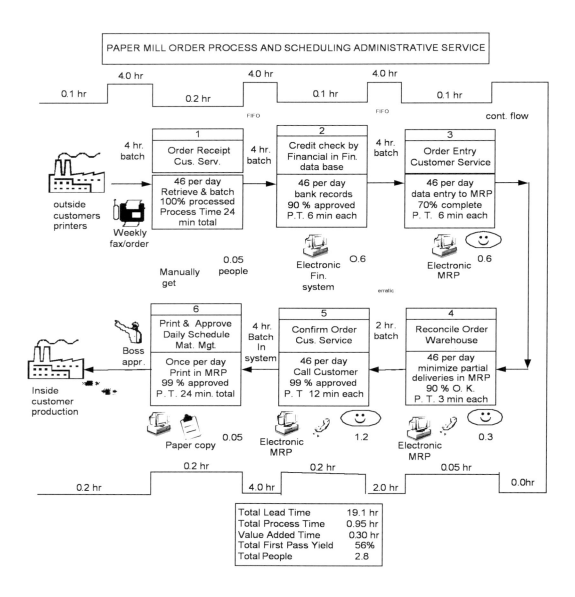

Process description includes:

- What activity is done
- Who does the activity
- How many people it takes to do the activity
- Time it takes to do one part or one transaction
- Technology and tools involved
- Percent of first pass yield
- Direction and flow of the product, service, and information

"Total lead-time" is the sum of all process and delay times between processes. "Process time" is the time to do one-piece or transaction. The "total process time" is the sum of all the process times. "Value-added time" is the time to do those processes where the service or product changes in nature or character for the benefit of a customer. For example, receiving an order and checking credit are non-value process times. Turning the order into a Manufacturing Resource Planning (MRP) entry and developing a production schedule are value-added process times.

My fifteen years of experience with PRIDE show that large disparities exist between lead-time and process time in most administrative and product flows. During PRIDE, the objective is to reduce the lead-time closer to process time and to reduce process time closer to value-added time. On product families, PRIDE usually nets 30% improvement in time and resources and more than 50% on administrative services.

The number of people used in a process means how many people on average do an activity and for roughly how much of their working time. If four people spend 20% of their time doing an activity every day, that would equal 0.8 people fully used in the process. An alternative formula is to multiply the time to do one transaction, times the number of transactions done per day, and divide by eight hours. If one transaction requires two hours and three transactions are done on average each day, that also would be 0.8 people fully used. Creating the picture is an art, not a science. Estimates and averages are the order of the day.

The team starts tearing apart the current picture immediately upon its completion. The PRIDE system's next three steps, 4 through 6, start with the letters R and I. These steps focus on changing the way we do a job or process, produce a product, or provide a service.

PRIDE

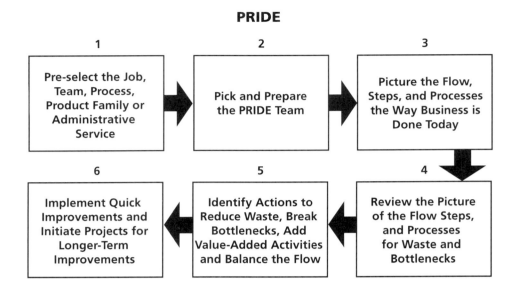

Reviewing the picture of the flow and processes for waste requires the PRIDE team to learn PRIDE thinking. A simple example of "PRIDE thinking" is, **"How do we create the most value for the customer while consuming the fewest resources?"** Resources are time, people, and material. Some of the keys for finding waste are answering the following questions about each process or activity that makes up the job, process, team role, product family, or service flow.

- Does this process or activity add value?
- Can we eliminate this process or activity without losing value for the company or a customer?
- Does this process or activity have too many steps? (redundant steps, multiple approvals, or double data entry)
- Does this process or activity need correction in any form? (product defects or paperwork errors)
- Does this process or activity involve waiting before, during, or after activities? (lack of inventory, lack of available resources, or batching of transactions)
- Does this process or activity have excess motion or transportation? (walking to get a tool or walking to archive documents in a file cabinet)
- Does this process or activity over-produce, causing in-process inventory?

- Does this process or activity under-produce, causing delays further on in the process flow?
- Is the flow of parts, material, or paperwork pulled as needed or pushed as produced on the next process or activity?
- Does this process or activity cause an imbalance in the flow of the product or service?
- Does this process or activity have unneeded or double inspection?
- Does this process or activity repeat what is or could be done more efficiently elsewhere?
- Could we automate this process or activity to save time and resources?
- Can we reduce the time required for this process or activity?
- Does this process or activity involve a lack of trust, causing excessive approvals and associated delay?
- Is only part of the job done in this process or activity because employees do not have all the skills, information, tools, or training for doing a more complete job?
- Can this process be combined with other processes and activities to save time and resources?

Part of reviewing for waste is to identify bottlenecks. Bottlenecks may occur where parts or paperwork gather, in processes that must run on overtime regularly, on operations that process every piece of paper or every product, and on the jobs nobody wants to do. The four types of bottlenecks are speed, quality, reliability, and lack of resources (people or material).

Look at the waste and bottlenecks identified on the simple paper mill order processing and scheduling flow chart that follows.

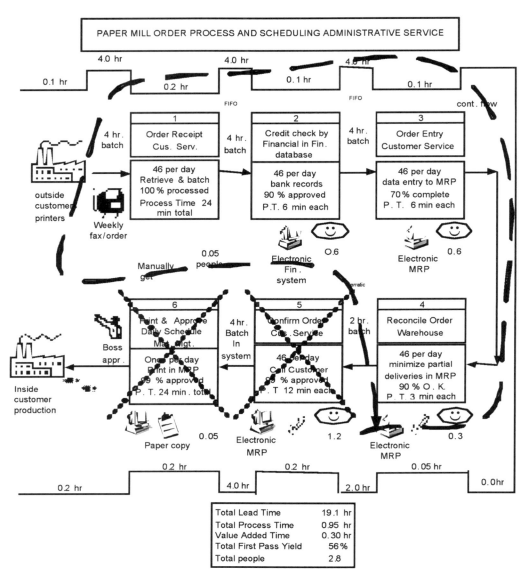

PAPER MILL ORDER PROCESS AND SCHEDULING ADMINISTRATIVE SERVICE

Total Lead Time	19.1 hr
Total Process Time	0.95 hr
Value Added Time	0.30 hr
Total First Pass Yield	56%
Total people	2.8

Wasted Time
between customer and
step 1 and between
steps 1 & 2 and 2 & 3

Wasted Motion
manually getting
paperwork in steps
1, 2, 3, & 4

Wasted Material
making a paper copy of
schedules

Quality Bottleneck
only 70% of the orders
received are
complete

Lack of Training
separate operators
retrieve, receive, check
and schedule

Lack of Trust
Verified orders still must
be approved

Wasted People
1.2 people used up
confirming orders

Combine Steps 1 - 4
all tasks can be learned
by one person

Eliminate Steps 5 & 6
completely non -value
added

Next, the PRIDE team develops suggestions on how to combine activities, remove waste, break bottlenecks, broaden tasks, automate, cut out steps, or reduce the resources used in a step. Each suggestion is either an immediate or a longer-term improvement. We use thirty days as a limit for the time necessary to complete an immediate change. Going back to our example of the paper mill, here are suggestions of the PRIDE team analyzing the company's order processing and scheduling service:

- Link financial software and MRP to avoid double-data entry. (longer-term)
- Develop a Web site for customers to enter orders to eliminate receiving faxes and incorporate electronic order confirmation for existing customers. (immediate)
- Have the Web site require all the information before order acceptance to eliminate errors in the quality bottleneck. (immediate)
- Develop a patch so the Web site will dump orders directly into the integrated financial and MRP software to eliminate order entry altogether. (longer-term)
- Train employees to do multiple tasks, including credit check, reconciling orders, developing the schedule, operating in MRP and the financial database. (longer-term)
- Provide job skill training and verification to employees running the new system as well as Pay-for-Skills to recognize them for becoming more versed and versatile. (longer–term)
- Electronically post the schedule on the Web site and update every four hours to accommodate just-in-time delivery to the customer. (immediate)

Now, see the final draft of the current picture with all the suggestions made at the paper mill.

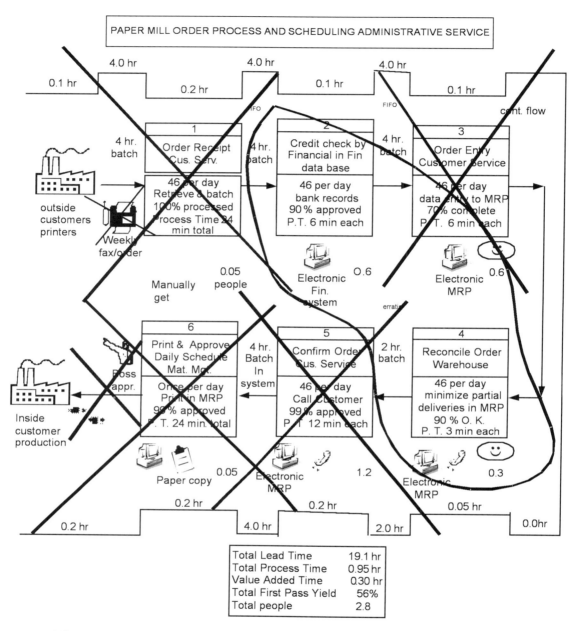

PAPER MILL ORDER PROCESS AND SCHEDULING ADMINISTRATIVE SERVICE

Total Lead Time	19.1 hr
Total Process Time	0.95 hr
Value Added Time	0.30 hr
Total First Pass Yield	56%
Total people	2.8

The next two steps of PRIDE are action steps. Implementation of immediate changes occurs within thirty days following an approval meeting. Where necessary, use *Project Implementation Worksheets* to organize implementation of the changes. Assign natural owners responsible to develop the steps and responsubilites for each improvement project. The ranking leader of the area most affected conducts a weekly PRIDE project completion meeting until all projects are completed. The champion of the PRIDE process will assure disciplined implementation and accountability in meeting target dates on the *Project Implementation Worksheet,* just like in CI.

PRIDE

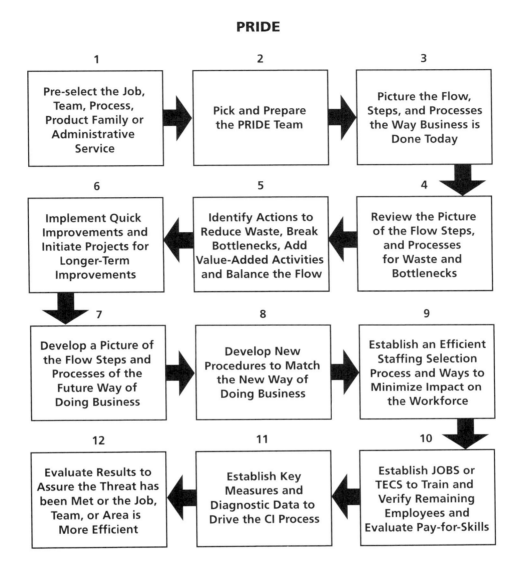

The final six steps of PRIDE, 7 through 12, address preparing for the future. Step 7 pictures the processes and flow of the future way of doing business. The future picture is important to visualize the changes, show the improvement, and help develop the new operating procedures in a reactive PRIDE and operating guidelines in a proactive PRIDE. New procedures or guidelines developed in step 8 of PRIDE are necessary to assure consistency and allow the company to achieve ISO and or other certifications necessary in its industry. Depicted next is the paper mill's future way of doing business in the paper ordering and receiving department.

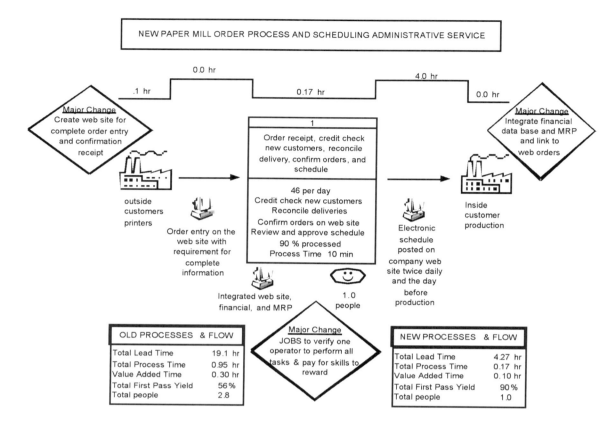

In Steps 9 and 10, the focus of PRIDE moves to people. This is where PRIDE differentiates itself from *any* other short-term improvement process. People are the key to making any new process work, and PRIDE has several steps to assure a positive result. The key people-related activities are advanced by:

- Efficient staffing
- Selecting the people most likely to succeed
- Minimizing any negative impact on the workforce
- Training and skills verification
- Evaluating Pay-for-Skills

For example in the paper mill, efficient staffing for the new way of doing business, shown above, moves from 2.8 people to 1 person. The timing of resources reassignment depends on the timing for completing the required changes and training of the remaining resource.

Behavioral skills assessment will help select people with the best chance for success. In the paper mill, the posting of a new position in customer service preceded a behavioral skills assessment. The assessment determined which candidate had the best computer and personal skills for success.

The advisable way to minimize the adverse impact of a staff reduction is to do it by attrition. In the paper mill, two people who were no longer needed in their area were given six-month assignments to train customers on the new Web site ordering system and to train and verify the person selected to perform in the new system. At the end of six months, the mill had two openings from attrition which absorbed displaced resources.

In a reactive PRIDE, it is not always possible to rely strictly on redeployment and attrition when facing a business survival threat. In this case, the PRIDE analysis includes exploring every ring of defense possible before directly reducing employees. One important message that must come through from the leader is that reducing the workforce is an agonizing last resort, rather than the first tactic a false leader uses to cut cost. The second important message is that sometimes it is necessary to lose one job in order to save ten and to position the company to grow in the future.

The most common mistake made in short-term directed improvement processes other than PRIDE, is that they result in fewer people doing more work without the benefit of additional training or positive reinforcement. The unavoidable result is that the company loses the hearts and minds of its workforce as well as the potential of becoming a high performance organization. PRIDE, on the other hand, integrates with employee development by creating operating guidelines and training checklists to train and verify employees. Where possible, increasing the pay of employees who gain needed skills provides positive recognition.

Unlike most short-term, directed improvement processes that show early results and then decline, Step 11 of PRIDE integrates with CI to assure that consistency and ongoing improvement occur. Through CI, first pass yeild at the paper mill improved from 90% to 96% and the cycle time for order processing and scheduling decreased from 4.3 hours to 3.9 hours.

The last step of the process for a reactive PRIDE is to assure the changes were enough to meet the survival threat. The job, process, or team should be more efficient in a proactive PRIDE. Prepared to meet the just-in-time delivery needs of its largest customer, the paper mill stayed in business. Dramatically, the paper mill picked up three additional customers because of its new just-in-time delivery capacity. The mill added a shift to one of its paper machines to cover the increase in sales.

PRIDE is a positive and powerful weapon to assure competitiveness. It will protect your high performance workforce by assuring the organization will adapt in time to meet unexpected survival challenges and move to high performance necessary for long-term survival and growth.

➔ PRIDE initiatives involve the workforce in ad hoc teams prepared to describe the current flow and processes and the future way of doing business.

➔ PRIDE initiatives reduce waste and break bottlenecks to improve: a job, team responsibilities, work area, processes, products, or services.

➔ The PRIDE process minimizes negative impacts on the workforce and assures proper selection, training, and recognition of those who gain new skills and versatility.

Note

[1] Mike Rother and others, *Learning to See, 3rd ed.* (Cambridge, MA: Lean Enterprise Institute, 2003) provides a more complete description of process mapping and flow-charting.

PART SIX

Structure and Support Systems

25

High Performance Structure

> We trained hard, but it seemed that every time we
> were beginning to form up into teams, we would be
> reorganized. I was to learn later in life that we tend to
> meet any new situation by reorganizing; and a wonderful
> method it can be for creating the illusion of progress while
> producing confusion, inefficiency, and demoralization.
>
> Gaius Petronus Arbiter[1]

The fifth and final pillar of a high performance organization is **structure and support systems**. Three things change organizations: people, systems, and structure. Effective leaders and high performance employees are the people who change organizations. The five Pillars of High Performance are the systems that change organizations. An organizational structure that supports rather than inhibits development, empowerment, accountability, and speed will help organizations become high performance.

This chapter starts with a remarkably intuitive quote usually attributed to Gaius Petronius Arbiter (210 BC), although the earliest reference was not until 1970. The quote explains that changing structure to meet every new situation, or to accommodate individual strengths or weaknesses, is a quick road to ruin. It is essential to design a structure to match strategic directions and strengthen high performance, and then evolve into the structure with the growing competence and skills of the workforce. To understand the concept, consider the difference between any structure and a high performance structure.

The design of a high performance structure supports the strategic direction of a company in terms of products, processes, or markets. A principle underlying the five pillars is: the company must fundamentally change products, processes, or markets faster than the competition.

The design of a high performance structure supports implementing the pillars because a high performance organization will improve faster than the competition. As Continuous Improvement is a team sport like football, not an individual sport like golf, a high performance structure must be team-oriented. This means a high performance organization provides for teamwork, team identity, and most importantly, team leadership. A principle underlying high performance is: everyone must be on at least one natural work group pursuing Continuous Improvement.

The design of a high performance structure also minimizes the numbers of levels and teams to support efficiency and speed by reducing bottlenecks and encouraging empowerment. Another principle underlying the pillars is: the organization must be efficiently staffed.

Like each of the pillar systems, a high performance structure is key, integrated, and adaptive. Structures either smother or foster growth, accountability, empowerment, and speed. A structure that supports decision-making and accountability at the level closest to the action accelerates leadership development, employee development, and speed.

It is both frustrating and time-consuming trying to move to a new level of performance with an inconsistent, fractured, suffocating, and inefficient organizational structure. Organizational structures usually change over years based on the talents or lack of talents of one individual leader, addition of new products or processes, efforts to build power, or the latest fad. Rarely do old structures match and support the most important journey a company will ever take: the move to high performance.

In most companies, every time the structure changes, performance suffers. This is because organizations change structure for the wrong reasons and at the wrong time. Strategically designing and gradually evolving a high performance structure as the workforce and systems develop will remove turf battles, fragmented responsibility, clouded accountability, and resultant waste and delays. A high performance structure changes as people and teams develop and become more independent, just as the human body slowly becomes more trim and fit through regular exercise.

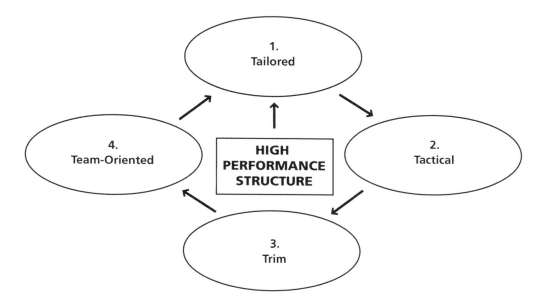

Designing and then evolving a high performance structure is a systematic process that follows the four T's: Tailored, Tactical, Trim, and Team-oriented.

A Tailored structure supports the five Pillars of a High Performance organization and focuses on strategic products, services, or markets.

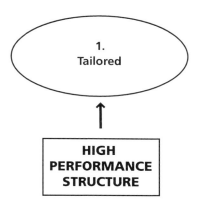

There is no ideal structure. However, designing a structure to support high performance depends on whether business groups are decentralized or centralized with confined control. Debates over the best type of structure, centralized or decentralized, have gone on for decades. Some companies have moved back and forth several times. I remember in the 1980s, when General Motors abruptly moved from independent car divisions to centralized platforms. Performance and identity suffered for years as a result.

A high performance organization, almost by definition, demands a decentralized structure. Having said that, some tasks demand centralization and combination to reduce cost and assure consistency. For example, it is a good idea to consolidate purchasing on widely used commodities to achieve volume discounts. However, a trim, decentralized organization does better if it consolidates buying a group of commodities for the company in one of the business divisions rather than create a central corporate procurement structure. Most central structures limit the responsibility of the business or operating divisions. Just as you cannot cut your way to high performance, you cannot control your way there either.

Decentralized means that operating locations have broad discretion and the skills necessary to conduct business without constant approval from corporate support groups. Centralized, functional structures with many silos, tight control, and fragmented responsibilities clash with the combined roles necessary to give a team the expertise and resources to run its part of the business.

To kill an old myth perpetuating silos in an organization, Engineers do not have to report to Engineering to become effective and developed. Maintenance Technicians do not have to report to Maintenance to become effective and developed, and and the same with Accountants to Accounting. In a high performance structure, workers report where they spend most of their time and effort and you rarely see a dotted line. Recently, one of our clients moved corporate accounting people trying to control the financial performance of several remote locations to the various operations leadership teams. Cost performance improved as the accountants helped their operating facility find and remove waste in running the operation.

The rapidly changing world market demands that, once designed, the structure be able to evolve as systems of high performance spread and people and teams develop. Small structure changes resulting from increased efficiency, growth, empowered teams, and waste reduction happen often and without trauma. This promotes greater ownership with immediate performance improvement.

Selecting the best overall structure begins by choosing the one that is best tailored to your company's strategic products, services, or markets. The chosen overall structure is then customized to accommodate the move to high performance. Do not design structure around the skills or lack of skills of individual people. First design the structure and then place, develop, or hire the people to match the structure.

A tailored high performance structure tightly focuses people to improve the products, services, or markets that are fundamental to the company's success. This means that high performance not only demands a speedy, decentralized structure, but also one with sharp focus on improving the company's core, strategic business.

There are many decentralized structures to choose from. The most common are functional, process, product, business unit, strategic business unit, market, geographic, and matrix. The following examples of each major structure type and the businesses they best support will simplify understanding. The first structure shown is a centralized functional structure with many silos or kingdoms that restrict high performance. This is followed by a decentralized functional structure, a high performance version of the functional structure.

CENTRALIZED FUNCTIONAL STRUCTURE WITH MANY SILOS OF RESPONSIBILITY

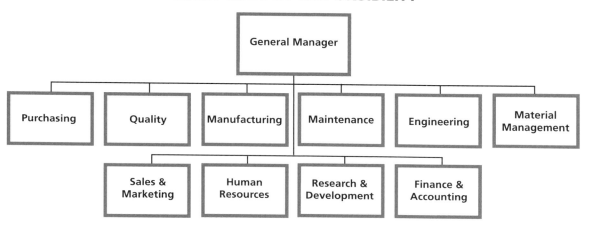

FUNCTIONAL STRUCTURE WITH COMBINED SILOS TO SUPPORT DECENTRALIZATION

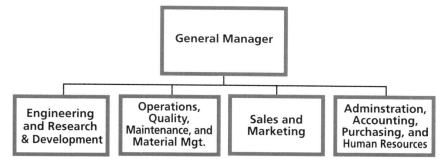

A decentralized functional structure works well in industries where the products or services are very stable and fundamental, for example, the steel industry or the hospital service industry. Change to the basic products and services is slow and evolutionary. It is important that the combined functions in the operations box or service to the customer box extend as far down in the organization as resources will allow. This will provide front-line operating teams with the people necessary to take responsibility for safely and efficiently building a quality product on time or providing a quality service in a timely fashion.

FUNCTIONAL STRUCTURE FOCUSED ON PROCESS

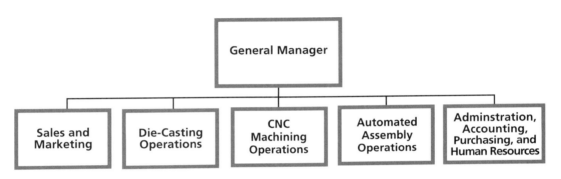

A decentralized, functional, and process-focused structure works well for smaller companies that have stable and similar products, such as aluminum water pumps and aluminum engine front covers, and also have technologically distinct manufacturing processes to make these products like die-casting and machining. An example in the service sector is a high school. Its distinct processes in providing a good education include mathematics, language, and history. As schools become larger, many are moving to "schools within schools" to promote decentralization and familiarity with their customers, the students.

PRODUCT ORGANIZATION

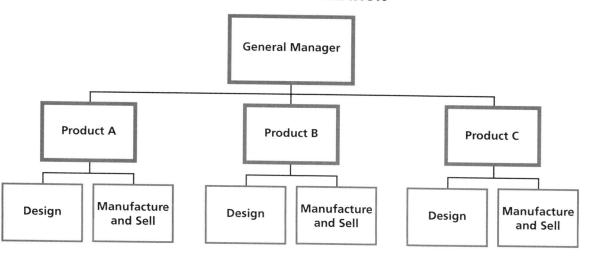

A product organization structure works well for companies that have several unrelated products or services. Each product and market, or service and market, is very different from the other products, services, and markets. An example would be an electronics company that makes cell phones, Doppler radar, and kitchen stoves. A service sector example with a product organization structure would be a company selling both life insurance and brokerage services.

MARKET ORGANIZATION

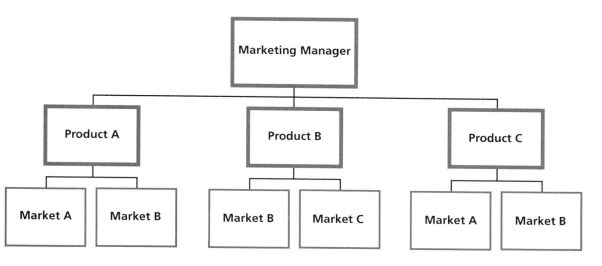

The market organization structure works well for companies focused on selling products that others make or services that others provide. The various products or services are unique but offered in some of the same markets. Examples would be: a company that sells cell phones that others build, a phone service that others provide, a television cable service that others provide, or a company that sells satellite television dishes that others build.

GEOGRAPHIC ORGANIZATION

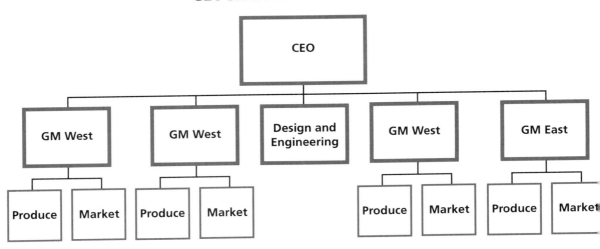

The geographic organization structure works well for companies that focus on selling a line of simple, stable, and related products or services to a single but wide market, such as injection molding and assembling swimming pool equipment. Selling pest control services is an example in the service sector.

DECENTRALIZED BUSINESS UNIT STRUCTURE

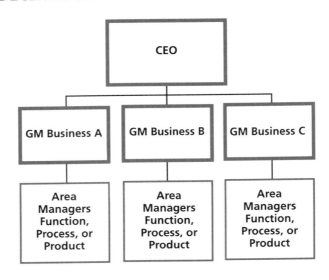

The business unit structure is an effective, decentralized, high performance structure for companies that not only have many unique products and services, but also many unique businesses. One example where this structure would be effective is in a company that makes and sells aircraft, ships, and all-terrain vehicles. Each unique business is led by a General Manager. The business unit structure works well when the unique businesses are stable, but still need to react quickly and independently to survive and grow in competitive markets.

DECENTRALIZED STRATEGIC BUSINESS UNIT STRUCTURE

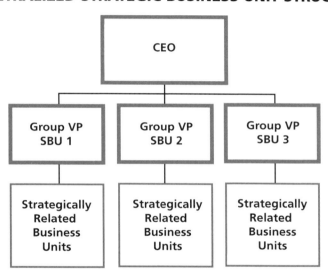

Closely related to the business unit structure is the strategic business unit structure. This structure suits a company focusing on the pursuit of many changes within several businesses that fall into one of its key strategies. The structure would fit a company that has a strategy to develop and sell wireless information technology and another strategy to develop and sell high-definition televisions, games, and computer monitoring systems. The strategic business unit structure works best when a company is pursuing several defined strategies and the businesses that fit into each strategy are rapidly changing and developing.

THE MATRIX STRUCTURE

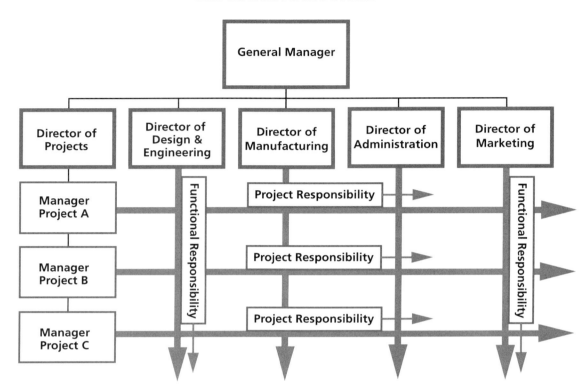

The matrix structure is the only structure with two chains of command and the dreaded dotted line. The horizontal line is the project line of responsibility and the vertical line is the functional line of responsibility. Project Managers have total decentralized responsibility for project success while Functional Managers are responsible to achieve and maintain high technical performance in their functions.

The matrix structure works well for companies whose products become obsolete quickly. Such companies survive by being the first to the market with the next generation of products. For employees to develop new products while simultaneously servicing existing products requires managers who are experienced at both of these disciplines. The need for speed and resource utilization outweighs the confusion that comes from two chains of command. An example is a company in the business of providing electronic games or state-of-the-art guidance systems for space travel.

After selecting the best overall structure for the top of the organization, complete the design for your first-level operating work groups, the ones that build your products or provide your services directly for or to external customers.

The best designs for first-level operating natural work groups center around a process, product, service, or customer. The best size of an effective work group is between 4 and 15 people. Properly sized and capitalized, an operating work team should produce 120% of scheduled demand on straight time. This will allow the team to recover from crashes, illnesses, changes in personnel, and demand increases. However, the main reason to give your first-line operating natural work groups enough capacity is to free them up to engage in Continuous Improvement and skill development, so you don't have to use expensive overtime or bring in staff to cover their CI or training time.

As is the case with business units, operating natural work groups should include, to the extent possible, dedicated support personnel. This will decentralize decision-making and allow the operating team to take the authority for managing the quantity and quality of their products or services.

Every natural work group needs stable membership and one well-selected, permanent leader. Together, the stable, integrated membership and one high performance leader will assure effective training, verification, and ongoing performance improvement. Recall that in a high performance organization, high expectations around consistency and CI demand team stability and effective leadership.

Often, you will design the first-level team and its work area simultaneously. When you have this luxury, do a proactive PRIDE analysis of the work and area before restructuring. The PRIDE analysis will provide for balanced, dedicated, and common equipment in a work area designed to remove, combine, automate, simplify steps, and overcome bottlenecks. The analysis will also reduce backtracking, crossovers, distances, inventory, and double handling.

After choosing the best, decentralized structure planning begins for effective, first-level operating teams, as you design your structure for speed.

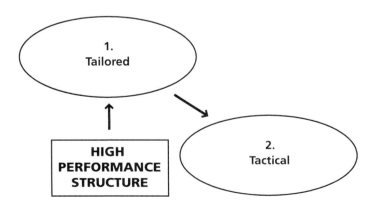

A **Tactical** structure is quick to respond because the lowest possible level in the organization solves problems and manages projects in its piece of the business. In a tactical structure, everyone focuses on building and improving the core products, or providing and improving the core services of the company. Tactical structures have many advantages: speed, ownership, better decisions, streamlining of costly central headquarters staffing, and clear accountability.

The closer a group and a leader are to the operation, the better suited they are to solve operations' problems, make operations' decisions, or implement operations' projects. They act in a more timely fashion than groups or leaders higher in the organizational structure. As leaders and employees develop in a high performance organization, they get more and more authority within the clear boundaries. This means that your tailored structure will evolve over time and become more tactical as your leaders and natural work teams develop.

Just as versed employees are expected to be less dependent on indirect or support groups, high performance operating groups should be less dependent on service groups. Operating groups are those that actually build the products or perform the services that comprise the core strategic business of the company.

Tactical structure means that every team at each level of operations has as many support people reporting directly to the Team Leader as possible. For example, instead of having Production Operators reporting to Production, Maintenance Technicians reporting to Maintenance, and Quality Inspectors reporting to Quality, it is more efficient and tactical to have one Operations Team Leader responsible for all three. All the people necessary to produce and improve the product daily should, to the extent possible, report directly to the Operating Group Leader.

Not all quality roles, maintenance roles, safety roles, or environmental roles integrate into operations. There needs to be some checks and balances, an independent internal voice of the customer, a central preventive maintenance role, an independent voice of safety and environmental compliance, and some combined purchasing. For example, the voice of the customer is responsible for external quality and can reside in a technical group, customer service group, or a separate quality group. The quality roles that remain outside direct operations' control are as follows:

- assuring component parts quality and supplier certification
- developing clear customer quality specifications
- developing inspection, testing procedures, and frequencies
- serving as the final voice on whether to ship products to the customer
- auditing the operation's inspection procedure and gauges
- adjusting inspection frequencies based on customer needs, com-

plaints, and internal defects, to assure quality and avoid non-value added inspection
- providing sophisticated product or service inspection that needs more time than operating employees can use or remote equipment
- implementing Continuous Improvement in measures of cost of quality, warranty, and customer complaints
- complying with external certifications, including ISO

Another example concerns maintenance. Many organizations need a group to manage central and non-operations maintenance. Non-operations maintenance includes repairs beyond the scope of dedicated Maintenance Technicians. Maintenance roles that remain outside operations are:

- complex maintenance tasks
- building and facility maintenance
- tool-and-die maintenance
- modification of preventive maintenance schedules based on unscheduled downtime
- Continuous Improvement in the cost of maintenance per unit measure, the percentage of preventive to reactive maintenance measure, maintenance-related downtime measure, and the change-over time measure

When building a structure, you will dedicate, assign, or designate support or service employees to assist operating groups. Support or service resources employees are those who are not actually building the core products or providing the core service.

In a tactical structure, support resources who provide the majority of their service to the same business or operations group are dedicated to and report to the leader of that operations group. Integration of services fundamental to an operations group increase speed and ownership while removing communication barriers, conflicting objectives, fragmented responsibilities, and clouded accountability.

Assign support employees that service two or more operating units, or groups to a similar extent, to each of the operation groups. These employees will report to a support group leader, but attend all the CI meetings of their assigned operation groups and will be natural owners of projects and problems. They are responsible to the Operating Leader to solve problems and complete projects. The Operating Leaders participate in their assigned support resources' 360-degree formal evaluation as customers.

Designate support personnel that do not spend significant amounts of time with any particular operating group, instead service many or all operating groups. Designated support employees can attend the CI meeting of specific operating teams by request. These support resources report to a support group leader. When operations need their specific expertise, they will respond to the Operating Leader's request for help in a timely fashion.

In a tactical organizational structure, all support employees understand that the operational groups are their internal customers. Now, you are ready to focus on trimming your high performance structure.

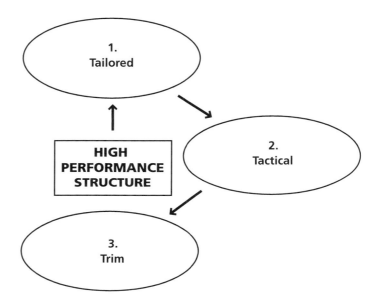

One of the components of a high performance organization is efficient staffing. A **Trim** organization is both lean and flat. Lean means as few distinct groups as possible. Flat means there are as few levels of teams and leaders as possible. Remember to design a structure that can evolve over years as your people develop.

After dedicating service or support resources to operation groups to the extent possible, you can reduce the number and size of service groups. This trims the organization and adds impetus for the drive toward decentralization, employee development, and service versatility.

To streamline central headquarters and central support groups, combine similar service groups. This removes fragmented responsibilities and reduces the need for group leaders. For example, instead of ticket agents, baggage handlers, and gate attendants, low-cost airlines combine these groups to trim the organization and fully use the workforce. When you trim service groups, you may want to automate or outsource such non-core tasks as payroll, insurance administration, or distributing boarding passes.

Before changing the structure by combining or removing one or several groups or levels of leadership, the first logical step is to do a PRIDE analysis. The PRIDE analysis reduces waste, streamlines, automates, outsources, assures proper training, and reduces potential trauma on the workforce. From the customers' perspective, our experience has shown that 50% of what service groups do is wasteful or non-value-added.

A flat structure has as few layers of groups and as few levels of leadership as possible. Extra levels of leadership and extra layers of groups become roadblocks to effective communication and delegation of responsibility to the lowest level. A trim organization has just enough levels of groups and leadership to carry out the core business and provide direction to the operation and service groups.

In 1982, the Cadillac Livonia Engine Plant, as part of the Livonia Opportunity, moved to a decentralized process structure that focused on a machining business group and an assembly business group. We dedicated support employees to each business process, and combined service groups. The levels of leadership from the Plant Manager to the workforce were reduced from 5 to 3, including an operating Team Leader. Soon after making these changes, the plant became the lowest cost and highest quality engine plant in General Motors. The Plant Manager from Livonia was transferred to GM's Ramos Arizpe engine and assembly complex in Mexico. With assistance from Workplace Transformation Inc., the feat was reproduced. Both the Cadillac engine plant and the Ramos plants became cost leaders and won their respective country's national quality award.

Because a high performance organization continually develops, more and more empowerment flows to individuals and groups. There is a slow and natural evolution in a high performance structure; as it needs less groups and levels because its leaders are more effective and the workforce more empowered. The best way to gain from this slow evolution is to redeploy to handle the growth, or through attrition, as people leave the company.

A decentralized, tactical, and trim structure will out-perform a centralized, functional, and hierarchical structure every time.

- ➲ A decentralized high performance structure is essential to support the development necessary to become a high performance organization.

- ➲ Tailor the structure to your strategic products or services and high performance. Tactically integrate support and trim levels and support groups.

- ➲ A high performance structure gradually evolves with the skills of the natural work teams and with the skills of their Team Leaders.

Note

[1] Quote usually attributed to Gaius Petronius Arbiter (210 BC), although the earliest reference to the quote was not until 1970 and the author is unknown to this day.

26

Team Structure

Natural work teams form the backbone of a high
performance structure.

Once again, the ultimate goal of a high performance organization is to innovate
and improve faster than the competition to secure the future of the organization
and its employees. Continuous Improvement and strategic planning are team
sports and therefore, a **team-oriented** structure strengthens high performance.

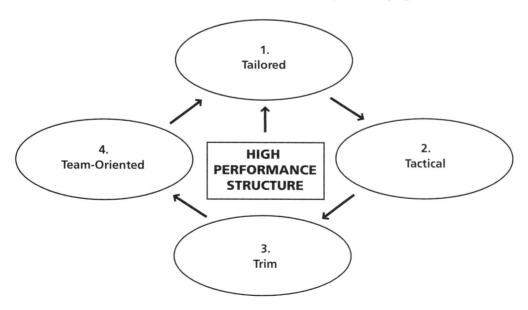

There is no more misunderstood word or more overused tool than "team." Confusion is caused by the failure to differentiate between the role of each type of team and the propensity of inefficient organizations to form a team every time they have a problem to solve, project to complete, or decision to make.

Understanding teams starts with realizing that the backbone of a high performance structure and the team engaged in daily Continuous Improvement is a **natural work team** or group. A *natural work team* is the group of people that work together every day to perform their piece of the business. They are not Kaizen teams, task teams, or even PRIDE teams for that matter. The natural work team has operating personnel and dedicated service personnel.

Even the most effective matrix companies have permanent groups with both project and functional chains of command. These organizations recognize the benefit of forming more permanent project teams that move together to implement their projects and move together to start the next project. Like any team, the more the natural work group works together, the better they get. The best matrix organizations recognize the value of keeping the same effective project Team Leader in place to lead the same project team whenever possible.

The natural work team is the group responsible for continually improving safety, internal quality, external quality, productivity, cost, training, orderliness, and environmental performance of their piece of business. A natural work team is a permanent team with a permanent leader and dedicated support resources. Assigned and designated support employees join the natural work team in their pursuit of CI.

Normally, an individual natural owner from an existing natural work team solves problems and oversees the completion of projects using the proper worksheet or tool. Input from others in person or by e-mail helps natural owners with problem-solving and project management. Forming expensive and time consuming ad hoc teams to solve problems or implement projects is a waste. Task teams take time away from the primary job of people and natural work teams. I wish I had a dollar for every time I have heard, "I am on so many teams, I do not have time to do my job." Resist the modern-day mania of "Let's form a team," which can burden even well-designed structures with unnecessary temporary teams.

In business, there are *operational* natural work teams and *service* or *support* natural work teams. The consistency, development, and continuing performance improvement expected in a high performance organization demands that each team have one effective leader. Natural work teams are already present in every organization. Just combine the people, develop their skills, give them an effective leader, implement CI and employee development, and get out of their way. There are no duplicate or artificial team structures in a high performance organization, only well-led natural work teams.

A team-oriented structure needs team leadership, another concept often misunderstood. Leadership of a natural work team is a permanent job. Schemes that rotate leadership or share leadership roles for different aspects of a natural work team's responsibility cause confusion, blur accountability, and do not work in a high performance organization. Recall that the first pillar of a high performance organization is effective leadership at every level. That means each layer of a natural work team must have one, carefully selected, and developed, high performance leader. When you succeed in developing a good leader, for goodness sake do not move the person, except to a higher leadership position.

Many organizations have turned over, or are considering turning over, the leadership of the front-line operating team to a working member of that team. Working Team Leaders are a way to trim mature high performance organizations. The best way to make this change is as an evolutionary change as leaders and groups develop. Unfortunately, many try to reduce cost by removing first-line Supervisors, regardless of the natural work team's readiness.

Rarely does a natural work group move successfully from ineffectively led to effectively self-led. The first step is to apply the leadership development process to existing first-line management Supervision. This includes verification of Supervisors in the JOBS process to first assure effective leadership at this level. Most moves to remove first-line Supervisors are premature and a disaster. Performance suffers for numerous reasons, such as:

- The natural work team is neither ready nor has it seen what effective team leadership is all about.
- The role of the working Team Leader is not well-defined, sufficient, or agreed upon.
- Team Leader selection does not include a leadership skills assessment.
- There is no training or verification for the new operating Team Leader.
- The working Team Leader is too busy with the operating job to perform the necessary leadership duties.
- There are no informal or formal evaluations of the Operating Leader's effectiveness.
- No method is in place to remove an unsuccessful Operating Team Leader.

The role of a first-line Team Leader in a high performance organization is important. The front-line operating natural work group builds the core products or provides the core services for customers; it is responsible for daily decisions to satisfy customers' needs. This is where the rubber meets the road! This level is where most injuries happen, productivity occurs, and quality is determined. Only effective first-line leadership can manage daily demands, train and verify employees, and direct the team's formal Continuous Improvement process.

We use the following list to help clients understand the role of high performance first-line leaders whether they are Supervisors, Operating Team Leaders, or Shift Leaders.

Beginning of the shift
- Arrive at least thirty minutes before the start of your shift.
- Meet and review problems faced by the previous Shift or Team Leader.
- Review the last shift or team's production and identify any potential customer-delivery problems.
- Assure all the material is available for the shift or team in properly marked containers.
- Assure proper staffing for each job, with verified Operators running at standard and producing quality product, before leaving the area or before operating yourself. Make the early round to greet each employee and do not leave until all machines are properly running or the proper people are on the scene.
- Assure that all employees are wearing the proper safety equipment, following safe practices, and that no safety hazards exist in the work area.
- Audit and assure that employees are performing according to JOBS or TECS operating guidelines.
- Assure that employees are correctly recording diagnostic data for CI.
- Manage attendance and tardiness problems and assure necessary follow-up.

During the shift
- Tour the work area and review the CI check sheets for any repetitive scrap or downtime problems. Notify up-stream operations of scrap found in your area.
- Assure that Maintenance or the Quality resources are responding to repetitive downtime or scrap issues.

- Take the machine offline for unresolved quality and safety concerns.
- Audit the check sheets to assure accuracy.
- Ask employees how the job is running and if they need any support.
- Assure that employees checked the parameters at the beginning of the shift and signed the check sheet.
- Review the parameter change log to see that it is current and the machine parameter settings to see if they are correct.
- Assure the maintenance log is complete and that preventive maintenance is being performed on schedule.
- Assure performance of visual and gauged quality checks.
- Review the area's housekeeping and resolve housekeeping problems.

Situational activities

- Orient new employees and assure they feel comfortable on the job. Make sure they have completed the orientation training and work with an experienced Operator until verified to the able level. Take part in verifying the Operator to the able level in the operating guideline before letting the employee work alone on the job.
- Check JOBS in the software to see if any Operators need re-verification and complete as necessary.
- Assure proper rotation of employees to keep Operator skills current and to preserve versatility. Assure jobs documents are complete for your area.
- Assure that all changeovers go smoothly. People and all parts must be in place and prepared.
- Work on CI problems and projects. Update progress in the software.
- Participate in 4-S housekeeping and orderliness audits and continually improve the housekeeping, safety, and ergonomics of your area.
- Lead the team's CI process, conduct the meetings, and be a successful and accountable natural owner of problems and projects as part of the team's Continuous Improvement process.
- Involve the team members in CI and teach them to use the tools.
- Create a proper environment for the workforce consisting of clear expectations, training to meet the expectations, and the time, tools, materials, and resources necessary to perform.
- Recognize performance that exceeds expectations and handle performance issues consistently using the *Human Performance Improvement Worksheet.*

End of the shift

- Assure the team met the production schedule and if not, take appropriate action, such as scheduling overtime to assure customer shipments.
- Document unsolved problems on the *Problem-Solving Worksheet*, including the description, interim actions, and possible causes. Leave the form for the next shift's leader.
- Meet with the incoming Team or Shift Leader and relay needed information to the next shift.
- Assure completion of operator check sheets.
- Print results of the previous shift from the software and post on the team production and CI board.

After developing the role of the Operating Team or Shift Leader, the first question to ask is, "Are our current management first-line leaders performing these tasks consistently?" If the answer is, "no," you are not ready for a successful move to self-leadership. Sometimes in represented plants, it is best to negotiate provisions allowing movement to Operating Leaders when the time is right through enabling language. In represented plants, always have at least one Management Shift Leader on every shift to assist Operating Team Leaders.

Some of these roles and responsibilities are controversial when moving to Operating Leaders in unionized companies. For Operating Leaders to make economic sense, there must be a matching decrease in the number of first-line management Supervisors. Without agreement on some important duties the Operating Team Leader must perform, it makes no sense to move from Supervisors to Operating Leaders. The most controversial changes are that the Operating Leader must assure that Operators use safety equipment and that Operators follow operator guidelines.

I can still remember my colleague, the late Ralph Fanelli, who was the union representative on our Livonia planning team, saying, "We want Operating Team Leaders to be union members. However, union brothers and sisters are not going to discipline or rat on union brothers and sisters."

I can still hear the response from management, "We want Operating Team Leaders as well. However, if they are not going to assure safe work practices, housekeeping, proper operating practices, they are not leaders. We still need Supervisors, and it is a waste to have both." It appeared we were at a stalemate.

Both the union and management were right. It takes careful joint planning to move successfully from well-led natural work groups to self-led natural work groups in a union environment. A clearly written procedure for Operating Leaders to follow and one management Leader on each shift, solved the stalemate at the Livonia Engine Plant.

When a performance problem was encountered, the Operating Leader first requested the employee to follow the proper procedure. If the employee refused, the leader referred the matter to the shift's elected union representative. If after talking to the employee, the person still refused or did not conform, then the Team Leader would report the performance problem to the Shift Manager. Management would handle the matter from that point forward.

Once workers understood the role of their Operating Team Leader and that the union would provide back-up, discipline decreased drastically. Livonia had only one written grievance in the second year of operating self-led natural work groups, while having the cleanest, safest, and highest performing engine plant in General Motors.

The United Steel Workers in its 2003 to 2008 labor agreement with United States Steel Corporation handled the issue differently. Their "Crew Leaders" are sometimes alone on shift and cannot give discipline. In cases of misconduct, the Crew Leader was given the authority to send fellow union members home for the balance of a shift or turn. Day shift management would then handle the matter.

Other necessary agreements concern selecting, paying, and removing Operating Leaders. The first agreement on selection concerns eligibility. The correct guidelines depend on the particular situation. For example, in a comparatively simple service or manufacturing setting, such as an insurance company or a plastic injection molding plant, everyone should be eligible to apply to become a Team Leader. Leadership skills are far more important than the technical skills for this position. In other settings including hospitals and paper mills, the technical skills are also critical, so only people with certain experience or performing certain jobs are able to apply. For example, in the paper-making industry, usually only machine tenders or back tenders become Operating Leaders.

There is a possible stalemate when the union wants seniority to prevail as the selection technique and management wants it based on demonstrated leadership skills, regardless of years of service. The answer is that both sides are right. The usual working compromise is to respect seniority as well as assure that a candidate has the prerequisite leadership skills. It makes no sense to select a person without the leadership skills and watch the leader and team fail. The most effective selection process is having candidates apply for and go through a thorough leadership skills assessment. This tool helps to assure that they have the requisite skills to be an effective leader. The job will go to the highest senior employee meeting the eligibility requirements and scoring high enough on the assessment to predict success.

If eligible employees choose not to become leaders or do not qualify, a Supervisor will remain as leader of that group until a leader emerges. Without union agreement on the proper duties, eligibility, selection, pay, time away from the operating job, evaluation, and replacement of operating Team Leaders, the company is better served with well-led natural work groups using Supervisors.

Many companies have removed Supervisors before they are ready, in pursuit of mindless, across-the-board cuts. However, performance suffers without proper Team and Shift Leadership in place. Instead of removing first-level Supervisors, what these companies have done is force second-level Managers to act like Supervisors to fill the gap. In essence, a process of reverse empowerment flows up the organization and chokes performance.

The building blocks forming the backbone of a strong high performance structure are natural work teams. The cartilage, tendons, and ligaments that hold the teams and team structure together, are effective leadership and common objectives.

Team-oriented structures give teams authority as they pursue a balanced set of objectives. Communication and coordination among teams flow from Team Leaders. An essential feature of effective team structures comes from the "link pin theory." In his groundbreaking book, *New Patterns of Management,*[1] Rensis Likert describes how to knit or link teams together through leadership. When designing a high performance structure, vertical linking is achieved when the Team Leader at one level is a member of the next higher-level team. Horizontal linking occurs when each leader of a service or support team also becomes a member of the operational CI team at their level.

Every leader in a linked organization leads one natural work team and its Continuous Improvement process while participating as an active member of another team's Continuous Improvement process. Linking leadership and CI double-weld the structure. Vertically and horizontally aligned key measures and objectives provide common focus. Linked leadership provides communication and coordination of efforts among different levels of operating teams and between service and operating teams.

Once designed, the high performance structure gradually evolves with implementation of high performance systems. A tailored, tactical, trim, and team-oriented structure, bonded together by CI and linked leadership, promotes empowerment, accountability, speed, and the common focus necessary to out-perform the competition.

⮞ A high performance structure is team-oriented because Continuous Improvement and strategic planning are team activities.

⮞ Natural work teams form the backbone of high performance organizations and are responsible for CI.

⮞ The most important ingredient of an effective team-oriented structure is effective team leadership.

Note

[1] Rensis Likert, *New Patterns of Management* (New York: McGraw-Hill, 1961).

27

High Performance Pillar Support Systems

High Performance, like a bridge, needs
support to allow safe passage.

There are two kinds of support systems in a high performance organization, **Pillar Support Systems** and **Operational Support Systems**. *Pillar Support Systems* facilitate implementation of the five key, integrated, and adaptive systems that define a high performance organization. *Operational Support Systems* help high performance workforces out-perform the competition by safely providing the external customers with high quality products or services on time and at a competitive price.

Although every company must fully implement each of the five Pillars of High Performance, the specific Pillar support systems needed vary with each organization. The seven most commonly needed Pillar Support Systems are as follows:

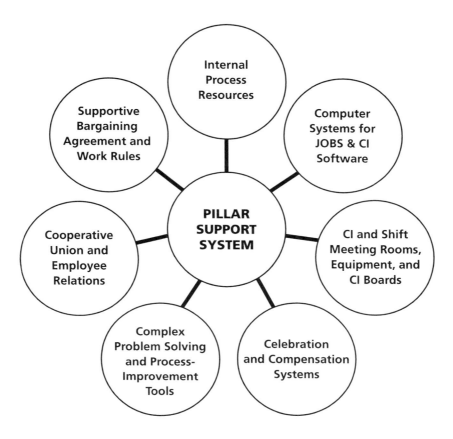

Internal process experts (Internal Resources), are essential to help organizations fully implement pillar and support systems. This is a full time job.

A demanding and specially configured behavioral skills assessment is the best tool for selecting those who become Internal Resources. Extensive training prepares the Internal Resources to help leaders implement all the systems, tools, and software necessary in a high performance organization. Internal Resources are in a position to become the company's key leaders of tomorrow. Because they help people in so many areas, Internal Resources either report to the top leader of the operations department, or entire facility. This is one position where adequate staffing means life or death for the organization's move to high performance.

In support of the first pillar, "Develop Effective Leadership at all Levels," Internal Resources aid with training, assessment, feedback, and retraining. Their most important role is in informal evaluation, as they help leaders hone their leadership skills.

In support of the second pillar, "Formal Continuous Improvement process," Internal Resources teach the three-step Continuous Improvement process, the forms and worksheets, and the software. Again, their most important role is to coach leaders and monitor the progress of teams.

In support of the third pillar, "Develop High Performance Employees," Internal Resources oversee the training and verification process. They interview employees and develop rough drafts of operating guidelines, develop training checklists, manage completion of training and verification documents, and set-up the JOBS portion of the Transformation Software. They take part in employee skills verification and train leaders to use and update the software. Additionally, Internal Resources coordinate new-hire behavioral assessments used for selecting new employees.

In support of the fourth pillar, "Short-term Directed Improvement," Internal Resources join with external resources to conduct PRIDE initiatives. They also attend and help run implementation meetings designed to assure implementation of PRIDE process improvement projects.

Perhaps the key role of Internal Resources is to become so knowledgeable about the Pillars of High Performance, that they can oversee implementation of high performance with minimal help from external consultants. Our experience suggests that Internal Resources can assume control over implementation in about three to five years, depending on the size of the company and the number of resources available.

The second Pillar Support System assures revealing diagnostic data and capable computer systems. Data, hardware, and software help leaders guide performance improvement using the three-step Continuous Improvement process and tools, and manage employee development using the JOBS training and verification system.

Diagnostic data paths focus improvement in CI. The necessary diagnostic data should be available in a readily usable computerized format to integrate with the CI portion of the Web-based Transformation Software. Computer capacity and the CI and JOBS modules of the Transformation Software reduce administrative burden in implementing these key systems.

Effective and regularly scheduled CI meetings help natural work teams coordinate their improvement efforts and assure accountability. They can replace quality, safety, cost, productivity, and training meetings once leaders figure out that CI is not something they are doing besides their job; it is their job. As Rensis Likert once said, "We have to start meeting like this."

The CI portion of the Transformation Software helps leaders run efficient CI meetings and natural owners run efficient problem-solving or project management meetings. The major focus of the meetings is to have owners of problems and projects review progress made since the last meeting and to assure accountability. The typical agenda of a CI meeting is as follows:

1. Review the performance trend and objective on each CI form.
2. Set new objectives when the team meets the previous objectives.
3. Present progress made since the last meeting from natural owners on open problems and projects in support of each key measure.
4. Assign new problems and projects as the team completes those previously assigned.
5. Assure accountability from natural owners and remove implementation barriers.
6. Refocus improvement when an area improves and is no longer the worst area.
7. Review meeting effectiveness and suggestions from the Internal Resource.

Teams need a meeting room with the proper equipment to run effective CI meetings. In addition, members will gather for start-of-shift meetings in an earmarked area, where a board visibly displays their CI forms and tools. The board will also show shift-by-shift results and be a place to post cross-shift communications.

High Performance Organizations begin every shift or day with a brief meeting and conclude each shift with employees updating the daily results board. The major points covered in a start-of-shift meeting and a list of end-of-shift responsibilities are as follows:

START-OF-SHIFT MEETING

- What were the results compared to requirements yesterday?

- What are the requirements for today?

- Where is today's bottleneck or potential bottleneck?

  › What are the reasons?

    —Quality: scrap or rework

    —Reliability: schedule machine downtime

    —Speed: staffing or cycle time

    —Resource: lack of material or verified operator

- What actions will break the bottleneck and who is responsible?

  › Interim actions list

  › *Problem-Solving Worksheets* and *Project Implementation Worksheets* to resolve issues or implement solutions where necessary

- What process changes, product changes, or trials occur today?

- What are the most compelling safety and quality precautions?

- What retraining and verification occur today because of changes in operating guidelines or verification requests?

END-OF-SHIFT RESPONSIBILITIES

- Record the shift's production.

- Record problems faced.

- Identify shortages to schedule and corrective actions.

- Start *Problem-Solving Worksheets* to define unresolved problems, specify interim actions taken, and identify possible causes; and then pass to the next shift for communication and completion.

The next Pillar Support System, Celebration and Compensation, accelerates CI and JOBS. To the extent possible, high performance organizations move away from annual across-the-board increases, subjective bonus systems, and obscure profit-sharing programs to compensation systems that encourage active involvement in skill development and achievement of specific CI objectives.

The celebration and compensation support system answers three questions for employees. The first question is, "We have acheived another CI objective, does anyone care?" Providing small celebrations for the team lets them know that you care. Some companies create boundaries for informal recognitions, such as cost, content, and participation. The celebration or recognition might be a free lunch, a hat, a pen, a trophy, a ticket to the ball game, or simply congratulations from the leader in person or in the company newsletter. Being recognized is what matters to people, not the value or form of the recognition.

The second recognition question is, "Why should I learn additional skills and jobs to become more versed and versatile?" The answer is a well-designed Pay-for-Skills compensation system. Note that the JOBS or TECS training documents, verification method and documents, pay families, and progression path must be in place before moving to a Pay-for-Skills compensation system.

A well-designed Pay-for-Skills system has the following advantages:

- reward and encouragement for learning
- elimination of favoritism and subjective rewards
- reduction and simplification of pay levels

- advancement within a job family based on employees' own skills and initiative
- employee advancement is at their own pace
- enhanced employee skills and versatility
- improved organizational performance in quality, cost, productivity, and safety
- consistent performance day-to-day and shift-to-shift
- re-verification immediately following improvements in best practices
- elimination of rewards simply for seniority which uncouples compensation from skills or contribution
- prevents older employees from blocking the progression of younger employees desiring to learn new skills and jobs

Complete job descriptions, sensible pay families, orderly progression, and practical versatility requirements make Pay-for-Skills a sound investment. Companies that have had bad experiences with the Pay-for-Skills systems usually did not have a solid operator training and skills verification process like JOBS or TECS and did not understand the importance of optimum versatility. The versatility formula presented in Chapter Twenty-Two, "Employee Development," avoids over-training, over-rotation, and skills loss.

A properly designed Pay-For-Skills System is a powerful engine that can drive needed skill development and versatility and help ensure survival and growth.

The last compensation question has to do with CI. The question is, "We have improved performance, the company is profitable, and they want us to continue to improve. What's in it for us?" The answer is a well-timed and well-designed variable compensation or gain-sharing system.

A well-timed variable compensation system starts after a company has a vibrant three-step Continuous Improvement process at the workforce level and after the company regularly exceeds an acceptable profitability level. This means everyone knows the measures needed to share in future improvements, they know how to get involved, and they know there is a likelihood of reward. With these conditions in place, money talks. The best-designed variable pay system implemented without CI is like a sailboat with a full set of sails deployed and no wind at its back.

Variable compensation or gain sharing is: a reward designed to encourage employees to improve profitability by improving certain CI measures. Employees share a percentage of profits or generated cost savings above the acceptable level, based on those improvements. Gain sharing measures usually include cost, productivity, quality, and safety or housekeeping. Well-designed variable compensation promotes trust, understanding of the business, ownership, responsibility, a sense of control, and higher levels of performance to improve competitiveness and security.

There are many variations in gain sharing plans, but integration with CI is imperative. One of our paper industry clients saw productivity in their pulp mill exceed the stated maximum capacity in tons by over twenty percent. The reasons, a strong Continuous Improvement process integrated with a gain sharing system.

The next Pillar Support System, Complex Problem-solving and Process Improvement Tools, helps advance the Continuous Improvement process in sophisticated or highly technical work environments. Techniques like design of experiments and Six Sigma are examples of complex problem-solving and process improvement tools. Use them only when needed and not as everyday tools.

In the case of a complex problem with many variables that combine, interact with, and compound one another, when the five-step Problem-Solving process cannot find the actual cause, do a design of experiments to find the cause. If CI cannot achieve needed consistency in a variable process, and reducing variability of the process would save money or customers, then use Six Sigma or statistical process control techniques to stabilize that process.

Companies that need complex process improvement and problem-solving should train a couple of black or green belts or better yet, have the Internal Resources expand their toolbox to fulfill this need. However, do not rely on complex tools, Six Sigma, or lean manufacturing as paths to high performance. Lean tools, like scoreboards and standard work, do not approximate the CI and JOBS processes necessary in a high performance organization. Complex tools have their place, but not as every day systems, because they are expensive, rarely needed, and not workforce friendly.

The next support system is essential for high performance. Effective employee and union relations, together with productive work rules, constitute major competitive advantages. Supportive work rules or collective bargaining agreements flow from positive employee and union relations. More than any other stakeholder, the workforce has more to gain from becoming high performance, and more to lose if they do not. What creates this disparity is the sheer number of people at the operating level and their relative inability to find comparable employment after a facility or company closes.

Some of our strongest high performance organizations have union-represented workforces. A high performance union is a driving force in implementing high performance systems, keeping management consistent, and assuring follow-through even though management leaders come and go. However, uninformed or misguided unions can unwittingly doom their membership.

The late Donald F. Ephlin, former Vice President of the United Auto Workers (UAW), was the man behind the Saturn process and contract, and a champion of union and management cooperation. After retirement, this colleague and friend helped Workplace Transformation, Inc. by training union leaders in the high performance role of the union. He told several groups, "The worst feeling I ever had as a union leader is when a worker I represented from my home plant in Massachusetts commented on a new contract I negotiated. The worker said, 'Thanks, Don, you forced management to agree to everything we wanted and negotiated a great contract. Unfortunately, my plant could not compete working this way and closed and I no longer have a job.'"

The union has a huge stake in helping make the company profitable. There are many companies without unions but no unions without companies. There is no artificial job security. There are only two ways to build lasting job security: 1) work for a profitable company, and 2) increase your individual skills and participation in that organization's success. Union leaders who stand in the way of workers gaining more skills and getting involved in improving performance, do their membership a disservice. These outdated attitudes are causing union membership to shrink and unions to become dinosaurs.

Understanding how a high performance union operates begins with breaking down the overall role of the union into three parts. The first role is negotiating a collective bargaining agreement. Two parts of every agreement have to do with economics and work rules. The economic portion is the "negotiating" part. This involves dividing the profits, the "fruit" of a high performance organization, among the workers, management, shareholders, and capital improvement needs. It is far easier to negotiate with a profitable company and debate how much goes to the workforce, than it is to negotiate with a non-profitable company about layoffs and wage-and-benefit concessions. By design, union bargainers seek to get as much as they can for their membership in spite of management's naturally differing objectives. Negotiation is the fitting process to resolve these differences.

Some pay practices and work practices innately interfere with a company becoming high performance. Most of these practices have little to do with how much money the workers receive. Rather, they are more about how little the workers do in return and who gets the money. With job banks in the auto industry, for example, thousands of workers receive close to thirty dollars an hour for doing nothing. In the same way, piece rate incentives divide some workforces, reduce quality and safety, and are incompatible with CI. Across-the-board increases and annual profit sharing do nothing to reinforce individual skill development or improved performance. Henceforth, when possible, negotiations should focus on moving to high performance compensation systems such as Pay-for-Skills and gain sharing.

The second part of the collective agreement role of the union is to set up work rules. In this area, there are many common objectives. The correct process is joint problem-solving, not negotiating. This area is fertile for common-interest bargaining.

Unproductive work practices exist because of years of abuse and mistrust. However, these rules must change in a high performance organization. Common objectives exist regarding issues like gaining skills, verifying on jobs, and selection of Operating Team Leaders. Not only do both parties benefit from improving the company's competitive position and profitability, they also benefit from respecting seniority to the fullest extent possible while preserving as many jobs as possible. Accomplishing these objectives means removing wasteful practices, unproductive jobs, and unproductive rules for the good of all members. Everyone gains when issues are solved together, rather than letting the courts sort out the mess in bankruptcy proceedings.

High performance unions are able to separate the issues and negotiate wages while jointly solving performance issues caused by unproductive work rules. Some examples of how to make changes and reduce the impact on employees are:

- Absorb needed cuts in over-staffed positions by attrition or early retirements to the extent possible.
- Redefine overtime eligibility provisions requiring companies to call in the "senior qualified" Operator to mean agreeing to use the senior JOBS-verified and current Operator.
- Allow higher seniority employees the opportunity to verify first for Pay-for-Skills increases.
- Select Operating Leaders by seniority after they qualify in a leadership assessment.
- Red-Circle people who are paid higher than their skills contribution and job would indicate.
- Create lay-off groups and shift preference groups that protect the variety of skills needed to continue performing on each shift, and follow seniority or reverse seniority within those groups, as the case may be.
- Create a bridge system to guard against pay losses when moving from incentives or profit-sharing to gain sharing.
- Reduce future legacy costs while the company is competitive, so that

the number of people working can support those retired or not working.

- Have technical employees concentrate on learning and performing complex jobs while routine jobs go to operating employees or get out-sourced.
- As a last resort, institute two-tiered wages to assure future competitiveness while minimizing the impact on current employees.

The second role of the union is protecting membership from the arbitrary actions of management. Unions have a legal duty to provide a good-faith defense for members disciplined by management. High performance unions will examine the facts, and decide whether management was right or wrong. If the union concludes that the management was wrong, they will pursue a grievance to the point of arbitration if necessary. On the other hand, if the union decides the management was right, it will step up to the membership and withdraw any grievance.

High performance unions recognize that protecting those who do not perform, do not follow operating procedures, do not come to work, or are not productive is not in the best interest of most of the workforce. This is where unions show whether they are part of the problem or part of the solution.

The final role of a union is to help management set up the five Pillars of High Performance. High performance union leaders attend CI meetings, take part in verifying Operators, and help with assessing new hires. The union's role is not just to keep management honest, but to set an example and encourage employees to join the move to high performance. A union alone cannot make a company high performance, but a union can block the move to high performance. Without union buy-in, their membership is robbed of its chance for growth and security.

The goal of a high performance union leader is the same as a high performance management leader, to have better trained, more versatile, and vitally engaged workers improving faster than the competition. Initially, becoming high performance requires effort, change, and waste reduction—expectations that are not immediately popular with most workforces. True union leaders will accept the challenge, regardless of its effect on their popularity. They put the good of the workforce, those who elected them, ahead of their own gain.

High performance management leadership is responsible to build effective relations with the union and with the workforce to secure the cooperation necessary to beat the competition. The union must follow the lead and participate to help secure the future of those it represents.

The sequential steps for developing effective relations with a union or a work-force are the Four O's, shown below.

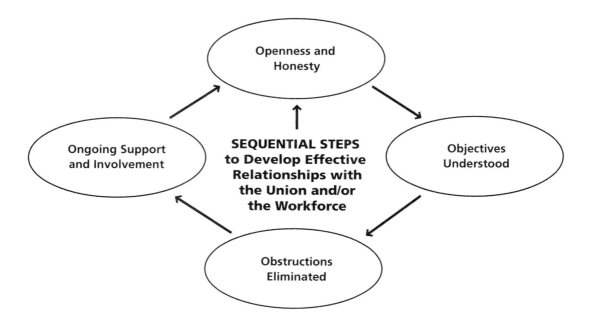

When management openly and honestly shares information about the good and the bad, the union and the workforce begin to respond positively. They stop saying, "We do not believe what management says," and "They never follow through on what they say." They start saying, "We do not like all they say and do, but they never lie to us or go back on their word." Once good relations become a part of your direction as a leader, you must set the example.

Management is largely responsible for how the union acts. Little things go a long way, such as sharing information with the union before telling the overall work-force, allowing the union to share good news with its members first, and publicizing positive gains like new business, jobs, or investment, resulting from improved performance. When a company has true union leaders, management should take every opportunity to improve their image with the workforce they represent.

When the union respects management's word, the timing is right to move to the second step, objectives understood. Management will educate the union and work-force about the compelling common objectives associated with becoming a high performance organization. The message is: "Neither the union nor management can create a competitive workplace alone, or despite one another, but they can by working together."

Again, management must understand that people, with their skills and involvement, are a company's only lasting competitive advantage. The union must understand that job security comes only from working for a profitable company, increasing individual skills, and actively participating in improving performance.

The workforce must understand the positive consequences of moving to high performance: an opportunity to control their own future, increased involvement, increased communication, better training and skills, an opportunity to advance based on their own initiative and, above all, increased security. Everyone must understand that, even in the face of short-term sacrifices, the main reason to become high performance is long-term job security and growth.

Once management, the union, and the workforce understand the common objectives, it is possible to begin a problem-solving or planning process to remove obstacles to high performance. Now the union and workforce might say, "We are still leery, but we have nothing to lose and everything to gain by joining in a planning process or problem-solving negotiation process to give ourselves a chance."

Many companies make a fatal mistake by trying to cure all the work rule ills at one time. There are essential changes and less important changes that are necessary. The priority must be on doing the important changes first, and only as many changes as the union and workforce can absorb at one time.

One of our saddest moments happened when the union and local management at a paper mill developed a plan to move to high performance. The local and international union moved from being against any changes to supporting changes in lines of progression, operator verification, versatility, and implementation of the five pillars. Corporate management in their arrogance and ignorance reasoned, "If the union is willing to make these changes, let's ask for everything we want."

The unavoidable happened when the union withdrew support, because the added requests were the straws that broke the camel's back. Over a decade later, thanks to a true leader in the Mill Manager's position and true leaders on the union committee, the same mill made many of the same changes proposed a decade earlier. One carry-over member on the union committee said, "Just think how far we would be if we had started ten years ago."

After jointly removing work rule obstacles, management is responsible to encourage the continuing involvement of the union and workforce. Some of the ways to do this are:

- Joint implementation team to oversee implementation and change of systems that affect the workforce
- Union attendance in leadership staff meetings and CI meetings

- Union and workforce involvement in systems that affect the workforce:
  - › Assessment hiring or selection
  - › Employee training and verification
  - › CI meetings
  - › PRIDE analysis
  - › Peer review in non-union companies

Former UAW Vice President Don Ephlin advised union leaders struggling to decide whether to become involved in helping save the company by jointly developing a plan to become high performance. As he said, "Management is too important to leave up to management."

Every company needs to implement all five key pillar systems of high performance; however, every company does not need all of the Pillar Support Systems. These systems help, encourage, and reward leaders and the workforce as they move to high performance. The Compulsory Pillar Support Systems include Internal Resources, CI meetings and facilities, diagnostic data, celebrations, computer capacity, software, good union and employee relations, and supportive work rules or bargaining agreement. Each individual company should decide if it needs to use Pay-for-Skills, variable compensation, complex problem-solving and process-improvement tools, and start-of-shift meetings.

➲ There are two kinds of support systems, Pillar Support Systems and Operational Support Systems.

➲ Pillar Support Systems speed up implementation of the five key pillar systems that define a high performance organization.

➲ Pillar Support Systems include Internal Resources, data and software, team meetings, recognition, and positive union and employee relations.

28

High Performance Operational Support Systems

There should be no magic in producing products
or providing your services.

A high performance business uses three fundamental yet simple Operational Support Systems to outperform the competition. They help a production or service workforce safely provide customers with high quality products or services, on time and at a competitive cost or price. Like the three legs on a milk stool, the three Operational Support Systems are each essential to forming a solid base to produce your products or provide your services. The systems are: safety, quality, and productivity.

Most companies have bits and pieces of each Operational Support System in place. High performance companies have complete operational systems. Just as importantly, high performance companies recognize that the safety, quality, and productivity systems are 90% complete simply by fully implementing the five pillar systems of high performance.

Arguably, the most important Operational Support System is safety. Different companies and countries place differing levels of emphasis on safety. A high performance company never compromises safety or quality for the sake of productivity. However, the reason high performance organizations are safer is that they recognize that safety is a system. They engage leadership, they engage the workforce, and they build their safety system from the Pillars of High Performance.

Many organizations with bits and pieces of the safety system in place will wonder why they still have injuries. When injury frequency goes up, or injuries get serious or fatal, they start another campaign and impose another set of tools. The companies do not see safety as one adaptive system integrated with leadership development, Continuous Improvement, and employee development.

The high performance safety support system is as follows:

Components of leadership development, employee development, and Continuous Improvement comprise the majority of a high performance safety system. The first step, as always, is to establish clear expectations. Clear and specific safety expectations are part of leadership development and employee development. In a high performance organization, examples of leadership safety expectations include:

- Set an example by wearing personal protective equipment.
- Look for safety hazards and unsafe acts every day.
- Take note of safety hazards or employees not wearing personal protective equipment or failing to follow proper safety practices.
- Handle safety performance issues in a timely, consistent, and appropriate manner using the *Human Performance Improvement Worksheet* or the *Injury Problem-Solving Worksheet.*
- Use the *Injury Problem-Solving Worksheet* every time an injury occurs and the employee was wearing safety equipment and following safety practices.
- Use the *Human Performance Improvement Worksheet* every time an injury occurs because the employee was not wearing safety equipment or not following safety practices.
- Lead the team's 4-S system and Continuous Improvement process, which includes fixing any housekeeping or orderliness problems you observe.
- Take part in injury and environmental CI efforts.

Employee safety expectations include:
- Wear personal protective equipment.
- Participate in the team's 4-S process.
- Take responsibility for personal safety.
- Report all injuries and accidents.
- Join in the team's CI process.
- Train, verify, and follow safe operating practices contained in the JOBS or TECS operating guidelines.
- Report potential safety hazards and unsafe acts. Suggest ways to make the job safer and more ergonomically sound.
- Remind co-workers of safe practices and procedures to help prevent unsafe work practices.
- Train on environmental compliance issues in the work area to help assure performance improvement.

Most organizations conduct annual and legally required safety training. High performance organizations, however, reinforce safety expectations by repetitive, "area specific" awareness training on the most dangerous aspects of a particular work environment. They reinforce the training with related signs, and appropriate protective equipment.

For example, repetitive training in the hot end of a steel mill includes quarterly Safety Captain training, annual Crane Operator training, quarterly fire prevention training, and training on safe recovery from a hot metal breakout. Safety signs clearly mark areas to avoid when working around hot metal, specify evacuation routes, and remind workers of the potential deadly affects of hot metal. Safety equipment includes respirators, carbon monoxide monitors, proper fire proof clothing, hard hats, safety shoes with metatarsals, safety glasses and shields, eye wash stations, first aid stations, fire fighting equipment, and trained emergency first-response resources and systems.

A safety environment is like any performance environment. Performance depends on clear expectations, training, and opportunity. Once expectations and opportunity are in place the training comes from JOBS or TECS. Operating guidelines and the skills verification process, not only provide training, but also assure and document the effectiveness of the training. Safe operating guidelines, including lock out, start up, operating, and stopping equipment, are the cornerstone of safety training. On-the-job training and the resulting safety procedures and check sheets tailored to match each job, are essential in a safe work environment. Employee training and skill verification on every job are to safety what bees are to honey.

Whenever a safety procedure changes because of an injury, observation, audit, or new technology, the JOBS or TECS guidelines change. All those performing the affected job re-verify on the new procedure the next day. The JOBS module of our Web-based high performance software controls the documents to identify individuals who need re-training and re-verification in a timely fashion in order to guarantee the safety of the workforce.

All the training and verification in the world is meaningless, if employees do not use it. The third major part of a high performance safety system is the use of the *Human Performance Improvement Worksheet*. The use of this tool by leaders strengthens the safety environment, assures accountability, provides consistency, and appropriately enforces safe operating practices.

The human performance problem-solving approach and worksheet are vital to a safe work environment. Whenever an employee is not following a safe work practice, leaders must examine the clarity of expectations, adequacy of training, and opportunity to perform safely. High performance leaders fix all deficiencies in the safety performance environment for the benefit of all employees, not just the injured person or the person observed not following safe work practices. The focus is on prevention as well as correction.

If the performance environment is in place and an employee is injured or observed not following safe work practices, there must be consistent and appropriate consequences to maintain the safety standards. It is far easier to discipline an employee choosing not to work safely than it is to live with the results of a disfiguring, disabling, or fatal injury that could have been prevented.

A formal 4-S audit system and key measure for the Continuous Improvement process, assures cleanliness, orderliness, safe practices, and proper ergonomics. Internal Resources coordinate 4-S audit teams, comprised of Operators, Team Leaders, Maintenance Technicians, and Safety Engineers. As previously described, the 4-S system produces a score, and every area improves their 4-S score using the CI tools.

A high performance organization responds both in an immediate and systematic way to injuries or accidents. When an injury, spill, or fire occurs, the first concern is to quickly respond to alleviate the danger and provide medical assistance. Most companies have trained personnel on each shift who can respond to spills, fires, and injuries immediately. In a high performance organization, this is part of the job for all expert Operators and skills are verified and kept current through the JOBS or TECS process.

After emergency response comes investigation, problem-solving, and preventive actions concerning the specific injury or accident. Our clients fill out an **Injury Problem-Solving Worksheet** every time there is an incident. They gather the necessary facts and quickly complete interim actions to protect the balance of the workforce. Problem-solving continues by identifying all possible causes. If an employee failure to follow proper safety practices is an actual cause, then the *Human Performance Improvement Worksheet* fixes the performance environment or assures consistent and appropriate consequences. If safety practices and procedures were followed, the *Injury Problem-Solving Worksheet* finds the actual cause, fixes the cause, and prevents recurrence.

The last part of a high performance safety system concerns the environment, including air, water, waste, and deforestation. Every organization in every industry has the responsibility to tell its workforce how the company's work affects the environment, and to reduce any adverse environmental impact. Company and industry actions affect everyone on the globe. For that reason, the environment performance area is rapidly becoming more important in every company and every country.

As a means of checks and balances in a high performance structure, the company's voice on environmental issues remains outside the operations group. The environment champion is typically responsible to:

- Create a safety procedure incorporating the tools of high performance for the environmental ISO requirements and other certifications.
- Conduct audits.
- Assure compliance using the *Project Implementation Worksheet.*
- Investigate any incidents using the *Problem-Solving Worksheet.*
- Sustain Continuous Improvement in environmental key measures.

The second high performance operational system is Quality. Like Safety, a high performance quality system comes about primarily from implementing the high performance pillar systems. The parts of a high performance quality system are as follows:

Just as in building a quality house, quality products or services start with the raw material and component parts that you buy from others. The first part of a high performance quality system assures quality of incoming parts and raw material. Purchasing, quality, or technical groups can manage this responsibility. The six major activities associated with component part's quality are:

- Identify and certify strategic suppliers.
- Optimize the number of suppliers to optimize adequate supply, consistent quality, and volume discounts.
- Set up purchased part inspection procedures based on supplier quality performance.
- Establish partnerships with strategic certified strategic suppliers and share gains from cost savings initiatives.
- Set up CI key measures in percent of certified suppliers, cost of purchased materials per unit, parts and raw material inventory turns, supplier on-time delivery, purchased parts or material defects, and downtime due to lack of purchased parts or material.

The second ingredient in a high performance quality system is product or service quality. The operating group controls, inspects, and corrects internal product or service quality. The JOBS or TECS training and verification system confirms that Operators have the skills to inspect the product or verify the service. Operators must know how to correct quality and be aware of the boundaries of their authority. The quality support system integrates with CI as operating groups continuously improve the internal quality of the product or service they build or provide. Manufacturing groups pursue CI in key measures of scrap and re-work, while service groups pursue improvement in key measures of service quality, speed, and accuracy. As a natural consequence, as internal quality improves so does external quality for the customer.

In a high performance structure, the quality champion resides outside the operations group and is the voice of the customer. Below are the key responsibilities of this quality champion:

- Process quality audit insuring that the operations group is following the inspection process and utilizing the correct tools and methods accurately and properly
- Quality tool and gauge calibration system and audit
- Customer problem reporting and problem-solving using the CI *Problem-Solving Worksheet*
- Natural owner of Continuous Improvement key measures on

warranty, customer complaints, 4-S in quality areas, and the cost of poor quality

- Develop specifications, operating parameters, and inspection process that operations will use to assure quality, based on customer requirements
- Change inspection practices, tools, and frequencies to reduce non-value-added inspection and increase inspection where defects occur or based on changing customer requirements
- Serve as the final arbiter of whether to ship questionable products or perform questionable services to and for the customer
- Set up a quality procedure incorporating the high performance systems for ISO and other certification processes, and conduct audits ensuring compliance

The final Operational Support System is Productivity. The five-part high performance Productivity system improves the effectiveness of the methods used to build products or perform services. The productivity support system, like safety and quality, is primarily comprised of the high performance pillar systems.

As rhythm is to music, so is flow to productivity. Balanced and uninterrupted flow is the key to productivity, whether it is to manufacture a product or provide a service. The following are ways to improve productivity:

- Continually reduce the time it takes for changeovers through CI
- Continually chase the bottlenecks that occur in every process using CI and PRIDE flow analysis
- Schedule to maximize utilization and minimize the number and complexity of changes
- Perform maintenance quickly and before the process crashes by pursuing CI in maintenance-related key measures
- Utilize material and inventory to assure supply, yet reduce cost and defects in the process by pursuing CI in material-related key measures

Technical support resources integrated into the operations group in a high performance structure are responsible for:

- production or service planning.
- efficient production and change scheduling.
- developing efficient changeover procedures and assisting changeovers.
- key measures of change frequencies, average time for a change, and 4-S tool repair areas.

Do not underestimate the impact that scheduling, balance, and flow have on productivity. One of our clients in the die-casting business increased efficiency simply by improving scheduling. Instead of having five products run on three machines, two machines were dedicated to the two highest-volume products and the other three products ran on the third machine. Product changeovers were scheduled on the third machine at 6 A.M., when a highly trained die-change team quickly changed the pre-staged and pre-heated dies. Of course, the dedicated machines never shut down again for a product change. This, combined with the Operators becoming more familiar with the products they ran, led to a fourteen percent increase in efficiency in only thirty days.

Using PRIDE in the service industry, we helped our clients cut the time from order to delivery of parts and services from 120 days to 20 days, and the number of days to close the books from 14 days to 2 days. Balance and flow of service greatly affect their timeliness, quality, and cost.

Every product or service flow has a chronic bottleneck. Unlike daily bottlenecks that may change every day, a chronic bottleneck slows or limits output more than any other operation over a period of time. The operations CI team identifies and breaks the chronic bottleneck.

Just like safety and quality, consistency improves productivity. JOBS and TECS provide needed operator training and verification in the most efficient procedures.

In a high performance organization, Maintenance Technicians, or Technical Support Resources in the service industry, strive to continually reduce unplanned downtime. It is better to fix an airplane on the ground than in the air. Likewise, it is better to update or back up computer systems on a weekend than to interrupt closing the books. Planned or preventive maintenance is always more efficient than reactive maintenance. Planned maintenance assures all the tools, materials, and resources are together to efficiently perform the maintenance and it is done when most convenient for operations.

Preventive maintenance is a shared responsibility between Operators and Technicians. Operators perform routine preventive maintenance, so that highly skilled Technicians can focus on sophisticated, preventive maintenance tasks.

High performance preventive maintenance systems change repair frequencies based on reactive downtime experience. This avoids unneeded repairs and replacements and reduces downtime because of reactive maintenance. For checks and balances, there is a champion of preventive maintenance, just like there is for safety and quality.

The maintenance champion is responsible to lead CI in maintenance-related downtime, average length of a breakdown, percentage preventive versus reactive maintenance, injuries in the maintenance group, 4-S in maintenance areas, and the cost of maintenance per unit produced.

Flow means more than how consistently a machine runs. It also means how well material flows through the operations process. Having a balanced flow of material and product pulled through the process with visible inventories will allow the operations group to build the right product at the right time, with low inventories and scrap rates. Visible inventories with clear minimum and maximum levels coupled with automatic re-ordering allow the operations group to manage inventory cost and reduce its dependency on support personnel.

Operational Support Systems, like all systems in a high performance organization, integrate with the five pillar systems. They flow from the pillar systems and are ninety percent complete when a company fully implements the Pillars of High Performance. There is no need for duplicative systems, tools, or interventions.

Like all systems, Operational Support Systems require disciplined implementation from effective leadership. So, we end where we began. The answer is always: "Effective Leadership." This is why the title of this book is *Lead the Way*. We have not just gone in a circle, we have traveled around the whole world of high performance. The next and final chapter puts it all together, so you can develop your own tailored travel itinerary and lead the way on your journey to high performance, growth, and security.

⮩ Operational Support Systems engage the entire workforce in safely providing customers high quality products or services at a competitive price.

⮩ There are three fundamental Operational Support Systems: safety, quality, and productivity.

⮩ Operational Support Systems flow from the key pillar systems and help high performance companies outperform the competition now and in the future.

PART SEVEN

Putting It All Together

29

Getting It Done

The systems are a science,
while implementation is an art.

Leadership, five pillar systems, principles, values, Pillar Support Systems, Operational Support Systems, and structure . . . are you a little confused? Like a science, the individual systems are complete, formulistic, and exact. Like an art, implementing the systems in the correct sequence takes creativity and intuition. This chapter removes the mystery and helps you "put it all together."

By now, you fully understand that high performance is the right and only path to long-term security and growth for your company. All you have to do now is get set and go. This chapter will help answer some of your questions, such as: "Where should I start?", "What systems do I need?", and "How should I sequence each step on the journey to high performance?"

All companies need to engage their entire workforce and implement the same key, adaptive, and integrated systems in order to survive in the world market. However, the starting point is always different for each company. Some companies start from a position of profitability, some start on the brink of failure. Some start with several systems in place, some have no systems at all. Some companies are large and some are small. Some companies have unions and some do not. Some companies have several effective leaders and some have only one leader starting the journey to high performance. Where to start, how fast to move, what to keep, and what to discard are unique to each organization.

Just as a doctor does a diagnosis before prescribing a cure, you need a diagnosis to get set before developing your road map to high performance. Start by analyzing all the systems in this book compared to the systems in your organization. Outside experts can diagnose your organization or you can do it yourself, if you believe you understand all the parts of high performance.

The flowcharts that follow show four different starting places and resulting implementation strategies. The four flowcharts depict the following:

1. A standard proactive implementation
2. A competitive emergency implementation or implementing when a company needs to recover from repetitive cuts and resulting loss of performance
3. An implementation in a difficult union or employee relations environment with restrictive work rules
4. A new facility or new opportunity implementation

Tailor one of these basic flowcharts to your company after a thorough diagnosis of its needs. Even though you know where you want to go, you have to understand where you are now, before plotting a course to get there.

To begin, no matter who you are, what you do, where you are, and what you have or have not done, the first ingredient for achieving high performance is enlisting the commitment of one or more true leaders. Actually, without them, there is no chance to achieve high performance. The true leader or leaders must have the authority and courage to carry out, or cause others to carry out needed changes in their team, area, facility, or company.

The first implementation flowchart is for the effective leader of a profitable or cost-effective team, area, or organization. Do not confuse results with high performance—high performance is about how the company achieves the results. Visionary leaders recognize that without changes, the competition will threaten the company in the changing marketplace. These leaders candidly admit that the company's profitability comes from being at the right place at the right time, and not from the strength of systems or the workforce.

In one sense, this is an easy change because the time, money, and people are present to complete systems sequentially. In another sense, it is a most difficult change because there is no visible or immediate compelling need to change. Leaders must do a great job presenting their vision of the future.

The proactive implementation allows the focus to start with leadership development and CI with top-down implementation. Leadership development and CI are prerequisite systems for many other changes. Tailor the exact timing and sequence of changes based on the strengths, weaknesses, and capacity of your unique group using the standard, proactive implementation flowchart as a basic guide.

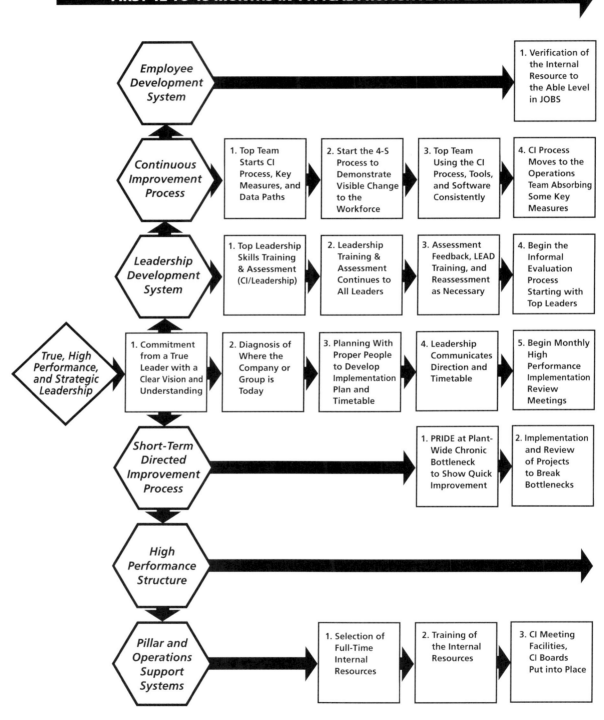

FIRST 12 TO 15 MONTHS IN TYPICAL PROACTIVE IMPLEMENTATION

Employee Development System

1. Verification of the Internal Resource to the Able Level in JOBS

Continuous Improvement Process

1. Top Team Starts CI Process, Key Measures, and Data Paths
2. Start the 4-S Process to Demonstrate Visible Change to the Workforce
3. Top Team Using the CI Process, Tools, and Software Consistently
4. CI Process Moves to the Operations Team Absorbing Some Key Measures

Leadership Development System

1. Top Leadership Skills Training & Assessment (CI/Leadership)
2. Leadership Training & Assessment Continues to All Leaders
3. Assessment Feedback, LEAD Training, and Reassessment as Necessary
4. Begin the Informal Evaluation Process Starting with Top Leaders

True, High Performance, and Strategic Leadership

1. Commitment from a True Leader with a Clear Vision and Understanding
2. Diagnosis of Where the Company or Group is Today
3. Planning With Proper People to Develop Implementation Plan and Timetable
4. Leadership Communicates Direction and Timetable
5. Begin Monthly High Performance Implementation Review Meetings

Short-Term Directed Improvement Process

1. PRIDE at Plant-Wide Chronic Bottleneck to Show Quick Improvement
2. Implementation and Review of Projects to Break Bottlenecks

High Performance Structure

Pillar and Operations Support Systems

1. Selection of Full-Time Internal Resources
2. Training of the Internal Resources
3. CI Meeting Facilities, CI Boards Put into Place

TYPICAL PROACTIVE IMPLEMENTATION

The first 12 to 15 months of implementation includes pieces from all of the Pillars of High Performance except structure. Emphasis is on top-down implementation of leadership development and Continuous Improvement. Prerequisite systems from one pillar precede systems from another as the synergistic power of high performance begins to unfold. The planning process begins to move from *Envision* and *Example* to *Encourage,* including use of the D2 leadership Style for employee involvement.

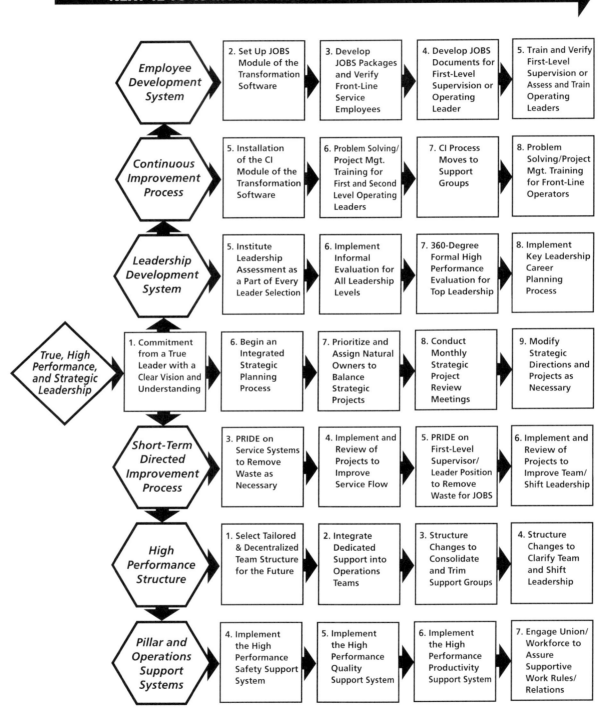

NEXT 12 TO 15 MONTHS IN TYPICAL PROACTIVE IMPLEMENTATION

Employee Development System
- 2. Set Up JOBS Module of the Transformation Software
- 3. Develop JOBS Packages and Verify Front-Line Service Employees
- 4. Develop JOBS Documents for First-Level Supervision or Operating Leader
- 5. Train and Verify First-Level Supervision or Assess and Train Operating Leaders

Continuous Improvement Process
- 5. Installation of the CI Module of the Transformation Software
- 6. Problem Solving/ Project Mgt. Training for First and Second Level Operating Leaders
- 7. CI Process Moves to Support Groups
- 8. Problem Solving/Project Mgt. Training for Front-Line Operators

Leadership Development System
- 5. Institute Leadership Assessment as a Part of Every Leader Selection
- 6. Implement Informal Evaluation for All Leadership Levels
- 7. 360-Degree Formal High Performance Evaluation for Top Leadership
- 8. Implement Key Leadership Career Planning Process

True, High Performance, and Strategic Leadership
- 1. Commitment from a True Leader with a Clear Vision and Understanding
- 6. Begin an Integrated Strategic Planning Process
- 7. Prioritize and Assign Natural Owners to Balance Strategic Projects
- 8. Conduct Monthly Strategic Project Review Meetings
- 9. Modify Strategic Directions and Projects as Necessary

Short-Term Directed Improvement Process
- 3. PRIDE on Service Systems to Remove Waste as Necessary
- 4. Implement and Review of Projects to Improve Service Flow
- 5. PRIDE on First-Level Supervisor/ Leader Position to Remove Waste for JOBS
- 6. Implement and Review of Projects to Improve Team/ Shift Leadership

High Performance Structure
- 1. Select Tailored & Decentralized Team Structure for the Future
- 2. Integrate Dedicated Support into Operations Teams
- 3. Structure Changes to Consolidate and Trim Support Groups
- 4. Structure Changes to Clarify Team and Shift Leadership

Pillar and Operations Support Systems
- 4. Implement the High Performance Safety Support System
- 5. Implement the High Performance Quality Support System
- 6. Implement the High Performance Productivity Support System
- 7. Engage Union/ Workforce to Assure Supportive Work Rules/ Relations

The second period of implementation continues leadership development and the spread of CI. In addition, implementation of many key support systems begins. By the end of the second period of implementation, all leadership development systems are in place and leadership focus starts to incorporate strategic planning. As leaders and teams develop, top leadership gradually spends more and more time on strategic issues. At least one front-line team is using CI. Emphasis shifts to verifying first-line leadership, structure, and implementation of essential support systems, including safety, quality, and productivity. Leaders are in the *Enable* phase and the use of D3 leadership Style begins.

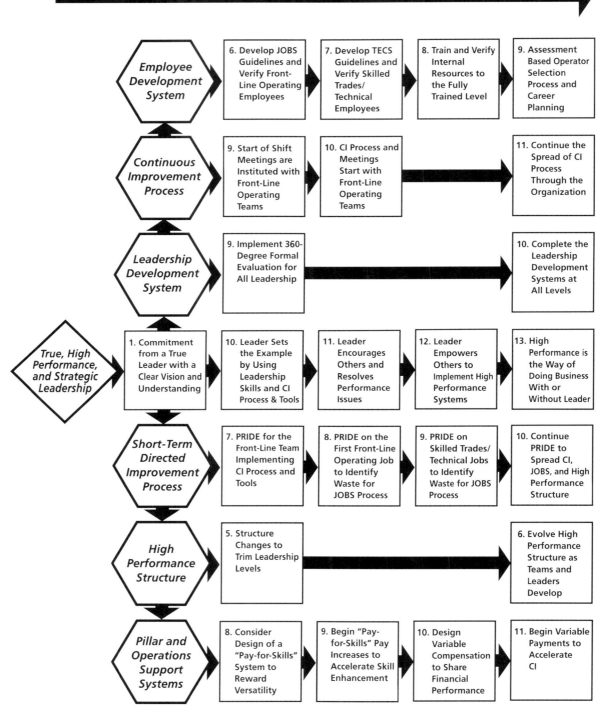

The third period of implementation focuses on employee development including front-line operating employees, skilled trades, and technical employees. Proactive PRIDE analysis, CI, and high performance structure spread through the organization. The company implements Pillar Support Systems needed to accelerate and reinforce the move to high performance.

The organization is now a high performance organization and the focus turns to preserving the systems and use of tools to assure constant progress. The leaders are in the *Empowerment* phase and frequently use of the D3 Style of leadership. The entire workforce owns and takes pride in the progress made.

The following series of flowcharts depicts implementation for a company in a competitive crisis or a company that has cut people and investment to the point of destroying performance. Since the first need is to show quick and dramatic improvement, a reactive PRIDE analysis is the first order of business. Need dictates that the company abandon the normal top-down implementation and focus first on meeting the immediate competitive threat. This is a difficult implementation. Dramatic changes including structure changes come early in the game. On the other hand, a clear compelling need for change helps the leader gain support.

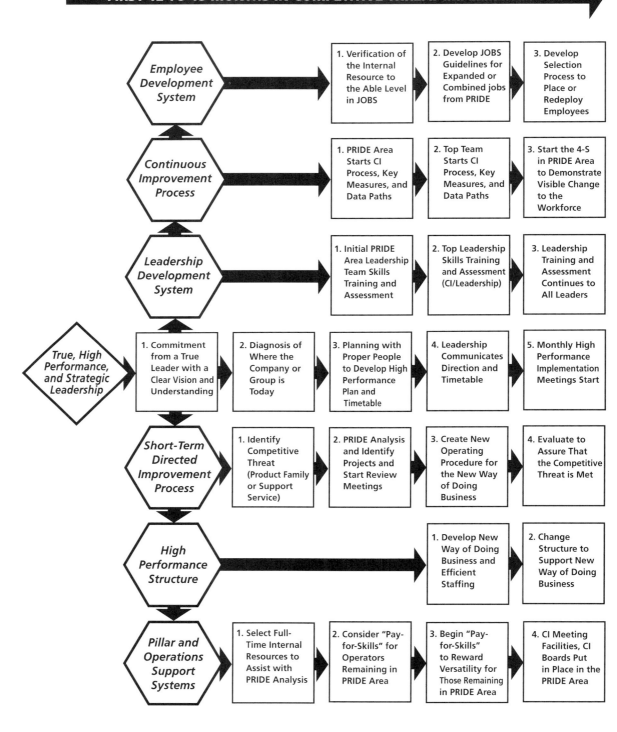

COMPETITIVE THREAT IMPLEMENTATION

During the first period of a competitive threat implementation, the PRIDE process is used to fix an immediate survival threat or help a reduced workforce perform. Survival dictates that these changes cannot wait for top-down implementation. Most often fixing one product family or administrative service will provide insight for company wide improvements. For this reason, the company focuses on fixing the most immediate need, and after the lessons are learned from those actions, system changes spread to other areas.

NEXT 12 TO 15 MONTHS IN COMPETITIVE THREAT IMPLEMENTATION

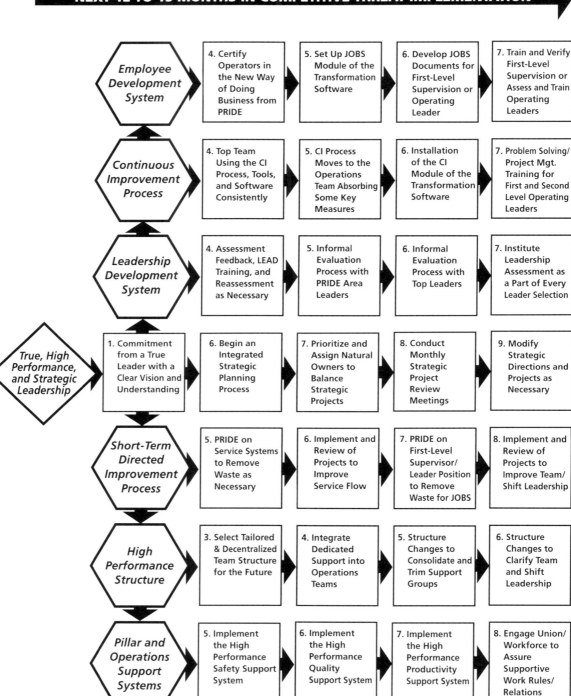

The first focus of the second period of a competitive-threat implementation starts by completing pillar systems in the area initially reconfigured with PRIDE. This assures training and recognition for employees needing greater versatility, and also that Continuous Improvement, not regression, follows quick-directed improvement. In the second period, the company begins to implement plans to move the entire company to high performance as the focus switches back to top-down implementation.

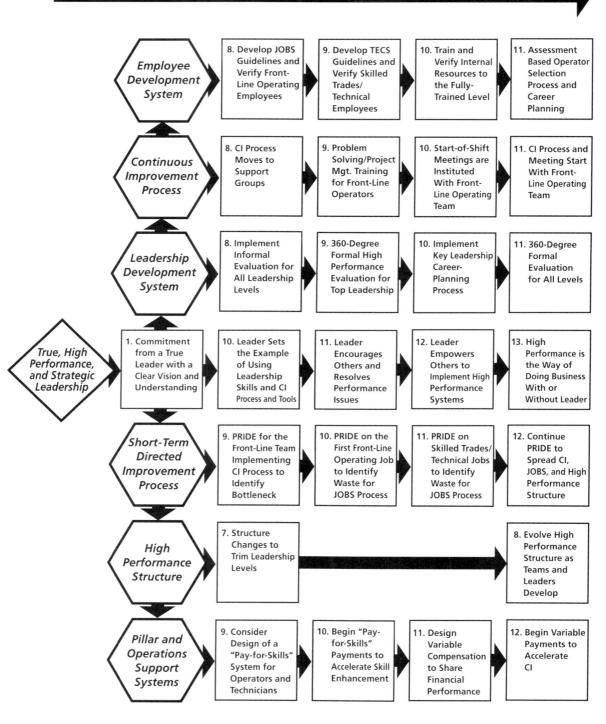

FINAL 12 TO 15 MONTHS IN COMPETITIVE THREAT IMPLEMENTATION

Employee Development System
- 8. Develop JOBS Guidelines and Verify Front-Line Operating Employees
- 9. Develop TECS Guidelines and Verify Skilled Trades/Technical Employees
- 10. Train and Verify Internal Resources to the Fully-Trained Level
- 11. Assessment Based Operator Selection Process and Career Planning

Continuous Improvement Process
- 8. CI Process Moves to Support Groups
- 9. Problem Solving/Project Mgt. Training for Front-Line Operators
- 10. Start-of-Shift Meetings are Instituted With Front-Line Operating Team
- 11. CI Process and Meeting Start With Front-Line Operating Team

Leadership Development System
- 8. Implement Informal Evaluation for All Leadership Levels
- 9. 360-Degree Formal High Performance Evaluation for Top Leadership
- 10. Implement Key Leadership Career-Planning Process
- 11. 360-Degree Formal Evaluation for All Levels

True, High Performance, and Strategic Leadership
- 1. Commitment from a True Leader with a Clear Vision and Understanding
- 10. Leader Sets the Example of Using Leadership Skills and CI Process and Tools
- 11. Leader Encourages Others and Resolves Performance Issues
- 12. Leader Empowers Others to Implement High Performance Systems
- 13. High Performance is the Way of Doing Business With or Without Leader

Short-Term Directed Improvement Process
- 9. PRIDE for the Front-Line Team Implementing CI Process to Identify Bottleneck
- 10. PRIDE on the First Front-Line Operating Job to Identify Waste for JOBS Process
- 11. PRIDE on Skilled Trades/Technical Jobs to Identify Waste for JOBS Process
- 12. Continue PRIDE to Spread CI, JOBS, and High Performance Structure

High Performance Structure
- 7. Structure Changes to Trim Leadership Levels
- 8. Evolve High Performance Structure as Teams and Leaders Develop

Pillar and Operations Support Systems
- 9. Consider Design of a "Pay-for-Skills" System for Operators and Technicians
- 10. Begin "Pay-for-Skills" Payments to Accelerate Skill Enhancement
- 11. Design Variable Compensation to Share Financial Performance
- 12. Begin Variable Payments to Accelerate CI

In the third period of implementation, CI, leadership development, and JOBS spread to the entire company. This completes the move from a serious competitive threat to high performance, growth, and security. Continued emphasis on strategic planning and CI will reduce the need for reactive pride and associated trauma.

The next flowchart series depicts implementation of high performance in a company with poor employee or union relations and resultant unproductive work rules or collective bargaining provisions. The underlying need is to create the understanding and relationships needed to change uncompetitive practices. The early focus is to inform, engage, and involve the workforce and union to gain support for necessary changes, while simultaneously implementing systems that engage management leadership in the pursuit of high performance.

Poor work practices are a result of deteriorated relations and mistrust between management and workers. It will take time to build healthy relations and support common objectives. Understanding and open communication must come before most unions or employees are willing to participate in planning the needed changes. Often an outside change agent is necessary to bring union and management together. Sometimes tours of other companies help union and management see that different ways of working are possible. The union and workforce must come to understand that there is no alternative, but to join management in a cooperative change process to pursue high performance, in order to garner growth and security. Management leadership needs to understand that it must set the stage for a joint planning and change initiative.

FIRST 12 TO 15 MONTHS OF IMPLEMENTATION WITH UNPRODUCTIVE RELATIONS AND WORK RULES

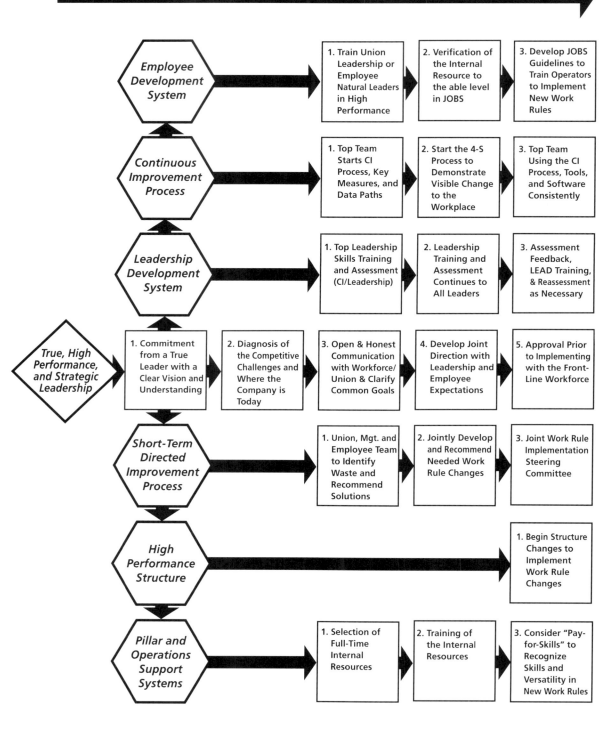

IMPLEMENTATION WITH UNPRODUCTIVE RELATIONS AND WORK RULES

The main outcome of the first phase is a change plan developed by a joint planning team empowered to develop recommendations for assuring competitiveness and growth. The plan in represented companies is usually subject to employee approval because the proposed changes usually modify collective bargaining agreements.

In a unionized facility, the best time to start developing the plan modifying the bargaining agreement is about 15 months before contract expiration. However, sometimes mid-term contract changes are necessary as a way to save the company and as many of the associated jobs as possible. In other cases, companies extend existing contracts to allow time for planning.

In a represented facility, union and management must understand that neither entity can preserve the company and accomplish high performance alone, or in spite of each other. Learning to work together to meet the competitive challenge is not an option.

Starting leadership development and CI at the management team level will save valuable implementation time as the joint change plan is developed and approved. Inviting union or employee leaders to participate in leadership training and the 4-S process will help build understanding and stronger relationships.

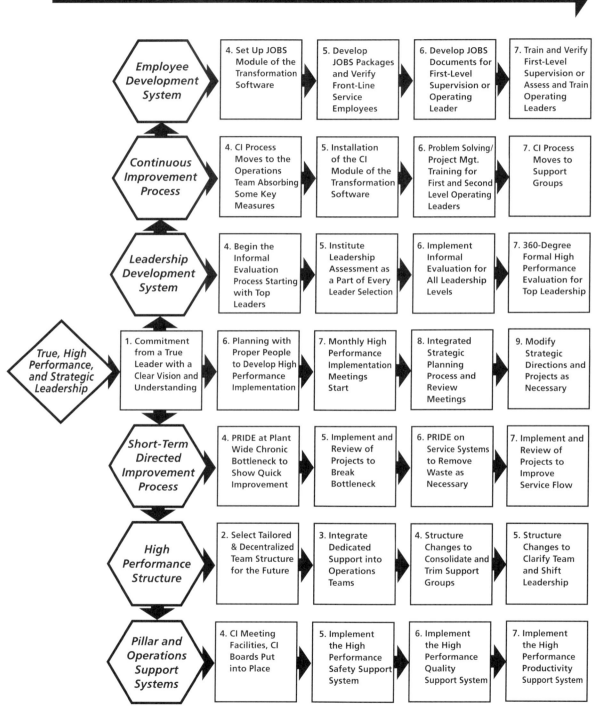

In the second implementation period, the focus switches away from work rule changes to moving the entire company toward high performance. Employee development begins while expanding leadership development and CI with management teams. Support systems help speed up improved results. Selected and trained Internal Resources help implement high performance systems.

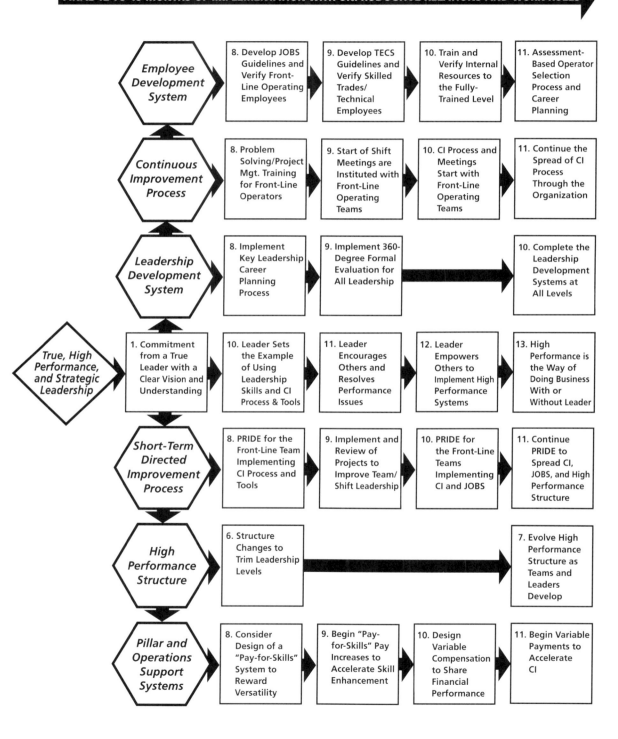

FINAL 12 TO 15 MONTHS OF IMPLEMENTATION WITH UNPRODUCTIVE RELATIONS AND WORK RULES

Employee Development System

8. Develop JOBS Guidelines and Verify Front-Line Operating Employees

9. Develop TECS Guidelines and Verify Skilled Trades/Technical Employees

10. Train and Verify Internal Resources to the Fully-Trained Level

11. Assessment-Based Operator Selection Process and Career Planning

Continuous Improvement Process

8. Problem Solving/Project Mgt. Training for Front-Line Operators

9. Start of Shift Meetings are Instituted with Front-Line Operating Teams

10. CI Process and Meetings Start with Front-Line Operating Teams

11. Continue the Spread of CI Process Through the Organization

Leadership Development System

8. Implement Key Leadership Career Planning Process

9. Implement 360-Degree Formal Evaluation for All Leadership

10. Complete the Leadership Development Systems at All Levels

True, High Performance, and Strategic Leadership

1. Commitment from a True Leader with a Clear Vision and Understanding

10. Leader Sets the Example of Using Leadership Skills and CI Process & Tools

11. Leader Encourages Others and Resolves Performance Issues

12. Leader Empowers Others to Implement High Performance Systems

13. High Performance is the Way of Doing Business With or Without Leader

Short-Term Directed Improvement Process

8. PRIDE for the Front-Line Team Implementing CI Process and Tools

9. Implement and Review of Projects to Improve Team/Shift Leadership

10. PRIDE for the Front-Line Teams Implementing CI and JOBS

11. Continue PRIDE to Spread CI, JOBS, and High Performance Structure

High Performance Structure

6. Structure Changes to Trim Leadership Levels

7. Evolve High Performance Structure as Teams and Leaders Develop

Pillar and Operations Support Systems

8. Consider Design of a "Pay-for-Skills" System to Reward Versatility

9. Begin "Pay-for-Skills" Pay Increases to Accelerate Skill Enhancement

10. Design Variable Compensation to Share Financial Performance

11. Begin Variable Payments to Accelerate CI

In the final implementation phase, the major emphasis is on employee development across the entire organization and spreading CI to front-line operating teams. With this work accomplished, the high performance organization is complete. All training and support should be in place and all unproductive work practices should be replaced with work practices that encourage skill development, improvement, waste reduction, safety, quality, and productivity. The organization is positioned to be profitable and poised to grow in the marketplace.

The last implementation flowchart series is for a new facility or opportunity. The first underlying needs are to design the structure, select the right leaders and employees, and train them to assure a successful launch. The early emphasis is different from any other implementation. This is the quickest implementation because it is easier to create something than to change something. Similarly, it is quicker to select high performance leaders and employees than to develop them from within the organization.

Tailor the exact timing and sequence of changes based on the strengths, weaknesses, and capacity of your unique group using the standard new plant or opportunity implantation flowchart. Notice that implementation begins well before start-up. Do not make the mistake of putting your new and often pivotal opportunities in the hands of ineffective leaders relying on old and unproductive systems.

FIRST 12 TO 15 MONTHS BEFORE START-UP OF NEW PLANT OR OPPORTUNITY

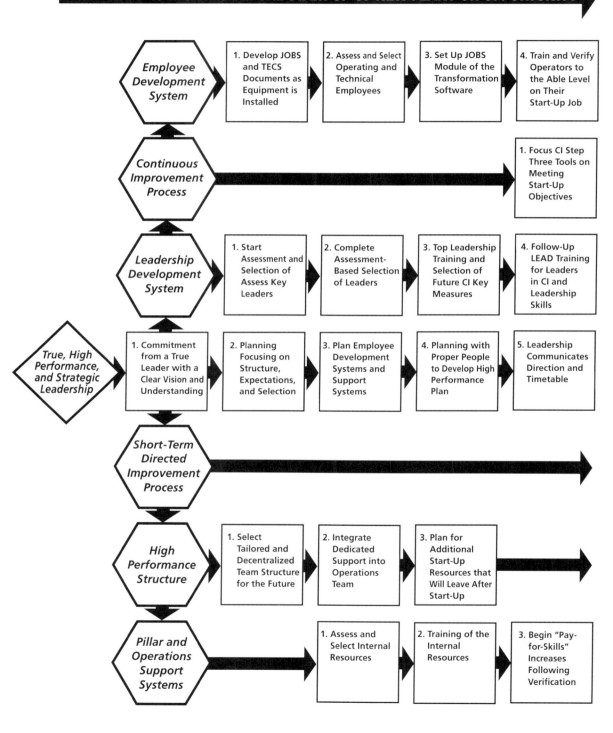

START-UP OF A NEW PLANT OR OPPORTUNITY

In the pre-startup period of implementation, the focus is on designing structure and selecting the right people for the new opportunity. The most common mistake made in the name of cost savings is waiting too long to place or hire leaders and employees. This forces hurried decisions, placement compromises, and inadequate preparation for the start-up. As a result, the start-up performance falls short of objectives and the move to high performance is inevitably delayed.

The new opportunity should begin with a high performance, decentralized structure and support systems, like productive work rules and Pay-for-Skills, as a part of the initial design. CI begins after performance and schedules stabilize following start-up. However, project management and problem-solving tools help extensively during the start-up.

The next period of implementation focuses on a successful start-up. After meeting start-up objectives, the focus turns to high performance systems to assure constant improvement and long-term growth and security.

NEXT 12 TO 15 MONTHS ACTUAL START-UP OF NEW PLANT OR OPPORTUNITY IMPLEMENTATION

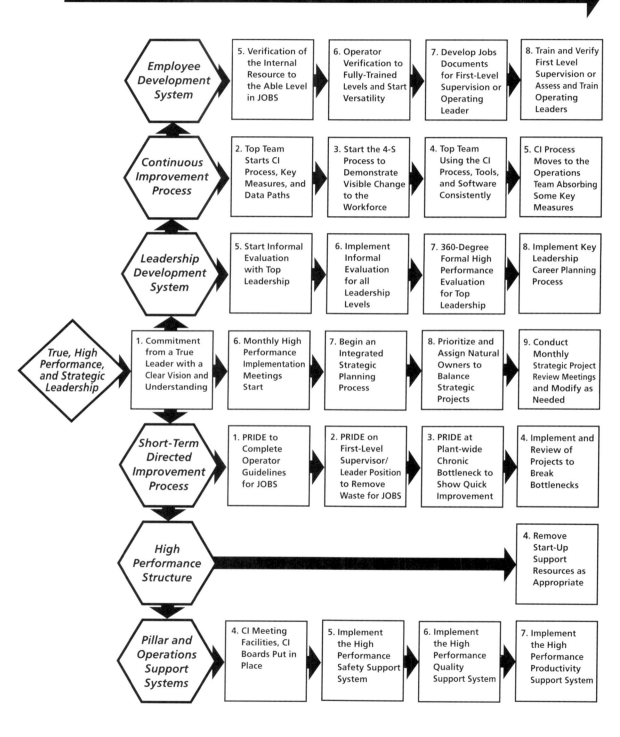

The start-up phase of a new location or opportunity focuses on training the people selected and accomplishing start-up objectives. In addition, support systems assure safety, housekeeping, orderliness, ergonomics, quality, and productivity. The balance of the high performance systems starts in the final period of implementation.

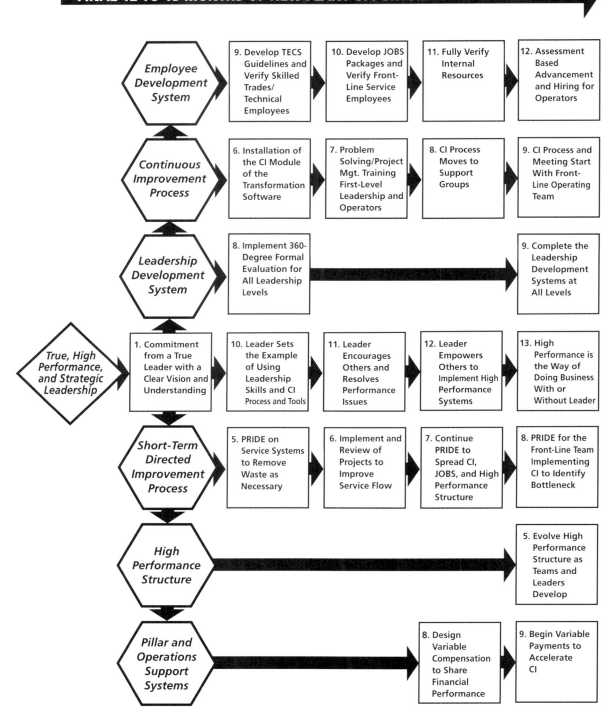

FINAL 12 TO 15 MONTHS OF NEW PLANT OPPORTUNITY IMPLEMENTATION

Employee Development System

9. Develop TECS Guidelines and Verify Skilled Trades/Technical Employees

10. Develop JOBS Packages and Verify Front-Line Service Employees

11. Fully Verify Internal Resources

12. Assessment Based Advancement and Hiring for Operators

Continuous Improvement Process

6. Installation of the CI Module of the Transformation Software

7. Problem Solving/Project Mgt. Training First-Level Leadership and Operators

8. CI Process Moves to Support Groups

9. CI Process and Meeting Start With Front-Line Operating Team

Leadership Development System

8. Implement 360-Degree Formal Evaluation for All Leadership Levels

9. Complete the Leadership Development Systems at All Levels

True, High Performance, and Strategic Leadership

1. Commitment from a True Leader with a Clear Vision and Understanding

10. Leader Sets the Example of Using Leadership Skills and CI Process and Tools

11. Leader Encourages Others and Resolves Performance Issues

12. Leader Empowers Others to Implement High Performance Systems

13. High Performance is the Way of Doing Business With or Without Leader

Short-Term Directed Improvement Process

5. PRIDE on Service Systems to Remove Waste as Necessary

6. Implement and Review of Projects to Improve Service Flow

7. Continue PRIDE to Spread CI, JOBS, and High Performance Structure

8. PRIDE for the Front-Line Team Implementing CI to Identify Bottleneck

High Performance Structure

5. Evolve High Performance Structure as Teams and Leaders Develop

Pillar and Operations Support Systems

8. Design Variable Compensation to Share Financial Performance

9. Begin Variable Payments to Accelerate CI

The final phase of the new facility or opportunity implementation focuses on CI after the start-up performance stabilizes. In addition, implementation focus turns to finalizing high performance systems.

Following a thorough diagnosis of your needs, you can use the four basic flow-chart series to design your own implementation plan. No matter where you start from, there is a path that will take you to high performance, growth, and security. The total time to get there will depend on the size of your organization, and the time, people, and investment available to help the move to high performance.

Every business in every country needs to journey to high performance for varying reasons. There is no acceptable alternative. The values, principles, and Pillars of High Performance have stood the test of time and will not change. There is only one choice left, and that choice is yours.

Now that you know the process, the pivotal question is: *Are you willing to Lead The Way?* The only ingredient missing for success is you! As the author Chester Bernard said in this quintessential quote, "To try and fail is at least to learn. To fail to try is to suffer the inestimable loss of what might have been."

⮑ Implementing high performance starts with leadership, diagnosis of where you are today, and a tailored implementation plan.

⮑ Where to start, how fast to move, what to keep, and what to discard, are unique to each organization.

⮑ You are now armed and dangerous, are you willing to make a difference? Are you going to *Lead the Way*?

References

Bossidy, Larry, and Ram Charan. 2002. *Execution: The Discipline of Getting Things Done.* New York: Crown Business.

Brethover, Dale N. 1972. *A Total Performance System.* Kalamazoo, MI: Behaviordelia, Inc.

Collins, Jim. 2001. *Good to Great.* New York,: HarperCollins Publishers.

Drucker, Peter F. 1954. *The Practice of Management.* New York: Harper & Row. 1993. repr., HarperBusiness.

Karrass, Charles L. 1970. *The Negotiating Game.* New York: HarperCollins.

Lencioni, Patrick. 1998. *The Five Temptations of a CEO.* San Francisco: Jossey-Bass.

———. 2000. *The Four Obsessions of an Extraordinary Executive.* San Francisco: Jossey-Bass.

Lombardi, Vince, Jr. 2002. *The Essential Vince Lombardi: Words & Wisdom to Motivate, Inspire, and Win.* New York: McGraw-Hill.

Maraniss, David. 1999. *When Pride Still Mattered: A Life of Vince Lombardi.* New York,: Simon & Schuster.

Maslow, Abraham H. 1943. A Theory of Human Motivation. *Psychological Review* 50:370–396.

———. 1954. *Motivation and Personality.* New York: Harper.

Oncken, William, and Donald L. Wass. *Management Time: Who's Got the Monkey? Harvard Business Review,* November–December 1974: 75–80.

Perrottet, Tony. 2002. *The Naked Olympics: The True Story of the Olympic Games.* New York: Random House.

Peter, Laurence J., and Raymond Hull. 1970. *The Peter Principle.* London: Pan Books.

———. 1982. *In Search of Excellence.* New York: Harper & Row.

G.R.F. Ferrari, ed., and Tom Griffith, trans. 2000. *Plato: The Republic.* New York: Cambridge University Press.

Sirracos, Constantine L. 2002. *History of the Olympic Games: From Antiquity to the Present Time.* Long Island, NY: Seaburn Publishing.

Skinner, B.F. 1974. *About Behaviorism.* New York: Random House.

———. 1971. *Beyond Freedom and Dignity.* New York: Knopf.

Taylor, Frederick W., 1911. *The Principles of Scientific Management.* New York: W.W. Norton & Company.

About the Author
John J. (Jack) Nora

Jack Nora is a co-author of *Transforming the Workplace,* a detailed case study about the Cadillac Livonia Engine Plant's transformation to a high performance work organization. He is also the author of *One Way,* which is an easy to read story about a major change effort in a fictional plant, using real world examples. *One Way* is in its sixth printing and published in five languages.

Jack has had a wide variety of career experiences. He progressed from an hourly employee at General Motors Cadillac Motor Car Division through many production supervisory positions. He moved from Human Resource Manager, to Cadillac Division's Head of Quality of Work Life. Jack led the planning team that transformed the Cadillac Livonia Engine Plant into the most innovative and successful plant of the 1980s. The Livonia Engine Plant made changes, twenty-five years ago, that other companies are only now beginning to make. Examples of these changes include assessment-based hiring, operator skills verification, Pay-for-Skills, multi-craft, reduction of management levels, and formation of business teams of Operators led by a Working Team Leader.

Following his career at General Motors, Jack joined a large law firm and eventually became senior partner of his own law firm. For over two decades, Jack has been President of Workplace Transformation, Inc., an international consulting firm that has helped over one hundred and forty companies meet their competitive challenges.

Jack's broad consulting experiences include major change efforts in manufacturing and service organizations in more than twenty different industries. His consulting clients include companies in the United States, Canada, Mexico, Argentina, Slovakia, Serbia, and South Korea.

Jack received a Bachelor of Arts degree from Michigan State University, an MBA from the University of Detroit graduating number one in his class, and a Juris Doctor degree, Summa Cum Laude, from the University of Detroit School of Law.

About Workplace Transformation, Inc.

Workplace Transformation helps clients identify, custom design, and deploy changes necessary to improve short-term measurable results and provide for long-term growth and security. We not only help implement needed changes, we also train and develop leaders and the Internal Resources necessary to continue independently.

What separates Workplace Transformation from the sea of other consultants is:

- Our consultants have extensive industrial as well as consulting experience
- Our long-term, proven, comprehensive, value-driven approach
- Our understanding of the key to success: building effective leadership that engages a skilled workforce in becoming a high performance organization
- Our proprietary, proven systems, tools, and software, all of which are essential in a high performance organization
- Our ability to custom design a change intervention for each unique company or location and to build on past improvement efforts
- Our experience with union-represented companies
- Our extensive "hands-on" implementation support
- Our ability to transfer the skills necessary to enable your organization to complete successful implementation without unending reliance on external consultants

If you would like more information about Workplace Transformation, Inc., please visit our Web site at *www.workplacetransform.com* or call 1-800-783-2026.

Index